A History of Popular Culture

This lively and informative survey provides a thematic global history of popular culture focusing on the period since the end of the Second World War.

A History of Popular Culture explores the rapid diffusion and "hybridization" of popular culture as the result of three conditions of the world since the end of World War Two: instantaneous communications, widespread consumption in a market-based economy and the visualization of reality. Betts considers the dominance of American entertainment media and habits of consumption, assessing adaptation and negative reactions to this influence.

The author surveys a wide range of topics, including:

- the emergence and conditions of modern popular culture
- the effects of global conflict
- the phenomenon and effects of urbanization
- the changing demography of the political arena and the work place
- the development of contemporary music culture
- film, television and visual experience
- the growth of sport as a commercial enterprise.

Now updated by Lyz Bly to include major developments such as blogs and social networks, YouTube.com, and enhanced technologies such as the iPhone, iPod, and iPad as well as the way in which the internet has reshaped the ways we consume media. The book provides an engaging introduction to this pervasive and ever-changing subject.

Raymond F. Betts was Professor of History at the University of Kentucky and the author of many books on culture and empire, including *Decolonization* (Routledge 2004).

Lyz Bly is Instructor of History and Gender Studies at Case Western Reserve University and Cleveland State University. She is co-editor of *Make Your Own History: Documenting Feminist and Queer Activism in the 21st Century* (2012) and *Generation X and the Invention of a Third Wave Feminism* (forthcoming).

A History of Popular Culture
More of Everything, Faster and Brighter

Second edition

Raymond F. Betts with Lyz Bly

Routledge
Taylor & Francis Group

LONDON AND NEW YORK

First published 2004, this edition published 2013
by Routledge
2 Park Square, Milton Park, Abingdon, Oxon OX14 4RN

Simultaneously published in the USA and Canada
by Routledge
711 Third Avenue, New York, NY 10017

Routledge is an imprint of the Taylor & Francis Group, an informa business

British Library Cataloguing in Publication Data
A catalogue record for this book is available from the British Library

Library of Congress Cataloging in Publication Data
Betts, Raymond F.
A history of popular culture : more of everything, faster and brighter /
Raymond Betts, with Lyz Bly. – 2nd ed.
p. cm.
Includes bibliographical references.
1. Popular culture – History. I. Bly, Lyz. II. Title.
CB427.B46 2012
306 – dc23
2012021526

ISBN: 978-0-415-67436-2 (hbk)
ISBN: 978-0-415-67437-9 (pbk)
ISBN: 978-0-203-07948-5 (ebk)

Typeset in Times New Roman
by Taylor & Francis Books

MIX
Paper from
responsible sources
FSC
www.fsc.org   FSC® C004839

Printed and bound in Great Britain by the MPG Books Group

To the Many Students We Have Taught and
Who in Turn Have Taught Us

Contents

Preface

Raymond F. Betts

Few subjects range as far and vary as frequently as does popular culture. It seems to embrace all and to discard much. Its consistency is change. Like the escalator that is now so essential to shopping center, sports arena and airport, it moves regularly, conveying us all up and down to different levels of engagement and distraction, to goods and pleasures regularly rearranged to attract, to appeal, to entice.

Unlike the elevator that encloses and limits our immediate vision of things, the escalator opens out and provides a particular panoramic view of a carefully arranged environment. Contemporary popular culture is all about movement, about seeing things, about buying and having, about being distracted and entertained. At one time, the word "transported" suggested a psychological or spiritual change of condition, an imaginary movement from one state of consciousness to another. Today, of course, being transported means being moved swiftly – and usually effortlessly – from here to there and back again. Up and down the escalator, on the plane and in the car, we have a form of spatial freedom not known before the late twentieth century. The pace of life has changed dramatically, as has the space in which we now move. We also see more than did the people of previous cultures. Popular culture is about mass-produced images changing their form in seconds, popping up as advertisements on the computer screen, elegantly laid out in photographs in trendy niche publications.

My effort has been to situate all this activity within the institutions and among the devices where it moves, captures attention, allows diversion and assures entertainment. I therefore have concentrated on transportation and communication, and the new environment they have created. Megamalls and cyberspace, automobiles and movies, tourist destinations and airports provide much of the structure of the text. They suggest the changes in both pace and space that have become so pronounced in the last half century. Entertainment pervades all: there is no denying that it has become a major industry, and many of its performers and producers form a new class of the wealthy.

Prior to 1937, when Walt Disney made his first full-length animated film, *Snow White and the Seven Dwarfs*, the appearance of characters populating fairy tales was still largely left to the reader's or listener's imagination. Today, we see all. Our visions, of course, are less internally inspired than projected inward. Our culture is manufactured, machine-made and machine-guided. Once motivated by steam, as were the factory whistle and the carousel, our culture is now charged electrically. Widely wired in the twentieth century, it now is moving to the wireless, an obvious response to ever-increasing personal mobility and intensifying ease (not really an oxymoron) that also condition our daily lives. The multi-purpose hand-held entertainment and communications center, the cell phone, is obvious proof.

After I decided on this approach, just briefly described, I came across the twining of the expressions "kinetic" and "cinematic" by the French sociologist Jean Baudrillard, who used these terms to sum up the dominant qualities of contemporary American culture. Baudrillard's assertion of this complementary approach to the appearance of the world about us being fast and visible was recently confirmed in the wild comedy film *Rush Hour*, in which that ever-bouncing ball of energy, the Hong Kong movie actor Jackie Chan, did his thing gloriously.

In emphasizing the visual, I knowingly restructure the audible and audio in their new visible form: the rock concert, the DVD by way of MTV. Whether performed by Luciano Pavarotti and his two associated tenors or by Mick Jagger and his Rolling Stones group, the contemporary musical experience is a bit like the sound-and-light (*son et lumière*) shows that gained in popularity after World War Two as a means of dramatically illustrating historic sites. The popular "concert experience" is music presented as an audio-visual experience. The first time that Jimi Hendrix set fire to his guitar, the first time that Michael Jackson did (his now patented) moon walk, the audiences were dazzled.

I come to this subject as a long-lived spectator of much of it and as a historian who has viewed the world at large in years of research on the subject of modern imperialism which included its own show-and-tell. The famous encounter of Stanley and Livingstone in "darkest Africa," for instance, was theatrical. Stanley wondered how he should greet the long-searched-after Dr. Livingstone. Stanley was, among other things, a newspaper reporter. He therefore knew the value of dramatic encounter. He determined that his greeting should be formal and devoid of emotion, thus assuring a proper dignity for local Africans to observe. "Dr. Livingstone, I presume?" he therefore inquired. Nearly a century later, American presidential candidate Bill Clinton appeared on a television talk show, wore shades and played the saxophone. Encounter and presentation were still the same, although tone and idiom had changed.

I have written much based on traditional scholarly research: documents and texts found in libraries and archives. The bibliography of this book still contains proof of that. However, I have made great use of the World Wide Web in gaining information on, and insight into, analyses of and attitudes toward popular culture. Sites on figures as diverse as Elvis Presley (the rock star) and Santiago Calatrava (the Spanish architect) give some indication of the range of materials quickly retrieved.

Never before have the attributes of culture – its artifacts, idioms, iconography, social and spatial arrangements – been so plentiful, so widespread and so changing as they are today. Moreover, in our time, described as post-modern, the service industry is dominant. It is decidedly marked by its production of entertainment with high visibility at home on computer monitor and television screens; out and about on the stage of the rock concert, in the museum exhibit, among the carefully arrayed products in the supermarket and shopping mall, on the tattoos that the singers Eminem and Ozzy Osbourne sport; in the garish lighting along The Strip in Las Vegas at night and in the grounds of any theme park.

It's all to be seen.

Like the Ghost of Christmas Past in zest and enthusiasm, the United States looms brightly over the global scene of popular culture. The text takes a similar, but critical, approach to an appreciation of the American role. Moreover, it is a narrative account that gives little space to the lively theoretical debates that have marked the newer academic fields of culture studies and semiotics, and that have been principally informed by a post-World War Two generation of French philosophers interested in deconstruction and postmodernism.

The British author Robert Hewison (Hewison 1986) defined popular culture as collage culture. That is a good term but one that cannot account for the luminescence, the bright electric appearance of so much of it. I therefore prefer the qualifying adjective "kaleidoscopic." Today's popular culture is visual, highly visible. Strobe lights, laser beams, glass tubes aglow with neon and argon gases, fireworks and the blue luminescence of television screens are the constituent elements of light by which popular culture commands the night sky.

In respect for popular culture, its informality, intensity and incessant rhythms, I have departed somewhat from the traditional academic approach to historical style, where the author is the Grand or Omniscient Narrator who attempts to remain out of sight (hence the stylistic use of the third person and the avoidance of editorial asides). That approach is similar to the one played out by the Wizard of Oz who spoke sonorously and appeared sternly until the little dog Toto spoiled the trick.

I have been fortunate to enjoy continuing family support of my projects and thank my daughter Susan, a long-time cheerleader of my academic enterprises, for the benefit of her computer savvy, her on-the-scene assessment of popular culture as it plays out in San Francisco, and her assistance with organization of the bibliography, so heavy in Web references. My son Jim, a generous and good-humored critic of my academic writing, has also cast a critical eye over parts of the text and offered insights, particularly from the perspective of one who was growing up when rock-and-roll was at its most popular.

My two older grandchildren, Jimmy and Andrew, neither one nor the other yet bearing a dozen years, helped school me in current popular culture

developments. Jimmy, an enthusiast of the *Harry Potter* series, encouraged
me to read the books that he just finished; and Andrew, who has made his
Game Boy something of a prosthetic device, has helped me understand the
intricacies of the Pokémon characters and games. My long-time friend and
patron of the University of Kentucky humanities center that bears his name,
John R. Gaines, has read the entire text, offered helpful insights and acted as
enthusiast-in-residence. I also rejoiced at hearing his hearty laugh when some
off-the-wall item aroused his curiosity. To the University of Kentucky reference librarians, and in particular Roxanne Geralds and Shawn Livingston,
I express thanks for their good spirited searches for arcane facts. And to the
librarian of the University College of Architecture, Faith Harders, I also
express such thanks.

And then to the students whom I have had the privilege of teaching, all of
whom have made both conscious and unwitting commentary on popular
culture that I found exciting and beneficial, I express appreciation. Of that lot,
in class and out, I want to thank two groups in particular. The first group
consisted of those who were fellows in the Gaines Center for the Humanities
at the University of Kentucky and who both warmly supported and critically
assessed my efforts to make sense of the contemporary world. The second was
that group of students in the Semester-At-Sea program of the University of
Pittsburgh who, during the fall semester of 2000, arrived at 8:00 a.m. for the
course on popular culture that met on alternate days with the other course on
world cities. Such a class hour aboard a ship out of sight of land provided a
novel twist for teacher and students. Students in both classes deserve particular thanks for their attention and inspiration, to say nothing of their good
humor.

I have saved to last my expression of heartfelt appreciation for the support
of Jackie, my wife of many years, my intellectual companion who has helped
curb my tendency to write lengthy sentences. It is, however, for being an
unflagging supporter of my research enthusiasms, for long serving as my
loving but just critic, that I deeply thank her.

Preface

Lyz Bly

As I relished my newly completed doctorate degree during spring semester 2010, I celebrated by focusing my energy on teaching. One of my seminars, a course devoted to the history of late-twentieth-century popular culture in the US at Case Western Reserve University, comprised 18 undergraduates who devoured Guy Debord's *Society of the Spectacle* and Michel de Certeau's *The Practice of Everyday Life* as eagerly as they did Lady Gaga and David Bowie videos, Alan C. Martin's and Jamie Hewlett's graphic novel *Tank Girl,* and Jim Jarmusch's indie film classic *Stranger Than Paradise.* The course was a rare instance where almost everyone and everything jived; there was rarely a break in discussion, most students related even the most theoretical of concepts to the popular culture that they were consuming in their free time, and their final research papers were engaging, smart, and well written.

The experience reinforced what I already knew – that teaching history through the lens of pop culture can inspire students who have little interest in the humanities, much less history, to engage in the concrete and the theoretical aspects of the field. For instance, there may be no better way of illustrating the ways in which gender and race are historically constructed than by looking at David Bowie's early seventies performance of "Ziggy Stardust," Richard Roundtree's character in the classic 1970s Blaxploitation film, *Shaft,* Madonna's "post-feminist" performance of her 1985 hit, "Material Girl," and Nicki Minaj's 2010 video for "Massive Attack." While popular culture is never a perfect reflection of society's vision of itself, it shows us what the general population is, what – to use the more academically elitist phrase – "ordinary people" are tolerating at any given moment in time. Beyond that, instances of pop culture, like Roundtree's uber-hip performance of John Shaft, stoke – and perhaps shape – viewers' visions of what is possible, or, conversely, what is limiting about categories of identity such as race and gender.

In the twenty-first century aspects of popular culture have had broader implications for political discourse and social justice and activism. Blogs and Twitter are digital versions of what pamphleteers such as British-American thinker Thomas Paine, who wrote and self-published missives on his theories and ideologies during the period of the American Revolution, and feminist riot grrrls of the 1990s who wrote and circulated fanzines on gendered oppression put forth in paper form. Self-publishing has historically and contemporarily been a powerful tool for shaping opinion and inciting change. The scope and range of this expanded considerably in the digital realm. In the 2011 uprising in Libya, mobile phones, Facebook, and Twitter played a key role in getting images, videos, and personal accounts of the Gaddafi administration's violent backlash and propaganda to the global news media. Banal Facebook posts or Tweets about what one is eating, where one has arrived, and what music one is listening to are complicated by posts and images of military violence, mass protests, and social uprising. In an instant, these avenues of self-expression can become important tools of revolution. This rung especially true in 2009 when 26-year-old Iranian Nedā Āġā Soltān was murdered by gun fire on June 20 as she got out of her car to view a protest against the disputed election of President Mahmoud Ahmedinejad. The video of her bleeding to death on an Iranian street was video-recorded and distributed across the internet, becoming an iconic symbol of the struggle of Iranian protestors and activists. *Time* magazine writer Krista Mahr described Soltān's death as "probably the most widely witnessed in human history." In this context, popular culture has significant political and historical, as well as personal, implications.

Whether we use popular culture to galvanize, inform, or entertain, it is a significant, weighty tool for understanding ourselves, our cultures, and our values and ideologies. As Raymond and I address throughout this text, it is, nonetheless, an apparatus connected to powerful agents such as corporations and governments. As evidenced by the comments of my students – many of whom tell me that after taking my classes they can no longer passively enjoy Disney films, rap videos, and MTV's *Jersey Shore* – critically studying pop culture is a serious endeavor. Because it shapes the way we understand the world, if we are merely passive viewers of it we let ourselves succumb to highly influential forces. As students and scholars of history one of the best ways to challenge power is to study it, understand it, and take it apart. In doing so we counter French theorist Roland Barthes' assertion that "the image always gets the last word."

As is the case with any scholarly endeavor, one does not complete it without significant support from family and friends. I am indebted to my best friend and husband, R. A. Washington, for creating the space for me to work, for reading my revisions of Raymond's already trenchant scholarship, and for making me laugh when I was burned out from teaching numerous courses across three campuses and writing/editing two books at once. Thanks are also due to all of my students for their willingness to critically explore their favorite forms of entertainment, to read complicated theoretical texts, and connect the pop culture of the past to more "codified" historical events. Mostly, however, I appreciate them sharing their knowledge of their generation's popular culture with me and for their patience with my Generation X cynicism of all of it – their articulations of, as well as my own generation's versions of mass culture. Finally, I thank my son Gabe Bly for introducing me to new music (including his own) and re-engaging me with my own generation's music, some of which I overlooked "back in the day," and my daughter Xoe Bly, who, as a young girl, reminds me of the sway the media has on her and her peers' conceptions of girlhood and femininity. My work on this project is dedicated to her and her brother.

Introduction

Contemporary popular culture is almost without definition, so all-embracing are its subjects, so far are its effects. It has occupied the space of the traditional art museum – as a 2011 exhibition of Disney Pixar animator Sanjay Patel's illustrations, titled "Deities, Demons and Dudes with 'Staches," graced the galleries of the Asian Art Museum in San Francisco demonstrated – and it has made a more visceral appearance in the form of the "meat dress" that pop artist Lady Gaga wore as a paradoxically pro-vegan political statement at the 2011 MTV Music Awards. It consisted of the estimated one billion television viewers and radio listeners who formed a worldwide audience for the wedding of Prince Charles and Lady Diana in London on February 24, 1981, as well as the 27.6 million television viewers who watched the Canadian soccer team beat the USA three to two in overtime in the game that was the sensation of the 2010 Winter Olympics (website "Olympic Hockey Finale Drew Huge Ratings" 2012). Add to this the consumption of McDonald's hamburgers, the attendance at Disney World (Orlando, Tokyo, Paris or Hong Kong), and the more than 800 million active Facebook users, and the sum of it all seems to be that contemporary popular culture is without fixed dimensions, even if in many ways it is quantifiable (website "Number of Active Users of Facebook Over the Years" 2012).

What most obviously sets contemporary popular culture apart from anything preceding it is the mass-produced means of pleasure and entertainment that are now being enjoyed by multitudes never reached before. Moreover, contemporary popular culture is about market-directed activities intended to yield large profits, while personal success is certainly assigned to those individuals who enjoy huge incomes in providing that entertainment. Author of the *Harry Potter* book series J. K. Rowling was worth more than $1 billion in 2012 (earning $1.6 million every three days), and Major League soccer player David Beckham earned $6.5 million in 2011 (websites "Pottermore: How Rich is J.K. Rowling?" and "M.L.S. Salary Figures Released" 2012). Furthermore, popular culture frequently measures its successes either in exquisitely refined statistics (the Men's Double Luge gold medal winner in the Salt Lake City Olympics of 2002 was 0.134 of a second faster than the winner of the silver medal) or in gross numbers (the billionth hamburger produced by

McDonald's was celebrated by its presentation to Art Linkletter, the host of a popular American television program, in 1963).

Folk-like, local activities on the periphery of mass production, which reflect market-driven culture, such as garage sales in the United States or flea markets in Europe, become global endeavors in the virtual space of the internet. Popular culture, which some contend can be traced back to cavemen drawings and Roman graffiti, has been radically altered in the last century principally by the technological changes in communication and transport that have provided billions of consumers with television sets, computers and smart phones; and that have made widely accessible the personal means – the automobile – and the public means – the airplane – to drastically reorder our sense of distance and the nature of travel.

What follows then is a historical interpretation of this development, which is a development of global proportions. The agent that makes most of it possible is unseen and silent but all-pervasive. Electricity gives popular culture its charge. Laser lights and neon signs, electric guitars and microphones, Game Boys and digital cameras – all these devices are obviously dependent on electricity, and the list could easily be extended. The modern home is arranged with numerous electrical outlets, while AAA and cadmium batteries assure portability. And so the underlying premise of this history becomes as obvious as the light bulb – fluorescent or incandescent – by which you are probably reading these words: popular culture is highly visible. We all see more, if not better, than our ancestors or our grandparents, for that matter.

It is estimated that the city dweller sees between 15,000 and 20,000 images a day – on billboards, in shop windows, in magazines and newspapers – images of people and things flashing past as they drive, on the grocery carts they push, and – for a time in New York – projected on to the sidewalks on which they walked; images processed from television, the movies, the computer. Pornographic images, now accessible instantly online in the privacy of one's home, have been critiqued for their portrayal of women and for setting beauty standards that encompass the most intimate arenas of the body; one of the fastest growing cosmetic surgeries of the 2000s – labiaplasty, which involves trimming the inner labia so that they are smaller and symmetrical. Google image search any celebrity – Miley Cyrus, the late Michael Jackson, or Lebron James, for instance, and hundreds of millions of images appear. Ultimately, there's a lot for two eyes to see in any given time.

"More of everything, faster and brighter" thus becomes a meaningful subtitle for this book, chiefly concerned with the proliferation of goods and services delivered at a fast pace and in a brightly illuminated environment.

There is little purpose here in trying to date the origins of popular culture, considering that the Mayans invented popcorn and Queen Elizabeth I's court was introduced to smoking tobacco. However, the abbreviated term "pop" as a qualifier is modern, appearing in England in the 1950s to describe art inspired by consumerism and then music directed to the young. Pop art was best defined by the British artist Richard Hamilton, who provided a list of adjectives to describe the term: transient, expendable, mass-produced, young, witty, sexy, gimmicky, glamorous, big-business. All of these terms apply equally well to contemporary popular culture. However, the one other that Hamilton lists – low cost – certainly is a variable, as suggested by the income figures for Beckham and J. K. Rowling.

Hamilton had shown his hand before he wrote down these qualifying words. His collage "Just what is it that makes today's homes so different, so appealing?" was laid out as a poster announcing an art show in 1956. The collage consisted of crowded and competing images from advertisements, for products ranging from vacuum cleaner to body builder (or vice versa), in an attempt to demonstrate that art – hitherto generally considered as set apart from the clutter of everyday life – now found its subject matter in the advertisements for ever-proliferating consumer products.

While indications of this fusion – or confusion – of art subjects can be found earlier on, most notoriously in the French artist Marcel Duchamp's 1917 sculpture *Fountain*, which was actually a urinal, the embrace of on-the-shelf products as sources of still-life art became widespread only after World War Two, just at the time advertising agents enthusiastically turned to graphic design and color photography. Unquestionably the most celebrated practitioner of such pop art was the American Andy Warhol, famous for his painting of Campbell Soup Company cans and his multiple silkscreen renditions of Marilyn Monroe and Elvis Presley. Warhol, who called his place of work a factory not a studio, rhapsodized that "good business is the best art." He died a wealthy man.

Whatever credence the old expression "art for art's sake" may have had, it certainly was discounted in this turbulent pop-art environment. It was also overturned in academic analysis. Scholars seeking to understand the new phenomenon of globalization, extending beyond the regionalism and internationalization of the previous exchange of goods and services, frequently declared it to be a conflation of economics and culture. Analyzing the various approaches to globalization, Fredric Jameson, a noted literary critic and culture analyst, wrote that in one sense "it means the export and import of culture" (Jameson 1998: 58). To many, then, culture was treated as a commodity, marketable and susceptible to global distribution. CDs, DVDs, and now MP3s and iTunes allow the global sales of music, films and television shows. Fast-food outlets and soft drinks have changed global geography and have universalized certain tastes. There is no denying that popular culture is within easy reach in the form of an ever-expanding number of consumer products.

Although this study is intended to be a general assessment of the major elements of popular culture in the twentieth and early twenty-first centuries, it will not attempt a traditional chronological narrative but will approach the subject in a topical manner. Popular culture is chiefly marked by four characteristics: visualization, commodification, entertainment and technology – the last the means to an end, and hence the energizing and controlling force of the other three. It will therefore be considered first. But first, the setting or environment in which popular culture grew must be treated.

In a 1941 editorial in *Life* magazine, its publisher Henry Luce first labeled the previous century "The American Century." "It now becomes our time," he asserted, "to be the powerhouse from which the ideals spread throughout the world." The powerhouse was at that time also generating popular culture through its unmatched industrial organization, techniques and production. World War Two accelerated and intensified the process of such manufacture and distribution. And after that war, the United States became the creator and arbiter of much of popular culture, as its entrepreneurs expanded into new markets around the world, in a process derisively described as Cocacolonization.

It is difficult to grasp the enormity of the power, wealth and influence of the United States in cultural matters. Comprising just over 4 percent (http://www.census.gov/population/popclockworld.html) of the world's population, this country's percentages are overwhelmingly impressive in economic matters: it leads in high tech design and research (though according to Susan Hockfield, who wrote an Op-Ed for *The New York Times* on manufacturing, innovation and economic recovery there was a $81 billion annual trade deficit in the manufacture of high tech goods in 2011) (website "WorldPOP Clock Projection" 2012). Its economy is the largest in the world, and is approximately a quarter of the global Gross Domestic Product. The Stockholm International Peace Research Institute reports that the country spent $698 billion on its military in 2010, followed by China, which spent $579 billion less, in far second place (website "Military Expenditure" 2012). The English language is the most widely spoken language, even if it does not have the largest number of native speakers, as does China. American media (films, television, computer software) dominate world communications.

The French sociologist Jean Baudrillard makes an unusual case for this dominance in *America*, his most accessible and delightful book, critical ruminations on a trip he took across the United States in 1986. *America* is in large measure a comparison of the American and European cultural scenes. Accepting the notion of a "new world," Baudrillard finds the United States doubly unique: in its spatial expansiveness and in its lack of a configuring past. It is a country of the moment, of an ever-dynamic present. In California he finds the two defining characteristics of this cultural condition: the cinematic and the kinetic. Everything is played out in images, and everything is frenetically paced. What the American perceives of as reality is what is seen on the movie screen and through the automobile windshield.

America, Baudrillard insists, is the "original version of modernity" and all other places are imitations, "dubbed or subtitled versions" (Baudrillard 1988: 76). His emphasis on the visual, just revealed in the reference to films, is found throughout the book, as is his assessment of the kinetic activity, a culture without pause and not given to reflection but the opposite: "instantaneous, depthless refraction," the condition of the television viewer. In the

United States, he concludes, "Culture is space, speed, cinema, technology" (Baudrillard 1988: 100).

Of historical necessity, this text will therefore stress American activity. Soon other nations and enterprises joined in. These were the chief industrial nations of Europe, along with Japan, which remain in the forefront but now include China. The exceptional position of the United States has been determined by its market-based economy, by its widespread neophilia (love of new things), and by its increase of consumer buying power, particularly in the 1970s and 1990s. Where the nation was praised as the "arsenal of democracy" during World War Two, it is today the supermarket of the world: Wal-Mart is currently the most powerful corporation in the world, if judged by annual sales. Sale of consumer goods has become the main national economic indicator. Immediately following the tragic destruction of the twin towers of the New York World Trade Center in 2001, President George W. Bush urged the citizenry of the land to consume, to continue as before.

Today, the United States is in the anomalous position of being the richest and the most indebted nation of the world. It also is in the complementary position of being the greatest producer of popular culture, as well as its greatest consumer. And, it can safely be asserted, the USA has seen the development of more products, both useful and useless, than any other country in history. In the listing of such products would be found the artifacts of popular culture, for example, the computer and bubble gum.

What Jameson and Baudrillard provide – more than most other critics of contemporary consumerist culture – is an explanation of the environment in which popular culture runs loose. The "dynamic" is of images, a riot of things to see. Energy is directed to consumerism and, even grander, "commodification" – which is the marketability of all goods and services. Moreover, both Jameson and Baudrillard describe a contemporary world of a persistent present, unsettled in opinion and intention, accepting and discarding fad and fashion. It is a world of constantly shifting forms and arrangements. Along with other postmodernist critics, they have created a new vocabulary to suggest the departure in thought and theory from the dominant interpretation of the sources of knowledge fostered in the West since the Enlightenment. Terms like decentering, fragmentation, heterarchy and polyculturalism all deny a fixed order of things and a certain way of interpreting reality. These form a refutation of the traditional and dominant thought in the West since the eighteenth century: that collective human behavior was uni-linear in its movement toward improvement or betterment, and best analyzed at the comfortable distance of analyst from subject provided by detachment, therefore objectivity (the ivory tower perspective).

The term "meganarrative" was added to the vocabulary of dissent from this privileged position of Western culture and its supposedly detached, analytical observer. The idea of a particular guiding story line or narrative in which all human activity and all humankind were seen to be marching in the same direction, if at varying speeds and with varying degrees of success, was the particular "meganarrative" that caused the most discomfort. It marginalized or dismissed other cultures and imposed a standard of acceptability of what was fit and proper, to which all were expected to aspire.

Graphically described, the movement to betterment was upward as well as onward, perhaps at a 45-degree angle from the present to the future. The top of the trajectory was occupied by those concerned with the "pursuit of excellence," as the nineteenth-century English art critic John Ruskin put it. These people were the arbiters of taste, the seekers of "goodness and light," another popular term provided by Ruskin. In fact, they were the art and literary critics, the museum directors, the members of academies of art, the university professors and the wealthy patrons who created high or elite culture. Having a further filtered effect was the social order itself, which privileged some and disadvantaged many more. This knowledge/power relationship, as the French theorist Michel Foucault described it, largely determined what creative effort was encouraged, praised and then elevated to the status of "classic."

There is no end of examples in which this or that academy, this or that jury, discarded what was considered unworthy of consideration and yet what was later seen as outstanding. Consider only this now rather amusing declaration made by Paul Johnson in the February 26, 1964 issue of the *New Statesman*. "Those who flock around the Beatles, who scream themselves in hysteria, whose vacant faces flicker over the television screen, are the least fortunate of their generation: the dull, the idle, the failures." Now remember that just a decade and a half ago, Paul McCartney was knighted by Queen Elizabeth II. If the distinctions between high (elitist) and low (popular) culture have not been completely erased, they are becoming insignificant. Here's how Sir Paul recognized the change a few decades back. At the beginning of a royal command performance of the Beatles at the Albert Hall, London, in 1963, he urged: "People in the cheap seats, please clap your hands ... The rest of you, rattle your jewelry." In a jocular manner McCartney was simply suggesting, not declaring, that the distinction between high and low culture was gone; polyculturism, as it has been called, was now part of a decentered and fragmented world. Unity had given way to diversity as the desirable condition of things.

There is no fixed center, no easily measured distance from observer to object observed. The linear metaphors have given way to metaphors of movement, for which the word "swirl" seems an appropriate descriptive term. The swirl of things – characterized by pace, intensity, proliferation of activities and accessibility to goods and entertainment – explains the disappearance of so many of the distinctions made between high culture and low culture. Even such high-culture institutions as the museum, the art gallery, the concert hall and the university have opened to new and diverse audiences, just as they now offer programs that one hundred years ago would have been sternly rejected.

High culture maintained limitations, endorsed exclusivity, restricted membership and fostered excellence. It was circumscribed by formal rules and cherished traditions. Innovation and novelty found little favor; and measure, meaning no excess, was the prescribed pattern of social behavior. High culture grew in a pre-industrial world where land defined wealth, and class determined relationships, and where art, like all else, was limited in its availability.

Popular culture flourishes in a quite different environment. "The modern age," said the architect Frank Gehry in a 1999 television interview, "is an avalanche of stuff coming at you" – coming at you swiftly, inexorably, over-whelmingly. Such is this avalanche of goods and services with which we are all familiar, of which we all partake. It is made possible and widely distributed by industrial production and swift means of transportation and swifter ones of communication, all of which are governed by high technology – and, at the moment, by the microchip. However divided the occupants of the globe still are by political systems, religious beliefs and geography, most of us are living in what has been described as a "democracy of surfaces," where T-shirts and athletic shoes, television sets and smart phones, fast-food shops and auto-mobiles are as much a part of daily life as whatever previously persisted in the local culture. All of this is produced in vast numbers and with the realization that most of it will be quickly consumed or discarded.

The inconstancy and instaneity of popular culture make it a tricky subject to treat. As has been said by many, historical perspective is largely denied. Of the moment, popular culture – like the "pop" of a balloon or the uncorking of a bottle of champagne – indicates a quick change of condition. The expression "here today, gone tomorrow" now has a new urgency.

The première of *Gone with the Wind* (© Bettmann/CORBIS)

1 Popular culture in the early twentieth-century world

"Produce! Produce! Were it but the pitifullest infinitesimal fraction of a product, produce it in God's name!" implored the Scottish political philosopher Thomas Carlyle in 1834. And so the century did through the development of an industrial system that made the factory the center of production, steam the motivating force and iron the construction material of the new age. Railroad lines criss-crossed the countries of Europe and by 1869 bound together the United States. The Brooklyn Bridge spanned outward, and the Eiffel Tower rose skyward in testimony to this constructive age that shortened distances, crowded cities and facilitated comfort in domestic life to a degree hitherto unknown. Canned food and cotton clothing, cakes of soap and bars of chocolate candy were obvious signs that an economy of scarcity (think of a fairy tale like "Hansel and Gretel") was being replaced by an economy of abundance, with the department store, appearing first at mid-century in Paris, offering particular testimony.

All this activity was celebrated as progress, especially in the world's fairs, those nineteenth-century showcases of ever-increasing and ever-innovative products. For all that, no previous technological changes were so tightly clustered together as the industrial advancements that appeared in the first dozen years of the twentieth century. They initially defined the dimensions of contemporary popular culture and also provided the instruments that would form it. In this brief period, inventions and technical improvements moved the industrial base from steam and iron to gasoline and electricity. The bulkiness of the first phase of industrial development, so evident in the steam train, a powerful but inefficient instrument, was succeeded by swifter and less spatially restricted means of communication.

In 1901, the first Mercedes appeared, a well-built and highly maneuverable automobile soon to become an enduring brand name. It was a vehicle that helped convert the automobile from a novelty to a new form of individual transportation. A few years later, in 1908, Henry Ford introduced his Model-T, the world's best-selling car for nearly a half century until the Volkswagen Beetle came along. Heard but not seen in that year of the first Mercedes was the first transatlantic wireless (radio) message, the contribution of the Italian scientist Guglielmo Marconi. Seen but not heard in that year were the photographs produced by the Eastman Kodak Company's Brownie camera, the first camera mass-produced for personal use.

Now add to the list of technological changes two other items: a new invention and the popularization of an earlier one. In 1903 the Wright brothers left the ground briefly in their airplane. In 1909 the Frenchman Louis Blériot crossed the English Channel in his, suggesting that the machine could traverse long distances while avoiding down-to-earth obstacles. In 1910, the Gaumont Palace opened in Paris, a 5,000-seat movie theater, the first of its kind and the model for a new form of ticketed entertainment: the movies or cinema. Pictures projected on a screen were the contribution of the French Lumière brothers who introduced the technique in 1895.

All these developments increased the pace, the visual range and the forms of modern popular culture. They were cinematic and kinetic, the terms Jean Baudrillard used to describe the late twentieth-century American scene. They were not, however, dominantly American. What understandably gave the sparkle and dazzle to America at the turn of the century was electricity or, more accurately stated, its practical application. Some of the basic electrical terms, ohms, amperes and voltage, were derived from the last names of European scientists investigating the properties of electricity, after Benjamin Franklin, flying a kite in a thunderstorm, got the shock of his life.

In the United States and in the year 1879, Thomas Alva Edison had successfully concluded his search for a durable filament that would burn long and bright so that electricity might serve widely as a new means of illumination. Yet the really dazzling announcement of the electric age came in that busy year, 1901. The Pan-American International Exposition in Buffalo, New York had its several hundred thousand incandescent lights, the most impressive light show of the time, illuminated by a new generator placed at the base of Niagara Falls. The wires running the twenty miles between the Exposition site and the Falls were the first of what is everywhere called a national grid, a network of wires reaching hundreds of miles and assuring that electricity would be the silent servant of the vast majority of people. The Exposition itself recognized the potential of electric light in its Electric Tower, nearly 400 feet high. One commentator declared that the structure "shines like diamonds." What the creators of the exposition had succeeded in doing was to make electric light an integral part of architectural design. The buildings were bathed in light, not spotlighted, previously the dominant form of night illumination.

Jean Baudrillard follows a long tradition in calling the United States he visited in 1986 "dynamic." What stood out brightly in the night sky of Buffalo a century ago was the work of heavily humming dynamos. Artificial light changed night from threatening darkness to attractive brightness. It became the signature of American – and then of all – contemporary popular culture. The Japanese architect Toyo Ito wrote that, after twilight, Tokyo becomes a "jungle of lights," in distinct opposition to its daytime appearance (Ito 1997: 32).

Las Vegas presents a similar contrast, a desert town that blooms in neon colors at night. Everywhere the daytime city invites, everywhere the nighttime city beckons. Contemporary popular culture bathes in the nightly spectacular.

Unlike mercy, which Shakespeare's Portia said falls gently as the rain from heaven, electricity now zooms through space and strongly charges popular culture. It is no exaggeration to say that all contemporary popular culture depends on electrically powered developments and practices. Entertainment, travel, telecommunications – the major popular culture industries – are all energized electrically.

Wheels and reels start rolling

In 1911, Henry Ford opened a car assembly plant in Manchester, England, where he produced his famous Model-T. Charlie Chaplin, born in London in 1889, migrated to the United States and first appeared in tramp garb in a 1914 Mack Sennett film titled *Mabel's Strange Predicament*. A decade later the Model-T was the most widely distributed automobile, and Charlie Chaplin was the most widely recognized film actor. Car and star were major elements in the internationalization of popular culture. Each commodity was widely appreciated. In much of the world, the noisy Ford and the silent Chaplin required no knowledge of a different language, customs or habits to assure much pleasure.

The name Ford was less identified with the man and Detroit than with new personal convenience and a novel method of production. Aldous Huxley satirized the assembly line in his dystopian novel *Brave New World* (1932) where Ford was worshiped as a deity ruling over a new religion: a system of earthly organization in which efficiency was the goal and manufactured happiness the implied mood. Huxley's acid criticism was not mentioned when in 1999 the Ford Motor Car Company received the "Car of the Century Award" for its Model-T. The organizer of the event, Dick Holzhhaus of the Netherlands, declared: "It was Henry Ford's vision to give people unprecedented mobility that changed the lives of millions throughout the world." Introduced in 1908, the Model-T accounted for 56 percent of global automobile production by 1927.

Chaplin had a similar global effect: he became the modern Everyman, making film comedy into skillful pantomime and graceful acrobatics. This was predominantly a visual experience in the days before the "talkies" were introduced. Even in his 1936 film *Modern Times*, a parody of Ford's industrial process, sound was primarily limited to music, the dialogue maintained as subtitles. Chaplin strongly helped to internationalize movies through his gestures and identification with the "little man" caught up in a world marked by economic and political uncertainty, with the dehumanizing influence of World War One and the industrial system.

The dream factory

Movies were an industrial art, produced for both entertainment and profit. Chaplin was living proof of the fact: he was the first star to receive a $1 million contract, that in 1918. Because movie production was an expensive undertaking, it quickly became the work of large companies, and the film became a new variant of the industrial corporation. Some have said that the movie industry, like the Ford Motor Company, was organized vertically: all activity from script writing, to casting, to filming and editing placed under single control. Equally significant was the further control imposed through what has been called the "studio system." By the 1930s five major companies had gained an oligopolistic control of the industry. Not only did they produce the films, but also they controlled distribution through the movie houses they owned. Paramount Pictures, for instance, owned 1,000 movie theaters.

A new palace of pleasure, unlike any seen before, the movie theater became the centerpiece of popular culture, far exceeding its only rival at the time, the seasonally restricted amusement park. Movie theater architecture was a new hybrid. Its once garish and now celebrated marquee – the dazzlingly lit front overhang – was more tantalizing for most who frequented the movies than that of the opera house and hotel. Its neon lights and incandescent bulbs were used to spell out the names of the features. Its façade was kitsch on the grand scale, imaginative pastiches of Arabian or Venetian palaces, Egyptian or Chinese temples. Lobbies were equally grand, as indeed was the theater itself. Some, like the theater of Radio City, New York, were done in the Art Deco manner with sleek lines and indirect lighting, impressive in itself, but enhanced – again, as was Radio City – by its stage presentations, particularly the long line of long-legged girls tap-dancing in unison as the Rockettes.

To add a further sense of drama to the movie theater scene, Sid Grauman, showman and entrepreneur who built several of the finest movie theaters of the time, introduced the idea of the première. As the name suggests, this was the first showing of a new film, attended by Hollywood's celebrities and carried on radio, in newspapers and newsreels as a major "event," a sterling example of the new phenomenon, the celebration as newsworthy. Even the Nazi propaganda film *Triumph of the Will* had such a première in Berlin in 1935. In attendance were, among others, Adolf Hitler and his propaganda minister Joseph Goebbels.

From the red carpet frequently rolled out for this occasion to the same rollout for an awards ceremony required little imaginative leap. The industry's newly established Academy of Motion Picture Arts and Sciences held its first awards night on May 16, 1929 at a hotel banquet, when award-winners received recognition for what were voted to be the best pictures and acting of the previous year. In the following year, the ceremony was carried on local radio. But it was not until 1944 that the Oscar Awards ceremony was made a network theatrical "event" – hosted by Grauman at his Chinese Theater in Hollywood – and broadcast overseas to America's military, then fighting in World War Two.

In 1940, as a result of news leakage, the announcement of awards gained new suspense: the names were sealed in envelopes, to be opened during the ceremony. Hardware had by then been made the essential part of the event. In 1934 the Oscar made its appearance. A 24-carat gold-plated, bronze trophy in the form of a medieval knight, the statuette was presented to actors and actresses of "merit." An annual blend of pomp, kitsch and fashion show, the Academy Awards were a twentieth-century spectacular, joined by other such film ceremonies elsewhere after World War Two.

Certainly there were many films and actors to choose from each year. With the introduction of double-feature shows in the 1930s and the growing popularity of newsreels and cartoons, production was maintained at a fast clip. And stars were distributed as were cars, through extensive advertising and publicity. Not surprisingly, many stars were photographed standing by the splendid cars they owned, testimony to new wealth and to the new mobility of the age. Their homes, spread out on well-manicured lawns, soon created a new geographical exercise for the sightseer, that of following the readily available maps of the homes of the stars. The emergence of movie magazines and fan clubs also added to Hollywood's growing reputation as Tinsel Town.

Even though movie production was an international activity in the interwar period, with European countries developing national production companies and creating films of great merit, Hollywood dominated. The magnetic attraction of the studios was so strong (money, facilities, national and international markets) that film directors and actors from abroad gathered in the Los Angeles suburb. Greta Garbo and Ingrid Bergman from Sweden, Hedy Lamarr and Paul Henreid from Austria, Cary Grant and Laurence Olivier from England, Charles Boyer from France and Marlene Dietrich from Germany – to name a few – settled in. Alfred Hitchcock, thoroughly English, was only the most famous of a series of European directors who made films there. And the popularity of the sub-genre of American-made British Empire films, of which *Gunga Din* (1939) eventually became the classic, led to the establishment of a British colony of actors there. Only one other film center rivaled Hollywood in scale of production and distribution: the Indian. Primarily settled in Bombay (now known as Mumbai), the name "Bollywood" was attached to this major film-manufacturing site.

Since the early work of D. W. Griffith (director of the Jim Crow-era racist epic *Birth of a Nation* [1915]), who introduced the moving camera trolley and the fade-out, Hollywood was acclaimed for its innovative techniques and practices. The feature film (a major production running about 90 minutes), genres (cowboy, South Sea romance, gangster-urban – forerunners of today's action films – and *film noir* which used lighting and effective use of the black-and-white medium to create a brooding or sinister atmosphere) defined Hollywood's stock-in-trade.

For sheer dramatic achievement, great credit must go to Walt Disney who turned crude animated cartoons into doubly fabled productions – the consummate skill of the animators and the use of animals as characters. No other Hollywood star approached and then exceeded the international reputation of Charlie Chaplin except Mickey Mouse. Making his screen debut in *Steamboat Willie* (1928), Mickey took on his definitive form by 1930. He became a feature actor in Disney's *Fantasia* (1940). Popular with all ages and in many places, Mickey even – unwittingly – made an appearance in Nazi Germany. He served as the "mascot" of a German fighter pilot, who had the mouse's likeness painted on the fuselage of his plane.

The automobile and the film, the one running on wheels and gasoline, the other on reels and electricity, were the most significant early twentieth-century technological advancements in the internationalization of popular culture. Film reels and car wheels epitomized speed and rhythm, as the film moved at 24 frames a second and the car engine turned at something like 3,000 revolutions per minute. Such speed created new allusions and illusions about reality. Both devices emerged from the industrial environment. Just as Henry Ford perfected mass production, Hollywood created a "dream factory."

The open road

The automobile promised a new freedom, or so Henry Ford said, the freedom of the road. The movie promised escape too, from the confines, the cares and the cacophony of the modern industrial city. Together, they created a new vision of things, of speed, of pleasure, of fun on-the-go. This relationship was particularly established in the romantic films of the 1930s where the convertible, ragtop down, served as the perfect intimate setting in which the debonair hero could engage in love-talk with the heroine, as her long hair was sensually caressed by the breezes stirred up by the powerful car rolling along the uncluttered road.

More often than not, the car stood still in the film studio with the countryside rolling by on projected background film, while breezes were generated by fans and wind machines. The car did indeed roll along the road in other films of other moods, the generic gangster film, most obviously, but also in *The Grapes of Wrath* (1940) in which a makeshift old truck conveys the hardship of the Depression days. Today, it is impossible to think of an action film that does not have a major car wreck or explosion in order to assure brilliant destruction.

As some of these connections might suggest, the automobile was not only utilitarian but also admirable. It became an industrial art form, its shapely contours engendered by the attraction for men (the vast majority of owners and drivers) of its fine curves and appealing lines. Thus viewed as a new graven image to be worshiped, the automobile invited pilgrimage to the annual automobile shows, notably in the United States and Europe. Perhaps the most famous was the Salon de automobile in Paris, an international event that continues to this day. These shows might also be considered new forms of theater featuring bright and sparkling models, with chrome for decoration, the automobile itself often placed on a revolving pedestal. As at the beauty contests that entered the popular culture scene at the same time (the first Miss America contest was held at Atlantic City in 1929), the automobile received the ardent male gaze.

The Romantic poet John Keats rhapsodized that "a thing of beauty is a joy forever." Not so in this modern world, where the physical beauty that aroused joy was the quality of youthfulness, while the automobile was manufactured on the principle of newness. To assure the appearance of change, cars were manufactured according to what was called "creative obsolescence," hence the idea of "model years" and the annual automobile show, where the shape of fenders, the size and location of headlights and the grill, of course, were all regularly redesigned and realigned to suggest further change toward better, more powerful and more graceful movement ahead. Remember that among the adjectives Richard Hamilton listed when he defined "pop art" was transitory. Popular culture, like all industrial activity in the twentieth century, sought and praised the new. Someone coined the term "neophilia" to express this sentiment.

The automobile also became an instrument of social change, notably in the United States. A driver's license was a young person's rite of passage, a "jalopy" was often his means – and occasionally hers – of detachment from family dependency. The closed sedan, an interwar innovation, gave the woman a comforting independence as well, some historians have asserted, as she drove herself to her own activities and also drove to accommodate those of her children. Youthful sex was enacted in the car, thus replacing the barn with an easily moved venue offering greater seclusion and intimacy. On the sober side of things, the traffic light, invented in 1923, altered road behavior and soon made drivers pavlovian in their responses worldwide. In 1935, the parking meter made its appearance, to regulate parking and gain revenue in Oklahoma City. Automobile advertisements now rivaled those for cigarettes in the space they occupied in magazines, and excelled cigarettes in the poetry of their copy. Automobile races – the Indianapolis 500 perhaps the most famous – became a new form of spectator sport; the gasoline station was a new architectural feature; and the parking meter added to the complexities of the motorized city street. Incidentally, the French boasted of having the remotest of gasoline pumps, one situated in the Sahara desert.

This automobile culture was certainly predominantly an American condition of the interwar era: Americans owned 17,481,000 automobiles in 1925. However, the automobile was also transforming the land forms and life forms of other peoples as well, if not on a comparable scale. The four other major automobile manufacturing countries – Britain, France, Germany and Italy – collectively counted only 1,631,000 car owners. Japan had 25,000.

Certainly, the automobile was the most recognizable and celebrated instrument of modern industrial technology. It was praised in poetry and art, was the subject of cartoons and children's stories. Perhaps the best known of these were *The Wind in the Willows*, a story written by the Englishman Kenneth

Grahame in 1908 and centering on a car-struck Mr. Toad; and the story of an unusually talented and cleverly anthropomorphized mouse who drove his flashy red convertible about in E. B. White's now classic *Stuart Little* (1945).

By this time, the automobile also became a literary trope expressive of modern power and authority. F. Scott Fitzgerald made a white Duesenberg just such an expression in his novel *The Great Gatsby* (1925): the heroine Daisy is driving it when she hits the wife of the owner of a small gasoline station. Warren Penn Warren, in his Pulitzer Prize-winning novel *All the King's Men* (1946), begins the narrative with a description of the American South as a place " ... where the age of the internal combustion engine has come into its own ... Where the eight cylinder jobs come roaring around the curves in the red hills and scatter the gravel like spray ... " The German author Ernst Jünger used a large, sleek automobile as the metaphor for destructive Nazi power in his *On the Marble Cliffs* (1939).

Cars and films were the two primary examples of a popular culture that was altering the social order with greater personal mobility and intensifying, formal entertainment. The automobile soon included a new element that made that formal or manufactured entertainment available "onboard." This is the car radio.

The invisible companion

Radio transmission had begun in the early 1920s and was sufficiently widespread and popular that in 1932 King George V started the annual royal custom of giving a Christmas message to his subjects, followed shortly thereafter by Franklin D. Roosevelt when he introduced the idea of "fireside chats" as informal talks to the American public. During World War Two, Winston Churchill used the radio to project to the British public a voice of strength and encouragement. No one, however, made more effective use of the radio than Adolf Hitler who harangued the Germans and the world at great length on his policies. As such the radio became a major instrument of the new state policy of deception: propaganda.

That trajectory of radio popularity rose higher with the car radio. First made commercially viable in 1930 by Paul Galvin, head of Galvin Manufacturing Company, this car radio was given the name "Motorola," which, according to the company's history, inferred a combination of motion and sound. In the following year, the company started making police radios.

The radio was the first electronic device to enter the intimate space of the individual: it sat grandly in the living room, soon assumed a more discreet position on the bedroom table, and became a major feature in the dashboard of the automobile. The radio could potentially be heard anywhere, soon broadcasting at great ranges. For instance, the British Broadcasting Company began its "Empire Service" with broadcasts to Australia and New Zealand in 1932.

What gave radio the edge over print as a source of information was its ability to bring news quickly to the public. The term "news flash," popularized in the 1930s, is verbal proof of this fact. The other radio advantage was its ability to extend the range and quality of entertainment. Music, ranging from grand opera to popular tunes, filled the airwaves. Then, there was the "theater of the air," radio dramas that commanded large audiences. The most famous of these and the most frequently cited as an example of the effectiveness of radio as an audible determinant of public behavior was Orson Welles' 1938 adaptation of H. G. Wells' science fiction novel *The War of the Worlds* (1898). Broadcast as one program on the weekly Mercury Theater of the Air, the episode began like a "breaking" news story; listeners assumed that's what it was and responded in fear and confusion. Many people in New Jersey, where the Martian landing was said to have taken place, fled their homes. Welles was propelled to fame by the broadcast, and the effects of it have provided a case history in books on social psychology.

But for sheer familiarity, as an invisible but regularly present companion, radio allowed the American housewife to leave the confinement of her home on airwaves. The serial melodramas known as "soap operas," because their sponsors were generally manufacturers of soap products, provided both dramatic distraction and involvement for the housewife as she did the chores of ironing, dusting, preparing meals. Cast in a 15-minute daily format, the shows pretended to dramatize ordinary travails of romance and home life, so listeners easily identified with them. With the advent of television, the "soaps" extended into 30- and 60-minute formats.

Although the longest-running of the radio soap operas, *The Guiding Light*, reached its 65th birthday in 2002, and was ultimately cancelled in 2009, this new audio art form has been outrun by sports broadcasting. Sports, played to national regulations on permanent playing areas, grew rapidly more popular in the late nineteenth century. More and more spectators were beginning to show "fan loyalty" just as radio was catching on. One of the very first radio broadcasts was of a major sporting event, the boxing match between the American boxer, Jack Dempsey, and a French war hero, Georges Carpentier. Held in an improvised stadium in Jersey City, New Jersey, on July 2, 1921, it was billed as the "world championship." Then on August 5, 1921, the first play-by-play baseball broadcast was aired by radio station KDKA in Pittsburgh. In a few years, American college football, Canadian hockey and British tennis at Wimbledon became broadcast features. In 1924, commentary on the Olympic Games first went out on the airwaves.

A symbiotic relationship between broadcasting and professional sports quickly grew. Radio, like television later, helped both generate and satisfy the growing popularity of major team sports.

The range of subject matter, from sports events to news commentary, by way of soap operas, made radio the most versatile medium of communication yet devised. Moreover, its direct and easy transmission assured it quick entrance into the individual household: no opening of the front door was required. The previous barriers – and safeguards – that stood between public and private space began to erode through this invisible but welcome intrusion. Radio was like the automobile, a technological development that enhanced mass communications in a highly personal way. Both were therefore frequently referred to as "liberating," even as they established new modes of conformity.

Showing off

Unlike most other parts of the world, the United States did not go for government-sponsored radio: it was given over to private enterprise. The federal government allotted licenses and assigned wavelengths, but the various stations and networks funded themselves through advertising (as the "soap operas" suggested). The activity began early: in 1923 Eveready batteries sponsored an entertainment program, and by 1926 commercial radio was firmly established. This pattern followed the print medium in which advertising had already assumed a major role. W. K. Kellogg, the cereal manufacturer, began newspaper ads in 1906 and spent $1 million on such advertising in 1915. In 1911 Procter & Gamble introduced its new shortening, Crisco, by way of newspaper ads.

None of this is to suggest that advertising was suddenly a twentieth-century activity. However, what distinguished the new advertising was threefold: the role of agencies, the development of campaigns and strategies, and the dominance of illustration. The three elements form a coherent whole.

"Albert Lasker," states a Lasker Foundation promotional piece, "can justifiably be called the founder of the modern advertising industry" (website "about albert lasker" 2003: 1). What Lasker established – and others accepted – was copywriting that asserted the primacy of the product in its field. This was a competitive approach to advertising, a sort of mine-is-much-better-than-yours assertion that has remained the fundamental principle of the ad business.

A corollary to "first in its field" was the "indirect copy approach" pioneered by Raymond Rubicam, who began as a copywriter and then in 1923 co-founded Young & Rubicam, which became the world's largest advertising agency. His well-known slogan of success – "Resist the usual" – was followed by the indirect copy approach, which focused on the reader, not the product. As a result, the advertising seemed to reflect the reader's interests or, as Rubicam advised, "Mirror the reader to himself." He strengthened this approach by research into public preferences, thus profiling readers' – and then listeners' – attitudes.

Rubicam also developed "picture-sequence copy," in the manner of comic strips. This concept became a significant factor in making advertising ever more dominated by pictures. The roots of contemporary illustrated advertising were in poster art. Posting ads on city kiosks and country fences (or barns, in the American tradition) was a familiar practice, and the posters themselves became an art form. The *fin-de-siècle* artist Toulouse-Lautrec is the quintessential poster artist. In the interwar period, the poster expanded into the billboard, and the illustration grew to occupy complete pages of magazines. Movie ads formed a new aspect of poster art and now are highly valuable "collectibles." Placed in theater lobbies and illuminated showcases outside, they graphically presented the drama, comedy or romance the film provided.

The three products most regularly treated to this expansive illustrating were the two already considered – automobiles and movies – and a third, which joined and even outpaced them: cigarettes. All three were fundamental elements in the chemistry of early twentieth-century popular culture. It's hard, for instance, to imagine the movie star – in film and advertising – without a cigarette. It is equally hard to imagine the success of the *film noir*, the brooding and mysterious detective or thriller film, without the intended effect of cigarette smoke adding to the uncertainty or obscurity of the plot. Humphrey Bogart, for instance, all but made the cigarette an external part of his personality. When Bette Davis, film sex symbol of the 1930s, ground a cigarette into an ash tray, the sense of anger or wrath was converted into a dramatic action. Paul Henreid added to cigarette allure when, in the film *Now, Voyager* (1942), he lit two cigarettes at once and then handed one to Miss Davis, an act found scandalous by some viewers.

In its own way the cigarette, like the automobile, became a symbol of power and a sign of sexual prowess. It was waved and wielded, lit up with grace or in anger, its smoke exhaled quickly in assertion, slowly in anticipation. It was a conversation piece by providing a visual interpretation of the pregnant pause, as in the dialogue of Humphrey Bogart (as Rick) in *Casablanca* (1942). It was an invitation to sexual intimacy, as when Anne Bancroft (as the sexually aggressive Mrs. Robinson) asks Dustin Hoffman (the uninitiated Benjamin Braddock) to light her cigarette in *The Graduate*. The jaunty air that President Franklin D. Roosevelt made popular was achieved by a cigarette holder held at an upward angle between his front teeth. The British actor George Sanders, playing the consummate cad Addison DeWitt – a theatre critic – in the film *All About Eve* (1950), enhanced his role by using a cigarette holder as a marker to underline his cynicism and verbal cruelty.

In quite a different context, advertisements frequently showed sports figures holding cigarettes, the suggestion being, of course, that cigarettes were enabling agents. Cigarette ads were among the most extensive and popular in the United States in the twentieth century. In an evaluation of the "Top 100 Advertising Campaigns" of the twentieth century, the publication *Advertising Age* in 2001 listed five cigarette ads. They were: the Marlboro Man (1959), the Winston ad "Winston tastes good like a cigarette should" (1954), the Camel ad "I'd walk a mile for a Camel" (1921) and the Lucky Strike ad "Reach for a Lucky instead of a sweet" (1923). The fifth ad showed the new temper of the 1960s: it was a Benson and Hedges ad captioned "The disadvantages."

Six automobile advertisements made that top-100 list, the earliest being a Cadillac ad of 1915. Automobile ads of the interwar period, unlike those now so widespread on television, were generally quite staid, showing the vehicle in profile or at a 45-degree angle from a head-on and down-low viewpoint to suggest the vehicle's power. The youth market was notably absent from such advertising, and the car as an instrument of carefree pleasure, so prominent in the movies, was little seen in advertisements. Its appeal was primarily directed to the typical American family, the Dick and Jane sort, with two soberly dressed parents – dad at the wheel. In a 1939 De Soto ad, though, Ginger Rogers – holding a tennis racket and standing before a four-door sedan – said: "I like action … I get it in my De Soto."

French ads for American cars tended to depict the vehicles in more nimble action, appearing to climb or descend quickly and surely. A Chrysler ad of 1927, ten years before the Ginger Rogers one (De Soto being manufactured by Chrysler), contained a broad-stroke sketch of a fashionable young French woman ecstatically holding on to the steering wheel; the text read: "The new pleasure provided by the automobile."

Visions of the future wheeled out

As in the movies, if not in the advertising of the interwar period, the automobile was envisioned as the major source of future urban movement and form. The comic book hero Batman, making his caped appearance in 1939, did not depend on superhuman powers. Unlike Superman, Batman got around Gotham City in a supercharged Batmobile. City planners and architects anticipated fast-moving city traffic, if not at Batman's rocket-like pace. Their future vision turned out to be our contemporary nightmare: those "spaghetti junctions" that serve as the entranceways to all major cities.

The motor city dream never appeared more attractive and real than in the downscaled form it received in the 1939 New York World's Fair "Democracity." Located in the globe-like "Perisphere," one of the dual Trylon and Perisphere signature structures, "Democracity" was described in the official guide book as an imagined city of one million, the "symbol of a perfectly integrated, futuristic metropolis pulsing with life and rhythm and music." The traffic moved swiftly and quietly around the geometric design of the cityscape, its orderly high rises marching one after the other. "Democracity" followed similar schemes of urban supermodernity sketched by the famous French-Swiss architect Le Corbusier who planned a comparable city of one million in which the automobile dominated, with sidewalks and pedestrians receding from the scene and buildings in effect serving as masonry channels through which the traffic moved.

This shape of things-to-come did come about – in greater frequency and intensity than the urban dreamers expected. The automobile arbitrated urban development after World War Two.

Razzle dazzle

Among the many terms entering the vocabulary of popular culture in the interwar period, one effectively describes the conditions of the time. It is "razzle dazzle." Often used to describe a sudden, unexpected and apparently confusing football play, the term had extended its meaning to explain any flashy and spectacular action that was forming part of spectator entertainment. It has, for instance, been used in discussion of Hollywood productions.

"Razzle dazzle" also serves well as a descriptive of the dramatic changes of rhythm and pace in the 1920s and 1930s. The dominance of urban life in the Western world was confirmed in the 1930s when France, last of the major industrial powers, saw its population shift from a predominantly rural to a predominantly urban base. Urban life, with its own rhythm, expressed the change noisily in the fad of tap dancing. Its rapid beat and metallic sound made it a near-perfect analogue of the industrial system and its efficient use of machinery. Frederick Taylor's time–motion studies coordinated the worker's actions with the beat of the machine. "Taylorization" was made artful by the movie team of Ginger Rogers and Fred Astaire as they whirled around and danced with seeming indefatigable coordination in a series of Hollywood musicals of the 1930s.

The machine-like precision of the chorus line was visually perfected by the film director and choreographer Busby Berkeley. Arguably, his most celebrated film was *Gold Diggers of 1933*. His use of the camera as a moveable instrument led to a series of overhead shots, his specialty. Berkeley's experience in the army during World War One – when he trained large numbers of soldiers in drills – inspired his technique; its appeal in film derived from the audience's ability to see human motion in which a whole flowed and undulated with a grace denied to its individual performers.

A comparable development in industrial design was in its initial phase often called "streamlining," an effort to create curvaceous, tear-drop forms to diminish the wind resistance to moving objects like cars, trains and airplanes. The angle of passenger ship funnels and the shape of car fenders swooped backward. The Union Pacific Railroad Company in 1934 introduced a special six-car passenger train pulled by a bulbous-fronted diesel engine, the unit called the "Streamliner." Household objects, from toasters to refrigerators, moved from the rectangular to the more curvaceous – and the best of these entered museums as examples of modern industrial art. These objects spoke of grace, smooth efficiency and an age on the move.

Pace, considered as increments of time, was altered socially as well. The 90-minute full length movie, the 15-minute soap opera episode on radio, the car moving at 35 miles an hour or the airplane at 190 miles an hour changed the long enduring sun-up, sun-down arrangement of diurnal life that seldom extended beyond the distance an individual could walk in daylight. Electricity altered the urban pattern of existence and gave popular culture its nocturnal hours of entertainment. Night clubs and cabarets became commonplace in the Western world; night baseball and soccer games, illuminated by pods of high-voltage light, changed the nature of spectator sports. Neon tubing added to urban nighttime glitz. Frenchman Georges Claude applied an electrical discharge to a glass tube of neon gas in the early 1900s, which caused neon and other gases to combine. The resulting blue, yellow and red coloring made electrical signage an art form and allowed the entertainment districts of cities as far apart as Tokyo, New York, London and Las Vegas to glow in a swirl of nightly color.

By the 1930s the so-called developed world had been electrified. It seemed that V. I. Lenin's famous definition was a truism for all social systems. "Communism," he declared, "is Soviet power plus the electrification of the whole country." Electricity flowed everywhere and in a vaster array of applications than all previous energy systems had provided. The vital juice of popular culture flowed through the wire.

Every element of contemporary popular culture depended directly or indirectly on electricity. Of course, talent and organization are partially exempt – but not even in the early 1920s would Rudolph Valentino have had any significance if his profile had not been filmed, while no one in the late 1930s could have imagined Frank Sinatra crooning other than into a microphone. Electricity charged the "celebrity," he or she became famous for being seen. Filmed and photographed, appearing in ads and in publicity releases, sought after for autographed photographs, the celebrity may have promoted the sale of breakfast cereal or cigarettes but primarily promoted self – or images of self. The publicity agent and the make-up artist, two new professionals, were responsible for assuring that the celebrity was presented in the best light. In a delightful aside in his book *America*, Jean Baudrillard wrote: "Americans may have no identity, but they do have wonderful teeth" (Baudrillard 1988: 34). The celebrity necessarily does today, as he or she did in the 1920s.

Brand recognition

Appearances extended to "brand recognition," a new form of promotion that would become a major characteristic of marketing after World War Two. Logos and symbols represented particular companies and corporations but also implied a distinctive quality not otherwise available. Ford and Coca-Cola, for instance, developed the print style of their corporate name – stylized cursives in the 1920s that they have retained ever since. Animals figured too: Mickey Mouse, recently renewed as a copyrighted figure, was quickly and then inextricably identified with Disney films and products. MGM had a roaring lion as its logo; the French film company Pathé used a rooster. Logos took wing with the airlines. Lufthansa used a sleek stylized bird in flight; Air France concocted a seahorse with wings; Pan-American Airways first used a winged arrow and later a stylized globe.

The most memorable incidence of brand recognition concerned no company, no product. When the Nazis took over power in Germany in 1933, they made the swastika the logo of their rule. Stark black, firmly rectangular, usually situated in a white circle in a field of bright red, this variant of an ages-old religious symbol, found both in Hindu and Native American cultures, came to represent the ruthlessness of Nazi power. On the flags everywhere present in Germany of the late 1930s, on armbands and party pins, on the huge vertical tail fins of the Zeppelin *Hindenburg* and on the foredeck of the battleship *Bismarck*, the swastika stamped the identity of the regime.

One of the most dramatic scenes in the Nazi propaganda film *Triumph of the Will* gives the illusion of a vast sea of flags moving inexorably onward. Here was a visual expression of Nazism as a "mass movement."

It was in the interwar period that the term "mass" entered the vocabulary of social theorists. Mass transportation, mass communications and mass entertainment joined older terms like urban mass and mass production to explain the quantitative effect on quality. Numbers added up to a qualitatively different social and cultural environment. This new statistical scale – in which newspaper circulation, box-office receipts and radio listener figures were measured in the millions – indicated a new spatial/temporal relationship. Spatially, popular culture engaged wider and more diversified audiences and participants than it ever had before. National and international markets now developed for its products, as movies and films clearly demonstrated. In an amusing comment on this development, a New Zealand movie critic said in 1945 that if New Zealand had a particular culture, it was "to a large extent a creation of Hollywood." Only drinking tea was more popular than going to the movies (Daley 2003: n.p.).

Temporally, everyone and everything closed in, became both more immediate and intimate – but less personal and direct – than the neighborhood or town had been. Telephone and radio joined to bring the previously faraway and out-of-touch into the intimacy of the house – and did so frequently, every day and even hourly. But the physical presence that neighborhood gossip and downtown politics had been based on – a whisper or an aside, a hand on the shoulder or a finger sharply pointed in anger – such tactile qualities – were absent. Disembodied voices now formed public opinion. Virtual reality was decades away.

Then World War Two occurred. In the early morning of December 7, 1941, two years and three months after Nazi Germany had invaded Poland and begun the world war, Japanese aircraft approaching Pearl Harbor homed in on the radio frequency of Honolulu radio stations playing popular music. The new war expanded the dimensions of popular culture.

The world goes to war: Bob Hope (1903–2003) entertaining troops on New Georgia in the Solomon Islands, January 1, 1944 (© Bettmann/CORBIS)

2 Popular culture joins the war effort

Along with the explosion of countless bombs and artillery shells, popular culture burst on the landscape of World War Two. Consumer products and entertainment, pleasure and diversion – particularly for the millions of young Americans who became soldiers – were introduced to large numbers of civilians in war-torn countries. Chewing gum and candy bars, the jokes of Bob Hope, and the music of Glenn Miller were such military exports. Like the simply drawn figure with nose and fingers appearing over a wall, with the caption "Kilroy was here," popular culture became widely familiar, if not commonplace.

As warfare expanded to new dimensions, so did the manufacture and distribution of military equipment. What was later called "globalization" – worldwide marketing, primarily of commodities, by multinational corporations – was first battle-tested. The most significant (if unintended) effects of the war effort on postwar popular culture were aspects of this spread of things. The two chief ones were spatial: proximity and mobility, an exceptional distribution of goods and services reaching most war fronts, and reaching them quickly, a phenomenon that would only increase after the war to become the vast commodification of our own age.

The goods of the good war

Declared by many historians to be the "good war," World War Two was also the goods war. In the Melanesian islands arose the "cargo cult," a belief in a forthcoming time of plenty that had anterior roots. Islanders, witnessing American landing vehicles discharging quantities of goods, assumed the beneficence was the gift of some offshore, unseen deity. The cult was built around the premise that the ships would come again in the future. For the Trust Territories, the Pacific islands placed by the United Nations under American trust for administration, the expression "Rust Territories" was soon coined in ironic humor about the vast quantities of war material left behind when the war was over.

War material both amazed populations around the world and littered their places of residence. President Franklin D. Roosevelt had none of this in mind when he referred to the United States as the "arsenal of democracy." Nor could he imagine that the country was becoming the proto-supermarket to the world. If any proof were needed of this "avalanche of stuff coming at you," to go back to Gehry's statement, it was easily and amply provided by Coca-Cola. Considered a refreshing means to boost morale (its 1929 slogan, "the pause that refreshes," was long the most successful and best remembered advertising line), Coca-Cola followed the troops wherever they went. By war's end some 64 Coke plants had been constructed around the world and five billion bottles of the beverage had been consumed. (One anecdote recounts that General Dwight D. Eisenhower had been photographed drinking Coca-Cola with a straw to the chagrin of company officials, who thought it suggested unclean bottle tops.)

A statistical advantage went to other American products as well. Cigarettes, chewing gum and chocolate candy found in American field rations developed a taste for such unnecessary products among young soldiers and civilians in war-torn countries. By the end of the war American cigarettes, appearing in packages of five in the field C-rations of American soldiers, were serving as surrogate currency in Germany. As for "durable goods," the omnipresent product then was strictly military: the Jeep. Both the most affectionately treated and the most versatile of war weapons, the Jeep raced across the North African desert, bounced along jungle trails in New Guinea and plunged ahead in heavy snow during the Battle of the Bulge in Belgium in December 1944. The Jeep was just about everywhere, the 586,489 produced during the war assuring that it was indeed commonplace, equally so because it was clearly an all-terrain vehicle, an SUV before its time. When produced after the war, it continued to be popular among American youth as the first sport utility vehicle.

The Jeep also suggested a further democratization of the technology that had made the automobile the conveyance of large numbers of people. The Jeep was driven by both corporal and colonel, a new equality of military position. And when the high-ranking officer was not at the wheel, he was at the side of the driver. Everyone drove a Jeep, and no one of consequence sat in the back seat. (The story goes that, during the Battle of the Bulge, a group of German soldiers wearing American uniforms had seized a Jeep and driven it behind American lines. Although they spoke English fluently, they were exposed because the soldier in a general's uniform sat in the back seat. Democratization, in whatever form, was clearly not happening in wartime Germany.)

And then there was military clothing. So much of it was produced that it became a postwar commodity featured in the army and navy surplus stores that flourished in the United States, Great Britain, Canada and even Australia. Surplus khaki clothing, the summer wear of fighting men, became popular casual wear of the 1950s. Clothing companies now also produced it, as it joined the blue blazer in the new style of "casual smart." Popular figures like the movie star James Dean and the author Jack Kerouac were seen in khakis.

The major production shift after the war was the obvious one: consumer goods replaced military equipment, reversing the earlier shift to military equipment from consumer goods. World War Two, if viewed as a commodity enterprise, a matter of statistical advantages, was able to assure mass destruction because of effective systems of mass distribution. Never before had so many soldiers and civilians died because never had the means of destruction been so widely amassed and quickly delivered. The on-demand and overnight delivery that we today accept as routine has its earlier analogue in the nightly bomber runs over Germany in the last two years of the war. World War Two was an accumulation of gross ironies as well as a dreadful compilation of wanton acts of waste and wasting, goods and human lives consumed.

The figures for military engagement were complemented by the figures for military disengagement or brief distraction from the agonies of war. Entertainment was also mass-produced and widely distributed. It is estimated that some 630,000 American troops abroad watched movies each night in 1943. By the end of the war, that number had risen to an estimated 3 million. The nightmare of war was relieved for an hour or two by products manufactured in Hollywood or in the studios of other war-burdened countries. Nowhere did the film industry remain idle. Even though production was necessarily cut back and sets altered because of wartime needs for raw materials (cellulose, a constituent of celluloid, was needed for the manufacture of explosives; and sugar rationing meant that fewer windows were broken in action films), the show went on.

The movie was a major element in this, the first spectacular war.

The first spectacular war

If World War Two was the first total war, encompassing all human activity on most continents, it was also the first spectacular war. The spectacular was new in two ways: first, it was extensively filmed – as fact in the battle scenes, shown weekly in newsreels, and as drama in the feature films that proliferated, well over 300 after last count – and second, the spectacular was principally enacted on a vertical plane. Scenes of the Blitz on English cities (1940), the attack on Pearl Harbor (1941), and the effects of the first atomic bomb dropped on Hiroshima (1945) showed destruction rained down and ruin rising in fiery clouds. These two characteristics distinguished this war as a visual experience unlike any before.

Modern wars had been amply illustrated before, in battlefield sketches and heroic paintings, in cartoons and posters. The first still photography at the battlefront was in the Crimean War (1854–56), and the first filming was by the French company Pathé of the siege of Fort Arthur during the Russo-Japanese War (1904–5). In World War One, movies were made abundantly of the battlefield, which soon after became a feature film genre. D. W. Griffith made *Hearts of the World*, depicting trench warfare, in 1918. The French filmmaker Abel Gance made his antiwar film denouncing its barbarity, *J'accuse*, in 1919. King Vidor in 1925 made what is considered one of the best films about the war, *The Big Parade*, in which the plot concerned the problems of a wounded American foot-soldier. These cinematic developments in and about World War One were minuscule and sporadic when compared with the outburst and output of World War Two.

The mobility of action in World War Two – tanks and aircraft allowing the creation of *blitzkrieg* or lightning warfare – and its near ubiquity on all of the major continents led to the introduction of a new American military term "theater of operations" to describe the military scene. Of the 2,500 training and information films created by the Army Pictorial Service of the American Army Signal Corps during the war, 1,500 were translated into languages other than English to serve nations allied with the United States in these theaters of operation. The figure indicates the significance placed on film-making and the manner in which the activity was structured into military operations. The British also had a special military film section, the Army Film and Photographic Unit that covered all the major military campaigns. The Germans also had special film companies that provided coverage of the war for the weekly news films that were designed to boost public confidence in the war. In preparation for the intended invasion of England, the German Ministry of Propaganda prepared a film titled *The Day of the Eagle*, which demonstrated the prowess of the German air force, the Luftwaffe.

Although every nation produced war-centered films, propaganda efforts to arouse and maintain public morale, the feature film remained designed to be entertaining and also diverting, projected in the movie theater, an enclosed environment that could easily exclude the war. Both Nazi Germany and Hollywood endorsed this idea. It was even championed by Joseph Goebbels, propaganda minister of Nazi Germany. And so, in 1943, after the Germans had lost the Battle of Stalingrad and were beginning their long retreat home, Goebbels authorized the making of *The Extraordinary Adventures of Baron Munchhausen* (1943), a glitzy, in-color production of the around-the-world adventures of the madcap eighteenth-century baron. The camera was used not so much to tell a story as to display the elegance, sumptuousness and sensuousness of the scenes Munchhausen encountered, including a harem.

Hollywood also looked back in time and at more scrubbed conditions than those so marred and rubble-strewn by war. *Meet Me in St. Louis* was a vehicle for Judy Garland (she joyfully rode on a trolley car while singing one of the film hits), released in the spring of 1944, just before D-Day. This film, in Technicolor, was a refreshing look at a supposed age of innocence and confidence, a reminder that technology could be still praised as being beneficial, as it was indeed during the 1904 St. Louis World's Fair, the setting of the movie.

Other films of the era reminded audiences of sacrifice and valor, now and then. The first American feature film of the war was *Wake Island*, put into production on December 23, 1941, unintentionally on the day the Japanese conquered the island. Among its war movies, Hollywood produced *Mrs. Miniver* (1942), a film about a comfortably situated Englishwoman now gently exerting herself to hold together an otherwise shattered country town after her husband had gone to war and the local church had been bombed. The film was well received on both sides of the Atlantic, with Winston Churchill remarking that in terms of morale it was worth a couple of battleships. As for other shipping news, Goebbels produced *Titanic* (1943), a film that depicted the English as both incompetent and cowardly. Quite the contrary in character assessment and more subtle as well was Laurence Olivier's film adaptation of Shakespeare's play *Henry V*, in which that English king led his faithful troops into battle at Agincourt against the more heavily armed and numerous French. Olivier's reading of the lines Shakespeare provided for the king on the day of the battle, St Crispin's Day, has become legendary as an expression of wartime courage and determination. The film, which was released in 1944, combined art with rhetoric to great effect.

Also looking back to a different time and a different landscape was another film classic that popularly served war purposes, the Soviet director Sergei Eisenstein's production of *Alexander Nevsky*, first shown in 1938. A sweeping war production of this Russian prince's defeat of invading German Teutonic knights in the thirteenth century, the film's international success was in part a reflection of a growing anti-German sentiment. However, the film was quickly shelved when the Soviets and Nazis signed a non-aggression pact in 1939. Sentiment again shifted with the invasion of the Soviet Union by Germany in 1941, and so the film was joyfully welcomed back as an expression of enduring Russian patriotism and determination to defend the homeland from invaders. As with the fortunes of war, so went the fortunes of wartime films.

Yet no one can now deny that the most popular and enduring of all the films produced during World War Two was *Casablanca*, released in 1942. In it Humphrey Bogart was cast as his screen self, quintessentially American, heroic out of determined resignation, not bright-eyed zeal. The English journalist and television commentator Alistair Cooke, a well-known sympathetic critic of American culture, has written that the new anti-hero – the one who gave strong if unusual encouragement to Americans looking for a type "to get the job done" – was Humphrey Bogart's character Rick, owner of the most famous non-existent nightspot, Rick's Café.

> There was nothing now to offend the most respectable suburban patriot in a hero who used the gangster's means to achieve our ends. And this character was suddenly very precious in the age of violence, for it satisfied a quiet desperate need of the engulfed ordinary citizen.
>
> (Cooke 1978: 227)

For sheer extravagance and benumbing purpose, however, no film of the era can come close to that final act of creative desperation in Nazi Germany,

Kolberg, the production of which was insisted upon by Joseph Goebbels. The film was a historical reenactment of a battle in which an undermanned German army fought valiantly but futilely against Napoleon's superior forces. To assure the visual grandeur he desired Goebbels took 10,000 troops from the war zone in order to enlist them as extras, which was a bizarre example of the mix of battle and ballyhoo. The film was given a première of sorts at the end of things for the Nazi regime. It was shown in bomb-pocked Berlin on April 17, 1945, just two weeks before Hitler committed suicide and three weeks before the regime collapsed in surrender on May 7, 1945. The film obviously had no box-office record.

As an effort unique in the United States, cartoons were drawn into war. Every major studio producing the short cartoons that accompanied every Saturday movie matinée now sent their fabled characters into the war zone. Donald Duck got called up (*Donald Gets Drafted*, 1942) and Bugs Bunny took on Hermann Goering (*Herr Meets Hare*, 1943). The madness of the Nazi regime was depicted in *Donald Duck in Nutzi Land* (1943) in which Donald has a nightmare that he is in Germany and worn to a frazzle by variously raising his arms to make bombs and to salute Hitler. Such films were a minor portion of Disney's wartime efforts. His firm produced 75 wartime training films for the military in which real life as well as animated characters made an effort to assure that these films were entertaining as well as informative.

Hollywood increased its worldwide influence during the war. Its facilities were undisturbed by the war and its production, even as they were used for war purposes. As a result, the American movie industry extended its audience and popularity. Although, shortly after the war, film production increased in several film-producing countries around the world and other countries began such production, nearly half the countries in the world had no film production unit. According to a 2008 UNESCO report, "85 per cent of the films shown around the world originate in Hollywood."

It was not foreign competition that caused the decline of Hollywood's fortunes but the rise of television. Although newsreel films brought scenes of warfare to viewers' eyes within days, the immediacy of the war depended on radio.

The unseen medium

During World War Two radio was the most nimble of the electronic media, easily jumping national boundaries and, via short wave, making the circuit of the globe. So readily – and usually cheaply – obtained, radio was also embraced and feared by the confrontational nations. Listening to broadcasts from England was an offense leading to imprisonment in Germany, where Hitler's speeches had been broadcast to millions of people before the war.

The most admired – and listened to – radio commentator on foreign affairs was the American Edward R. Murrow who assumed his responsibility was to present fully and carefully the news item he was discussing in order to leave judgments to his listeners. Murrow joined Columbia Broadcasting System (CBS) in 1937 and became its chief commentator in London in 1939. From there he described for millions of Americans the effects of the German bombing of London, the Blitz in 1940–41. His verbal local color commentary on the ordinary English as they struggled to maintain their pluck and routines in a war-scarred environment won sympathy for the British cause. And his soon assumed sign-on, "This is London" had an effect not dissimilar to Francis Scott Key's words "The flag was still there."

If Murrow was the most renowned of American newscasters in far-away places during the war, he joined his many colleagues in giving the American public an international, even a global, awareness that it had never had before. "Coverage" now meant the world-at-large, the first steps to CNN's "around the world every half-hour," so familiar today. It was also the first step in creating transnational media conglomerates that now control, for better and worse, so much of the news and entertainment distributed everywhere, primarily by television.

World War Two was unquestionably a "media event." Both those who fought in it and those who did not were tuned into it and visually conscious of it. Churchill's wartime speeches, so lugubriously but firmly delivered, were aural reminders of England's bulldog tenacity. The coterie of photographers who surrounded Field Marshal Erwin Rommel, the apparent romantic figure of the North African campaign, have left to posterity hundreds of photographs of the sun-burnished face of the "Desert Fox." One of the most famous wartime photographs was of that artful poseur General Douglas MacArthur, he nearly always with a corncob pipe as part of his regalia, as he waded ashore at the island of Leyte in the afternoon of October 20, 1944 and declared before a microphone, "People of the Philippines, I have returned." These words were uttered nearly three years after he had promised in high rhetoric, "I shall return," following the successful invasion of the Philippine Islands by the Japanese.

The early years of the postwar world

A little more than a year after MacArthur's declaration, millions of American service members returned to the United States. By then the conversion of swords into plowshares was moving forward at great speed. The austerity of war gave way to the new abundance of peace. Automobiles were quickly weighed down with chrome (in some instances 45 pounds of it) and their bodywork alluded to features of the aircraft that the automobile manufacturers turned out during the war. In the first decade after the war, automobiles sported rear fins and hood ornaments ("bonnet mascots" in British usage) suggestive of fighter planes. Buick even provided a chrome-plated variant of a bomb sight as a hood ornament, and named its new model Le Sabre after the F-86 Sabre jet fighter – with the French article inserted, one can guess, to suggest interior comforts a fighter plane never had.

Plastic, a new and soon-to-be major product of the chemical industry, began as the wartime substitute for battle-consumed metal. By the 1950s plastic was widely used in kitchenware, in furniture and in textile fibers, and made its dramatic appearance as a major automobile material in the first plastic body sitting on the frame of the 1954 Chevrolet Corvette. Easily produced, shaped and very versatile, plastic became the new building material of the age, as vinyl covered floors and outside walls and became the characteristic material of the first generation of McDonald's restaurants.

Through its Baby Boomer children of war veterans at home and through its service members serving as occupation troops abroad, the United States introduced new attitudes and practices easily grouped under the phrase "casual living." Clothing distinctions, so long the visual demarcation between rich and poor, gave way; and youth dress, formerly little more than a derivative of adult fashion, emerged as the new and profitable fashion line.

The two obvious items that expressed youthful rebelliousness against formality were T-shirts and jeans. Both quickly won acceptance, because they were worn by young ex-servicemen and popularized through the films of Marlon Brando (*A Streetcar Named Desire*, 1951 and *The Wild One*, 1953) and James Dean (*Rebel Without a Cause*, 1955). Through these films and extensive advertising campaigns by American companies like Levi Strauss and UFO, these clothing items found favor among youth world-wide. The UFO company proudly says of its sales in Europe in the 1960s: "From England ... to Italy, UFO reigned supreme" (website "It's in the Bag" 2003: 2).

One other element completes the current global fashion in clothing: the baseball cap. During World War Two, this headgear moved from the ball park to the Pacific naval theater of operations where it appeared as part of the on-ship wear of naval officers. (View the film *Mr. Roberts* for on-screen confirmation.) With deliberate irony about twenty years later the anti-war movement adopted the neo-military look as casual fashion. The hippies, youngsters who happily disengaged from the work-ethic society, laid back, as the term goes, in communes of simple self-sufficiency. Their counter-culture attire, mismatched and misplaced, consisted of army uniforms: jackets, overcoats with military regalia left sewn on.

Perhaps the most unusual legacy of World War Two has been the persistent and widespread fascination with the war in the one country not destroyed by it: the United States, of course. Here, production for that war continues unabated and forms a niche industry of contemporary popular culture. Books and websites far exceed in number the bombs the Germans dropped on Rotterdam in 1940. Amazon.com lists as currently available more than 13,000 books in which Hitler's name appears. The popular American historian Stephen Ambrose wrote more than 15 books on American battlefield activities, with one, *Band of Brothers*, made into a television show in 2001. The movie industry has geared up for war again, with Steven Spielberg's *Schind-ler's List* (1993) and *Saving Private Ryan* (1998) being the most prominent.

In part this has been the result of post-Vietnam reflection on the service-men of the 1940s who fought what was deemed a just war. Those military men called "grunts" were just recently labeled the "Greatest Generation." The fiftieth anniversary of the war's end precipitated the building of new war memorials and museums. The National D-Day Memorial in Bedford, Virginia, opened in 2001, and, after considerable debate over its location, a war mem-orial to the service personnel in World War Two began construction in 2003 in Washington, DC, on the Mall. More significant is the number of Holocaust museums, memorials and study centers around the country, from Maine to Florida, on to Texas and to California. The United States Memorial Holocaust Museum in Washington, DC is one of the city's top tourist sites.

The most unusual and dramatic of American probes into the past have been the recent maritime archeological searches undertaken by Robert Ballard, the famous deep-sea detective from the Woods Hole Oceanographic Institu-tion in Massachusetts who found the remains of the *Titanic* in 1985. Next he turned his attention and his submersible in a search of the sunken hull of the German battleship *Bismarck*, which he did successfully. More recently he has attempted to find one of the Japanese aircraft carriers that participated in the Battle of Midway (1942) and then sought to find the Japanese miniature submarine that was sighted off Pearl Harbor just before the attack on December 7, 1941. He failed in both of these efforts, but they nonetheless made compelling television programs.

The war also entered and continues to enter into the homes and pleasures of the children of a huge number of young American families. This develop-ment began in 1964 when the G.I. Joe doll, manly and agile with his twenty-one moveable parts, broke the gender barrier in an unusual way: he was the first popular doll created for boys. He also was the first of the "action toys" that are now a major product in the American toy industry. The name of the toy was derived from the 1945 war film *The Story of G.I. Joe*, largely based on the work of the famous wartime reporter Ernie Pyle who extolled the common infantryman. Over the years G.I. Joe was redesigned and re-uniformed as America's involvement in military campaigns continued. Moreover, he moved up the ranks as Hasbro, the toy company that manufactured the action toy, introduced famous figures like George Washington, General Eisenhower, John F. Kennedy and General Colin Powell as G.I. Joe figures. However, on recent decades, these figures have not joined the rank-and-file on the playroom floor; they generally occupy a higher niche as "collectibles" on shelves.

The war had a phoenix-like effect in those countries heavily wasted. Out of the ashes and debris arose reconstructed cities. Rotterdam, Coventry, Munich, Tokyo, Kyoto, Berlin – to name some of the most obvious – were the subjects of modern urban planning that had a democratic slant, building in low-cost housing and the amenities of new public spaces: parks, theaters, shopping facilities. Europe led the world in the immediate postwar era in modernist urban planning.

Yet of all the effects of the war on popular culture, none was more important, or more difficult to measure, than the displacement of populations. Slave laborers from Eastern Europe forced into Nazi Germany, refugees from defeated Germany and its formerly conquered areas and, later, people moving out of zones conquered and held by the Soviet Union: all were part of a wave of population shifts that continued through the rest of the twentieth century. While large numbers, an estimated 6 million, were repatriated right after the war, 1.5 million others chose not to return and sought asylum elsewhere. By 1952, some 330,000 displaced persons had sought refuge in the United States, another 300,000 in the United Kingdom. The new state of Israel (1948) was largely populated by those Jews in Europe who had escaped the Holocaust and those who fled the oppressive conditions in the Soviet Union. The collapse of the colonial empires shortly after the war, a result largely induced by the war, led to a surge of new immigrants, like Jamaicans and Pakistanis to the United Kingdom, Indonesians to the Netherlands and Algerians to France. With these refugees came new cuisine, new musical idioms and – tragically – new racial tensions.

The effect of long-term American occupation troops in Europe and Japan was also a conditioning factor of popular culture. The casualness of American social style and demeanor created the impression of the American as a *bon gar*, a good guy who was both affable and laid back. "The American lifestyle was fascinating for us young boys," wrote an Austrian many years later. "You have to imagine what a contrast that was. During the Nazi years, there had been a ban on gatherings of all kinds – and suddenly there were dances and music" (website "Salzburg" 2002: 1). In a brief article he wrote for *Time* on the American GI, General Colin Powell described a meeting he had had with a Japanese businessman who told Powell that in 1945, as a small child, he feared "the arrival of the dreaded American beasts. ... " Instead he was greeted by a smiling GI who gave him a Hershey bar. In a gesture of belated thanks for that gift, the Japanese man donated a large sum of money to the United Service Organization (USO). Powell continued: "After thanking him, I gave him as a souvenir a Hershey bar that I had autographed. He took it and began to cry" (Powell 2002: 2). Such sentiment was certainly not universal, but neither was it unusual. In the occupied countries, people found much to emulate from the United States: not only its consumer products, but also its social attitudes.

In the opposite direction, war brides now moved from the former war zones, Great Britain and France, even Germany, Italy and Japan, to the United States with their soldier husbands, creating a special form of international bonding and an enhancement of the growing tourist industry when these persons returned with their families to their native land on visits. Moreover, such displacement indirectly assisted the American travel industry. What effect wartime service by Americans created on interest in foreign travel is difficult to measure, but the "R&R" (rest and recreation) trips provided by the American army to its occupation troops (Switzerland was a great favorite) certainly was a contributing element.

In the last three decades of the twentieth century, the intensifying movement of diverse populations from their homelands to new locations affected or defined new characteristics of global popular culture, particularly in its urban setting: food, music, slang, clothing, all, like salsa, provided new taste. It has been said that there are more good Indonesian restaurants in the Netherlands than in Indonesia and that Indonesian cuisine is now the Dutch national one. A considerable immigration of Hungarian refugees to Vancouver, Canada, after the failed 1956 uprising against the Soviet Union's domination, gave the city a cosmopolitan air and sophistication it lacked before. Such examples can be easily multiplied if the global range of Japanese, Thai and Vietnamese restaurants is further considered.

It was thus that the worldwide distribution of information by the electronic media was matched by the worldwide movement of large portions of the population from defeated nation to victor, from poor nation to rich, from countryside to city. What was once proffered as the "bright lights" theory of migration still has appeal. To seek a better life, to find new opportunities, to join in the rhythm of the modern city as center of opportunity and entertainment, some people rushed and others patiently moved to the city. In 1950, only London and New York had aggregate populations of more than eight million.

Today, 25 cities now surpass that number, with many of them in Asia. Initially resulting from the dislocation caused by the war, accelerated by the collapse of colonial empires and the resultant stunting of rural development, this urbanization has changed the world irrevocably.

Furthermore, urban form underwent modification. In the United States, the suburb distended and then disconnected from the old city center. A nation given to the personal dream of a single residence on a manicured plot of land, the United States in the immediate postwar era went on a building spree. Mortgages provided to veterans at low interest rates, more young families as former GIs became parents, and the introduction of mass production to the construction industry led to a housing boom. From 325,000 housing units built in 1945, the annual number of houses constructed increased to 1,015,000 in 1946, then to 1,908,000 in 1950 (Bennett 1996: 15–16). Within this number, 17,447 were built in Levittown, New York, a creation of William J. Levitt who mass-produced inexpensive houses in two styles: ranch and Cape Cod. Workers moved from one house to another, in reverse assembly line procedure, performing a particular function. The technique allowed for a mushrooming community, both praised and denounced, but one of the first housing developments designed to accommodate the automobile. Indeed, it was the omnipresence of the automobile that made such housing development possible.

Perhaps another way to measure this global urbanization is to consider and count the number of newly emerging televisions shows that were suburban situation comedies, such as *Leave It to Beaver* (1957–63). The suburban-centered sitcom has subsequently become standard television fare around the world.

The war gave new emphasis to youth, not just the boys who fought it but the young men and their girlfriends at home who settled down to raise families. Birth rates rose dramatically in the United States and in many European countries as well. (The number of children between the ages of birth and four in France rose from 3.13 million in 1939 to 3.98 million in 1954; in the United Kingdom from 2.99 million in 1931 to 3.718 million in 1951; and in the Netherlands from 849,000 in 1940 to 1.14 million in 1950.) Such statistics in part explain the youth culture of the postwar era and the so-called "generation gap" of the 1960s, at which time these Baby Boomers were reaching young adulthood.

As leader in youth culture and youth benefits, the United States revolutionized the nature of higher education. A major response to the sacrifices made by the American troops was the approval of the Servicemen's Readjustment Act of 1944, commonly known as the GI Bill of Rights, which not only allowed veterans to get low-interest mortgages but also guaranteed higher education for those desirous and qualified. This benefit, however, was both questioned and denounced by many famous educators, including President Hutchins of the University of Chicago and President Conant of Harvard who thought a public works program made better sense (Bennett 1996: 21). Yet even those strongly supporting the legislation never imagined the effect it would have. By 1947, 1,150,000 veterans swelled a total college population of 2,338,226 (Bennett 1996: 18). The elitism that had generally characterized college attendance heretofore gave way to a democratic development. Now those who would previously never have dreamed of a college education succeeded in fulfilling its requirements and thereby acquired an upward mobility allowed only to Horatio Alger characters in previous generations.

Of equal significance was the Fulbright Scholarship program, established in 1946, and now considered one of the main institutions that led to a new dual appreciation: of Americans for other cultures, and of other peoples, principally European, for American culture. Senator J. William Fulbright from Arkansas asked the Senate on September 27, 1945 to give him "unanimous consent to introduce a bill ... authorizing the use of credits established through the sale of surplus properties abroad for the promotion of international good will through the exchange of students in the field of education, culture and science" (Johnson and Gwertzmann 1968: 108). Thus the tarnished hallmark of prewar global behavior, provincialism, gave way to an international exchange of previously unimagined proportions. Begun in 1948, the program soon expanded in numbers and countries participating so that twenty years later 82,585 students and faculty members had studied in one hundred countries (Johnson and Gwertzmann 1968: 112).

Not only did more young people, notably Americans go to college and university, but they did so in automobiles. People the world over took to the road. The vehicle which let them to do so, the most popular automobile ever manufactured, is the one developed under Nazi aegis, largely because Adolf Hitler liked cars. The Volkswagen, the model that evolved familiarly into "The Beetle," reveals its National Socialist origins in its name, translated as the "People's Car." It was designed by Dr. Ferdinand Porsche, an Austrian engineer who later did a job on tanks, particularly the formidable Panzer Tiger series.

This cheap car model would do for Germany what Ford's Model-T had done for the United States. With real economy in mind, Porsche originally had not included a rear window or windshield wipers, perhaps in the mistaken belief that the sun would never set on Nazi Germany. Hitler was enchanted and wanted to go ahead with production. He put together a dubious marketing scheme, promising Germans such a car if they made regular deposits toward its price through a governmental agency. A factory near Hanover in Eastern Germany was opened with fanfare in 1938, with a few of the forty-four prototypes then in existence standing bug-eyed, shiny black and at attention as Hitler cemented the foundation stone in place. He then joined Porsche in the front seats of a cabriolet. In another year the German army rolled off to war, the Volkswagen was made into a sort of German equivalent of the Jeep, and the German dream of a car for everyone was no longer visible in the thick smoke of battle.

When the war ended, and Germany was divided into occupation zones controlled by each of the major victors in Europe (United States, Soviet Union, Great Britain and France), the Volkswagen plant, badly bombed but not destroyed, was in the British sector. It was a British major, Ivan Hurst, who inspired the rehabilitation of the VW factory in Wolfsburg. Five hundred Beetles were constructed in 1945. Production soon expanded and the car was first exported to the Netherlands in 1947. The car came to the United States in 1949. The name "Beetle" was a New York advertising agent's idea, inspired by the rounded, beetle-like shape of the vehicle. The name caught on and soon became a term of endearment matching that of "Tin Lizzie" for the Model-T Ford.

One decade after the initial production, the millionth Beetle had been produced in Wolfsburg. By 1962, one million had been imported into the United States. Then factories were opened in Mexico, Nigeria, Australia, Argentina and South Africa. VW phased out production of the Beetle in Europe in 1978, but production continued until July 2003 in Mexico. The last Beetle built there, painted light blue, was no. 21,529, 464. This vehicle was not sold but instead was shipped to the VW Museum in Wolfsburg, Germany. This was a world record for manufacturing of a single car model.

That early model, Nazi memorabilia (medals in profusion and still found at flea markets) and film footage in which Hitler stars and appears with incredible regularity on American television, are all that remains of what was industrially initiated by the Third Reich.

In 1964, some 200,000 new VW Beetles hit American roads. In that same year, the first G.I. Joe hit the playroom floor. The small four-cylinder car and the little plastic figure with 21 moving parts suggested the range of the expanding market of popular culture. But its enormous dimensions were perhaps best demonstrated when 73 million American viewers saw the English group, the Beatles, perform on television in that same year.

The French statesman and army general, Charles de Gaulle once said that war was the unintended agency of social change. The statement holds true for World War Two. In the various theaters of war as well as in the domestic environment of so many countries, the pace and scale of life changed, markedly in some instances, subtly in others. Attitudes were altered. The provinciality and regionalism with which the world had previously been marked gave way to globalization, far-reaching networks of communication and transportation, the exchange of students and tourists as well as ideas and habits on a scale unimaginable before the war.

In the American variant of the English language, the word "stuff" quickly acquired its range of contemporary connotations. Descriptive of goods, of attitude (as in "the right stuff"), the word also served as an omnibus term for all that either defied detailed explanation or needed none. "Stuff like that" is the term used, a verbal sweep of everything readily accessible and available, the clutter of things, of attitudes, of habits that express a cultural environment in which abundance is assured in ever-altering forms. First milkshakes and now café latté, first single records, then DVDs – and now, again, among indie musicians, vinyl records; first the IBM electronic typewriter and now the iPhone. The "average" American woman now owns seven pairs of blue jeans. There are more than 1,100 McDonald's restaurants in France. Today, Volkswagen is Europe's largest car producer. And General Motors, once a fledgling US car maker, has replaced Volkswagen as the leading car maker in China. And on it goes.

Social media reframes 2011 revolution in Egypt (© Ron Haviv/VII/CORBIS)

3   Reconfiguring time and space

"Take your time to go fast" read an advertisement of the 1980s for the French high speed trains, the TGVs (Train à Grande Vitesse). It was a clever new slogan addressing an old human problem, found in Aesop's fable of the Tortoise and the Hare: how to make best use of the time available. The long sought-after solution was speed, achieved in the past only by mythical beasts like the Pegasus or imaginary devices like flying carpets. Even in the early twentieth century, when the automobile and airplane were becoming successful time machines, these fast-moving objects were primarily the playthings of the wealthy.

After World War Two, however, the cultural environment changed radically. The automobile was becoming a neighborhood fixture, as it had become a personal means of transportation, nearly everywhere. There were about 15,000 automobiles on the roads of the world in 1900; that number increased to 53 million in 1950, and then to 500 million at the end of the century. Airplane traffic increased enormously as well. In 1909, Charles Lambert, a student of Wilbur Wright, made the first airplane flight over and around the Eiffel Tower in Paris. He was alone. In 2011, more than 60 million passengers flew to or from Charles de Gaulle airport in that city (website "Statistiques annuelles" 2012). Yet Charles de Gaulle airport is only seventh in the 2011 list of the ten busiest airports, Atlanta ranking first with more than 92 million passengers (website "Year to Year Passenger Traffic" 2012).

In this heavily traveled world, time seems to stand apart, divorced from any spatial consideration. The laptop, the iPad and the PDA (personal digital assistant) have no fixed geography, no particular location. Nor do they require a panoply of support services in attendance. They are, quite literally, handy, making prestidigitation a matter of input, not trickery. Socially, these devices allow intimacy in the most public of places, the street, the airline check-in; and they even intrude into private places, the car and the dinner table. A call or an e-mail may be made or received from a soccer stadium in France, an automobile leaving Los Angeles, a safari camp in Kenya. The individual, regardless of place, has become the mobile command center of a global network.

Mobility and accessibility have become key features of contemporary life and have given popular culture distinctive qualities: it is fast-paced and geographically unconfined. Paved roads in Indonesia; long airport runways in Japan; Mercedes dealerships in Nairobi, Kenya and Lexington, Kentucky; cybercafés and cell phones answered in Swahili as well as in Finnish – all of these features may not have created a global village but they certainly have led to complicated systems of transportation and communication that empower much, even most, of the world's population. There is no longer a far away. Ted Turner, founder of CNN, the first twenty-four-hour news network, forbade his announcers in 1990 to use the word "foreign." Nearly three decades before, international agreement was reached on common symbols for major road signs, a silent expression of the same thought.

Car, plane, computer and PDA have become the contemporary means of popular interaction, the efficient devices that allow for easy personal and group movement through a culture that is transient and kinetic.

Car culture and its problems

The expression "car culture" has been widely used to describe the effects of the automobile on our individual and collective behavior. Initially a pronounced American phenomenon, car culture has spread around the world with surprisingly common effect. The automobile is, of course, more than a single moving object conveying a few people from one place to another. It is an extension of personality, a cherished possession, an art form. Advertisements in print and on television now seldom make allusion to the car as a means of transportation, emphasizing instead the appearance and agility of the car, its ability to give tangible expression to the desires of the driver. An ad for now obsolete Pontiac cars appearing in the March 2003 issue of *Men's Journal* had the caption "Unleash your nasty little urges."

Personal freedom and self-fulfillment are the understood meaning of most of the ads. Speeding carefree along a lonely road guarded by hills or racing before clouds of dust it has left behind across vast open space, machine and person are as one, joined in defiance of the natural and restrictive environment. Years ago, when the famous car designer Ettore Bugatti received a complaint about the brake system on one of his models, he forcefully replied that his cars were designed to go, not to stop. And so with contemporary advertisements, most of which show the car in unimpaired motion.

Yet car culture is now an unsatisfactory combination of mobility and constraint, of "go" and "stop." The automobile provides the maximum range of individual movement but also, because of its ubiquity, creates obstacles to that movement, the "bottlenecks" and "gridlock" that occur in and around every major city of the world. In Paris, for instance, there were an estimated 50,000 cars in 1939; by 1960 that number had leaped to 2,000,000. Within 18 years the number of cars in Moscow went from 60 per 1,000 residents to 350 per 1,000 in 2009. According to a recent article in *The New Yorker,* the increase presents an enormous traffic problem, causing hours-long traffic jam delays; a prominent Russian journalist documented the problem after missing a flight that he was scheduled to board with Prime Minister Vladimir Putin (website "Letter from Moscow: Stuck. The meaning of the city's traffic nightmare" 2012). The traffic in New York City moves at an average speed of five mph. The Robert Altman film *Nashville* (1975) took this problem of traffic congestion to its logical conclusion, when a minor accident on a major interstate leading from the airport to the city center brought traffic to a grinding halt. Frustration and anger were soon tempered by resignation, as drivers got out of their cars and engaged socially, thus forming a series of instantaneous communities of the oppressed sharing drink, food and off-the-road concerns.

The problem of "road rage" gained the attention of psychologists and journalists alike in the late twentieth century. In addressing an American congressional committee investigating the nature and significance of this rising phenomenon in 1997, Leon James, a social psychologist at the University of Hawaii, declared: "Automobiles are powerful, and obedient. They respond instantly and gratifyingly to our command, giving us a sense of well-being that comes with achieving control over one's environment" (James, "Congressional testimony by Dr. Leon James on road rage and aggressive drivers"). Inhibition or frustration of this control leads to road rage, anger at the anonymous Other, the driver in another car whose slow or careless driving is seen as an impediment to on-the-road progress.

Described as *rage du route* in France, the subject and its effects are international, with press commentary and institutional investigation adding to the degree of current concern. A report released at the beginning of the twenty-first century by the Royal Automobile Association Foundation in Great Britain revealed that road rage was a significant phenomenon, a more exaggerated and harmful expression of the inconsiderate and bad driving that had long marked the motoring experience. As an example, the report quoted a newspaper article in which the director of the RAC Foundation stated: "We had a case of a vicar's wife punching another female motorist for taking a parking place" (website "Roadrage" 2001: 3). The Foundation report also offered statistics, derived from the evaluations of 10,000 motorists in 16 European countries. In the United Kingdom 80 percent of drivers said that they had been "road raged," 77 percent in Greece, 66 percent in Austria and 65 percent in Ireland.

Not only personal behavior but urban form has been affected by the presence of the automobile. The most obvious problem has been spatial. The modern city, largely constructed before the automobile's omnipresence, is constrained from the widening of roads and streets to accommodate the ever-increasing flow of traffic. Elevated expressways (as in New York) and tunnels under major road intersections (as in Paris) have offered some relief. More drastic measures have been made to limit vehicular access to the city. Athens and Mexico City, for instance, have similar laws restricting cars to alternate-day city parking, as determined by the last digits of license plate numbers. New York has forbidden single-occupant cars from entering lower

Manhattan. Many cities, Bologna, Munich, Copenhagen, among them, have declared pedestrian zones in which cars may not travel. Singapore (since 1975) and London (since 2003) have imposed special fees on drivers entering city congested zones. The Singapore program has been very successful, reducing in-city traffic by 30 percent. Cities as widely separated as San Francisco and Paris have established bicycle, roller skater and pedestrian streets where on Sundays and holidays automobile traffic is prohibited.

Efforts to control automobile domination have also extended to street redesign. The street, after all, has been the main conduit of communications and urban discourse throughout history. Although much of that earlier function has been replaced by modern telecommunications and transportation, the street as the most likely axis of community convergence is now being strongly defended and rehabilitated. In the Netherlands and in Germany, such devices as the widening of sidewalks, the adding of small islands of greenery in the street, the realignment of the street with twists and curves, have been employed to discourage – indeed, impede – fast vehicular movement and to make the automobile share the street with the pedestrian and with children at play. The now nearly universal speed controller is the speed bump or the rumble strip.

"New architecture" proponents, particularly in the United States, see the answer to auto culture in the creation of small-scale communities, with basic facilities for shopping, governmental services and entertainment in a small center within walking distance of clustered residences. These residences, in turn, would have front porches facing closely to the sidewalks and with garages and access roads in the rear, such that the street would again be a place for social convergence.

In the United States the most cited and controversial urban planning experiment is one that seems to "go back to the future." Seaside, a planned community in Florida, is an attempt to reacquire the conditions of the small nineteenth-century American town, predating the advent of the automobile. Houses are clustered together, not separated by great swathes of lawn, porches are within easy hailing distance of the street, ostentatious structures with cathedral-high entranceways are disallowed, and public buildings are of inviting, not formidable form. A planned community of infrastructure and building codes, Seaside imposes no severe restrictions on architectural style. In its defense, one author has described it this way: "It is conservative, and it is democratic; it is élitist and it is populist; it is American" (Anderson 1991: 46).

The recent effort to give this contrived environment more lasting effect was realized in 1997 when the thoroughly engineered town of Celebration was opened, a short distance south of Disney World in Orlando, Florida. The official website for Celebration explains that it is "a place where memories of a lifetime are made; it's more than a home; it's a community rich with old-fashioned appeal and an eye on the future." It is a place attempting to force a sense of community by its spatial arrangements, everything designed to encourage pedestrian behavior. To achieve this, property is heavily regulated so as to prohibit any major changes in appearances. Being neighborly in appearance requires conformity, no serious deviation from the site plan or architectural design. To reverse the old modernist adage that form follows function, in the creation of urban space by the Disney Imagineers and the New Architects, function follows form: the structures are designed to induce a certain kind of behavior, one that is communal in thrust and strife-free. It is utopian and anti-democratic, harmonious and free of dissent or divergence – no place where a revolutionary tract would be written or a soap-box orator would speak. However, in 2010 the manufactured tranquility of the suburban never-never land was breached; over Thanksgiving weekend a 58-year-old resident was murdered and a week later another man in his fifties barricaded himself in his house and killed himself with a gunshot to the head. The latter incident brought SWAT teams and hovering helicopters to the town of shel- tered residents, many of whom felt shielded from violence. Beth Guskay, of Lakeland, Florida, and a regular visitor to Celebration who was interviewed by *The New York Times* for a report on the crimes, offered a candid obser- vation of the town: "I call it the 'Stepford Wives' community. As soon as you drive in it's creepy. I think it's for people who don't think anything bad is ever going to happen to them" (website "A Killing (a First) in a Town Produced by Disney" 2012).

The automobile has allowed – or forced – the reorganization of urban activities. Parking garages have added to the city's architecture and nowhere more dramatically than in Chicago where the twin Marina Towers, con- structed in 1959, accommodate 450 apartments, with parking for 450 cars in the lower third of the building. In major cities like London and Los Angeles, between 40 and 60 percent of urban space is now allocated to the needs of the automobile: parking garages and off-street parking at commercial establish- ments, modern expressways cutting into the older urban fabric and often rising above it, and the in-car services provided by drive-ins, popularized by McDonald's Speedy Service, initiated in 1957. By the early twenty-first cen- tury Speedy Service was introduced in Beijing, China, reflecting the country's adoption of car culture.

The automobile also engendered new architecture. Disproportionate to earlier urban features and frequently uninspiring in architectural form, but pervasive in effect, is the shopping center, afloat worldwide on a sea of asphalt designed to accommodate the automobile-driven consumer. More visible as a roadside feature is the motel. The most famous motel chain, started in 1946 and now worldwide in its locations, is Holiday Inn. Named after the fictional hostelry in the 1942 movie *Holiday Inn*, the new chain guaranteed the same features in all of its motels, so that the automobile traveler knew exactly what he or she would find wherever the motel was located.

"Gigantic. Spontaneous spectacle of automotive traffic," so wrote Baudrillard of the Los Angeles freeways. Further, they do not "denature the city or the landscape; they simply pass through it and unravel it." And they accommodate "the only profound pleasure, that of keeping on the move" (Baudrillard 1988: 53).

Jack Kerouac had earlier described this condition in his novel, *On the Road* (first published in 1957). As Dean Moriarty, sidekick of the narrator Sol Paradise, "hunched over the steering wheel and gunned the engine" of the Ford in which they are undertaking a cross-country trip, the narrator, Sol Paradise says of the travelers: "We were all delighted, we all realized we were leaving confusion and nonsense behind and performing a noble function: *move*. And we moved!" (Kerouac 2003: 134).

Car culture off the road

Kerouac's characters were not caught in the spaghetti junctions or super-highways that largely defined the car culture of the late 1960s. Nor was much attention paid to highways when the automobile was first displayed as an art object. It seems fitting that Los Angeles included, as part of the celebration of the 1984 Olympics in that city, a special exhibition titled, "Automobile and Culture." The exhibition was declared to be "the first retrospective of auto-mobile design." It certainly was not the first museum show given over to the automobile.

On a global scale, the automobile museum has become a significant feature of the tourist industry and popular culture. There are more than a thousand such museums in the world, from one in the Channel Islands with 20 vehicles, to the Autoworld Museum in Brussels with more than 400. The Netherlands and Australia have some half dozen such museums. Latvia has one, as does Turkey. Automobile brands have their own museums, such as the Corvette Museum in Kentucky and the BMW car gallery in Munich. The Imperial Palace Hotel in Las Vegas has an incredible collection of over 750 cars, with 200 of them regularly on display. If not a match in quantity, then certainly in quality, is the collection in the British National Motor Museum in Beaulieu, Hampshire. One of the oldest automobile museums, founded by Lord Montagu in 1952, the collection is a history of British motoring from 1895 to the present.

Hardly a history museum today does not have one or more historically significant automobiles on display, such as the Graf und Stift car in which the Archduke Franz Ferdinand was riding with his wife Sophie when they were both assassinated, an event often considered the immediate cause of World War One; the vehicle is now displayed in the Austrian Military Museum in Vienna. The Canadian Museum of Military History in Ottawa has the only one remaining of the seven Mercedes parade phaetons used by Adolf Hitler; and the 1938 Cadillac in which General Patton died as the result of a car crash in Germany in 1945 is now in the Patton Museum of Cavalry and Armor at Fort Knox, Kentucky.

Not all old cars are immobile, however. In 1966, the International Federa-tion of Classic Cars, FIVA (*Fédération Internationale des Véhicules*

Anciennes), was founded in Paris to coordinate the efforts of a large number of historical car clubs and thereby to "promote and protect our historical vehicle heritage for future generations," according to an official statement. As a manifestation of this wide interest in restoring and preserving cars, a series of *Concours d'Elégance* ("competitions of elegance") have been held around the world since the 1970s to the delight of many spectators, the numbers, for instance, reaching 10,000 visitors at the Nairobi, Kenya *Concours*, held in 2000. Although the *concours* are now held most frequently in the United States, they have dotted the globe elsewhere, notably in Australia, Germany, Britain and Italy. A variety of trophy awards is given at each event according to the conditions of various parts of the vehicle: engine, body (exterior and interior) and chassis. As publicity for the 2001 *Concours d'Elégance* of the Eastern United States stated, the *concours* is "a collection of the most elegant and mesmerizing vintage automobiles ever to grace the roadway." Certainly, that's the way most spectators see it.

On the other end of the automotive aesthetic scale is found the hot rod, the formerly slapped-together, junk-yard parts of engine, transmission, wheels and frame that led to today's straight-line hot-rod races of specially designed cars-as-racers that are popular in Europe, Australia and the United States. A visual pun on this makeshift car manufacture is found in the Australian film *Mad Max 2: Road Warrior* (1981) in which rival groups in a post-nuclear-war era build their new weapons of war from the equivalent of junk-yard parts. A sharp divergence from this inelegance is grandly exhibited at the annual Street Road Nationals, begun in the United States in 1969. The Minnesota Street Rod Association's 2011 Street Rod event drew some 100,000, where the sharply accoutered, painted and redesigned Fords and Chevrolets from the 1920s and 1930s provided a dazzling display of individual initiative and imagination.

Car art has become a widely expressed folk art. In its most commented-on form, low-riders, the vehicle redesigned with a hydraulic suspension system to ride low to the road but also to be raised in a rhythmic sort of prance, this is a regional art practiced by Mexican-Americans primarily in the Southwest and Southern California. Started in the late 1930s among migrant laborers needing transportation, "low-riding" has been called a baroque art form in its elaborateness of exterior and interior design, with murals frequently painted on the car bodies. Recently, however, it has become commercialized and has found some following among youth in Japan and Europe.

Another form of car art that has received considerable attention and has served well as advertising is the BMW Art Car Collection. It was initiated, with approval of the German automobile manufacturer, by the French race-car driver and art auctioneer Hervé Poulain in 1975. Poulain, who wanted to bring together the world of motorsport and art, convinced Alexander Calder to convert his BMW 3.0 CSL into a highly mobile canvas. The idea caught the public fancy – and that of BMW executives – so that a string of such cars rolled out and into the company's museum. David Hockney (England),

Matazo Kayama (Japan), César Manrique (Spain) and Esther Mahlangu (South Africa) have been among the artists who have been so engaged in this production.

What might be described as an accidental expression of car art occurred much earlier. In 1934 the three Mercedes racing cars entering a Grand Prix race – in which regulations on size, weight and engine capacity had been adopted – were each found to be one kilogram overweight. This was quickly rectified by stripping off the body paints and leaving the cars pristine in their polished aluminum. Dubbed the "Silver Arrows," the cars were so eye-catching that the silver color soon became identified with the Mercedes line – and so has remained. (In 2001 Mercedes issued a new "Silver Arrow" sports model.)

Road rally and race

The road rally and road race for vintage machines are not uncommon. Now the most spectacular and largest of these is the Great Race, begun in 1982 and properly sponsored by the American television History Channel throughout the first decade of the twenty-first century. With more than 100 participating vehicles covering 4,000 miles in 14 days, it traverses the continental United States and offers a prize purse of $275,000. More significantly, it follows a long tradition. The first car race was undertaken in France in 1895, over a distance of 750 miles, a circuit between Paris and Bordeaux. However, the most spectacular and praised race was the Italian *Mille Miglia* ("thousand miles"). An annual event held between 1927 and 1957, when it was stopped because of a tragic accident, the race was marked by the participation of almost all the major European car manufacturers and outstanding drivers. In 1955 Stirling Moss, Britain's renowned racing driver, drove his Mercedes along the 1,000-mile course, winding through Italy, at a speed of almost 100 mph (total time: 10 hours, 7 minutes, 48 seconds).

The first Grand Prix was held in France in 1906 on resurfaced roads outside Le Mans. The Grand Prix, later organized and regulated as Formula 1, was largely a European affair, with Americans seldom participating except as individual drivers until the 1960s. The famous racetrack at Indianapolis became the site for the American race.

In 1950, when the European car industry was being revived, the World Championship of Formula 1 car was introduced. The six Grand Prix races, plus the Indianapolis 500, were to be run sequentially, with the results tallied to determine the world championship. By then all of the races were held on purpose-constructed tracks, except the Monaco Grand Prix that still zips through the streets of the little principality. Today Formula 1 racing is a global sports activity, with 21 tracks including Malaysia, Mexico, Japan, Brazil, and Australia, as well as Europe and North America.

A more recent and now exceptionally popular set of automobile races is found under the acronym NASCAR, so well-known in the United States that the full name (National Association of Stock Car Racing) is seldom used. These races, begun with outgrowths of the "muscle cars" (mid-size stock cars identical to those in stock in car showrooms, but fitted with larger engines of greater horsepower) of the 1950s and 1960s, were a Southern dirt-track phenomenon. In the USA this has now become a national sport as popular as other professional team sports and currently enjoying the same type of television coverage previously reserved to them.

Air traffic

The romance of racing is seldom found in the air today. The interwar literature of the heroic flyer, chancing fate in long-distance solo flying, has been replaced only by the "top gun," the reckless air force pilot maneuvering the instrument-laden military fighter. The last of airplane romance was captured in Tom Wolfe's now famous description of test pilots, *The Right Stuff* (1979). In that book, the high-altitude flights of the two experimental rocket planes – the X-1 that first broke the sound barrier and the X-15 – were examples of daring efforts to "push the envelope," described with awe.

Popular interest in aircraft has shifted from old-fashioned (1920s) barnstorming and international flying feats (such as Lindbergh's) to the air shows, whether occasions for the display of new and vintage airplanes or the aeronautical trade shows that roll out the new models. The air shows provide dramatic aerial entertainment, even historical re-enactments, such as the "Korean era jet dogfight demonstration" at the Dayton, Ohio, air show of 2001. Like the county and regional fairs of the nineteenth century when homemade products, food stands and acrobats established a festive atmosphere, often marked with the sounds of audience appreciation, the contemporary air show is a summer affair, pleasing and enjoyable to the thousands or hundreds of thousands who attend.

In 1996, 216,500 spectators, including 75,000 trade visitors, attended the International Aerospace Exhibition in Berlin, the largest such attendance at the oldest of such air shows, originally established in Frankfurt in 1909. According to a survey commissioned by the International Council of Air Shows, air shows are demonstrably appealing to the young, with the average spectator being under 39 years of age, and the majority, 53 percent, of the spectators between the ages of 30 and 50. The same agency listed produced as many as 350 air shows in the United States and Canada in 2011, with attendance estimated at 10–12 million.

The military participation in such events demonstrates the publicity value of their presence. In Britain, France, Germany and the United States, military aircraft are featured prominently in static displays and aerial ones. In the United States, crack performance teams such as the Air Force precision-flying team, the Thunderbirds, and the Army's precision parachute team, the Golden Knights, make frequent appearances at air shows.

Today, however, the aircraft that dominate the news are the wide-bodied jet airliners. The two major manufacturers, Boeing and Airbus, compete to dominate the market with ever-larger aircraft that allow and encourage "jet-setting." Jet travel is now more commonplace than exceptional. This can be easily seen – and endured – at any major airport anywhere in the world today.

Even more than the major railroad station in the days before air travel, today's airport is both terminal and hub: the place to end travel, but also the place to await connections, often hours apart. The result is obvious: the airport has become something of a surrogate city, a collection of recognizable spaces or, as the cosmopolitan traveler Pico Iyer puts it, "an anthology of generic spaces – the shopping mall, the food court, the hotel lobby – which bear the same relation to life that Muzak does to music" (Iyer 2000: 43).

It can also be argued that the airport is one of the striking examples of once outdoor public space now moved indoors and highly controlled. The grand boulevards of Paris and the arcaded pedestrian shopping walkways in Paris, London, Brussels and Milan have their counterparts in the corridors of the major international airport. With its hotels, conference facilities, chapels and medical facilities, massage and communication centers, the airport bears a striking resemblance to the postmodern city, its chief commerce being the service industry of passenger care, comfort and accessible commodities.

In the aftermath of the September 11, 2001 terrorist attacks, the airport also serves as a site of surveillance and social and, in recent years, corporeal control. Shortly after the attacks, Congress passed the Aviation and Transportation Security Act, which created the Transportation Security Administration (TSA), mandating that federal employees be in charge of airport security and screening. What began as more extensive baggage checks in the days and months following the attacks became more and more invasive into travelers' personal privacy. More than ten years after the attacks, passengers and their carry-on bags and shoes are x-rayed, checked luggage passes through an explosive detection system and is randomly searched, and passengers are pre-screened and questioned for suspicious behavior. A report by the Council on Foreign Relations on airport security and its ramifications quotes airport security expert Norman Shanks, who believes that the changes "have raised the standard of security of all airports in the United States, which was long overdue" (website "Targets for Terrorists: Post-9/11 Aviation Security" 2012). However, critics argue that the security tactics are not effective, providing only the appearance of security, and that they infringe on the rights of individuals.

Post 9/11 airport security measures especially complicated the civil liberties of Arab-Americans and of "Arab-looking" men, as they were most often targets of suspicion among security agents and passengers. In 2011 Imam Al-Amin Abdul-Latif, leader of the Islamic Leadership Council of

Metropolitan New York, was prevented from boarding two flights to Charlotte, North Carolina, where, ironically, he was en route to a conference on Islamophobia.

Civil liberties aside, issues of personal privacy also emerged; in the same year, attorney and feminist blogger Jill Filpovic circulated (via Twitter) a photograph of a note from a TSA employee, referring to a vibrator the employee found while randomly searching her luggage. The photo of the note, which read, "Get your freak on, girl," went viral, and became fodder for discussion on the daytime program *The View* (website "TSA's 'Get Your Freak On Girl' Worker To Be Fired" 2012). Ultimately, the TSA employee was fired – an outcome that even Filpovic regretted, despite the invasion of her private life.

Another incident of security measures gone awry occurred in 2011 when a video of a three-year-old child confined to a wheelchair being searched went viral on YouTube. The clip of the visibly shaken boy being searched and swabbed for traces of explosives incited indignation among American and European travelers (website "Father's outrage as TSA subjects his wheelchair-bound three-year-old son to humiliating search ... on his way to Disney" 2012). While increased security following the devastating attacks was clearly warranted, critics question whether the policies and actions of the TSA properly address the actual threats and dangers terrorist pose. The reaction is akin to some of the programs that emerged during the Cold War era in the US. At best, public fallout shelters and 1951 Civil Defense films such as *Duck and Cover* provided a false sense of security, and likely added to Americans' anxieties during the Cold War. The film, featuring animated star Burt the Turtle, showed a generation of school children how to "protect" themselves by diving into doorways or under tables and covering their necks with their hands, a cloth, or a newspaper if a nuclear bomb was dropped. Like the US Department of Homeland Security's color coded alert system, which focused primarily on travelers, fallout shelters and civil defensive films provided little practical information on what to do following an attack (website "New terrorism alert system will offer specific warnings" 2012).

Despite their amenities, contemporary airports are colored with a sense of apprehension and frustration as security measures add preparation and travel time to leisure and business travelers' schedules.

No airport today rivals Amsterdam's Schiphol in the range of its services. Dating back to 1919 when the national carrier KLM was founded, this now very busy airport approaches being an airport city. With an annual traffic of some 49,800,000 passengers, the airport is one of the world's busiest hubs, a gate of aerial entry to Europe (website "Amsterdam Airport Schiphol's Network and Market Share in 2011" 2012). Its facilities include a number of hotels (two attached to the airport's single terminal), two chapels, a florist, a grocery store, a pharmacy, over fifty shops, numerous fast-food outlets and a casino. Unlike any other airport it also houses a national museum, the

National Aerospace Museum, with over thirty vintage airplanes on display. And, as nowhere else, the airport administration quietly insists on some formality: it requires all taxi drivers serving it to wear jackets and ties.

Quite differently attired are the handlers of air freight. The third largest cargo airport in Europe, Schiphol is less impressive when counted as the 17th largest in the world. First place belongs to Hong Kong International Airport, which eclipsed Memphis International Airport's (home airport of Federal Express) 18-year reign in 2010 (website "World Airport Rankings 2010" 2012). Modern air freight grew out of a term paper written at Yale University, which proves not all university matters are strictly academic. As he did research for the paper, Frederick W. Smith, founding president of Federal Express, determined that the current mode of shipping freight by regular carriers was "economically inadequate." Before Smith reached this conclusion, air freight was restricted to airmail and exceptional consignments of medical, exotic or perishable products. Perhaps it was the Berlin airlift of 1949 that proved the efficacy of flying in freight. At that time even flour and coal were part of an aircraft's manifest, the population of the besieged sections of the city being fed and kept warm by round-the-clock air arrivals.

What Smith introduced, when Federal Express began operations in 1973, was an airline totally devoted to freight. Its major predecessor, Flying Tigers Airlines – primarily given over to cargo but also flying some charter and regular domestic passenger services – was purchased by Federal Express in 1989. The company thereupon became the largest, worldwide all-cargo carrier. Its chief innovation, now a commonplace feature of all air cargo service, was overnight delivery. Now items that once were local and regional – foodstuffs especially, as well as durable goods from books to glassware – are flown.

A dramatic indication of the world's new airpower took place in Pittsburgh on the occasion of the publisher's release of the fourth volume in J. K. Rowling's *Harry Potter* series in 2000. Federal Express used 100 of its aircraft, 9,000 of its employees and 700 distribution stations around the country to assure morning delivery of the 250,000 copies of the book ordered from the internet book company, Amazon.com. Never before had "on-demand" delivery been carried out, in peaceful enterprise for children, of such a magnitude that it would have been the envy of the military in any war.

The world traveler

If Henry Ford's Model-T was the vehicle of change, leading to today's "autopia," it was the second generation of Boeing jet aircraft – especially the VLA (very large aircraft) or 747 – that re-arranged all air transportation. The first "jets" that made transcontinental and transoceanic air travel feasible and swift were the four-engine Boeing 707s, introduced in 1954 and inaugurating transatlantic service between New York and Paris in 1958. (The British Comet was actually the first passenger jet aircraft to make a transatlantic flight in that year, but regular service was postponed because of design problems with the aircraft.) These planes, capable of carrying over 100 passengers, quickly made obsolete the large ocean liners, like the French Line's *France* and the Italian liners *Raffaelo* and *Michelangelo*. However, it was the cavernous 747 with its capacity of 524 passengers that completely changed transoceanic flight. The aircraft was introduced on the New York–London route by Pan-American in 1970. The 747 was soon called "Everyman's Plane" because it catered to all classes of travelers and made long-distance travel more inexpensive than it ever had been.

Amid these throngs of passengers on business, on tours, visiting families or studying abroad, appeared the world traveler, one who might be called part of the "jet set" and part of that new social category, the frequent flyer. Film stars and rock stars, sports and television personalities, diplomats and world leaders added to the mix. One among them is the Indian-born, British-educated, American-and-Japanese-residing figure, Pico Iyer who described himself as a "global soul" in his book so named *The Global Soul*. Certainly in a minority, as he admits, he senses himself as a person who belongs nowhere but moves everywhere. Now living in Japan, he returns to Los Angeles for dental treatment. "[T]hough I spend most of my year in rural Japan or in a Catholic monastery," he writes, "I've nonetheless accumulated 1.5 million miles on one airline alone" (Iyer 2000: 23).

What Iyer has calculated as a single passenger, rock groups can tally up collectively. The global phenomenon of rock music was assisted by jet airplane travel as much as by the technology of modern music recording. The Rolling Stones have circumnavigated the globe several times; global sweeps have been done by Led Zeppelin, REM, and various "boy bands." However, no one excelled in world tours as did the late Michael Jackson, whose professional life was largely spent on the move. First touring Europe as part of the Jackson Five in 1972, he went on five other earth-girding tours until he reached the penultimate one: the HIStory Tour of 1996–97, during which he gave 82 concerts while visiting five continents, 39 countries and 58 cities. Michael Jackson was a global force, an air-age entertainer who endeared himself to audiences as no other entertainer before him.

Individual movement in ethereal space

Adele's 2011 hit "Someone Like You" is (at the time of going to press) currently available as one of the several dozen ring tones for iPhones and other cell phones. How far removed the current mobile phone is from the cumbersome, wooden-boxed, wall-fitted instrument of 1901 – celebrated in the song, "Hello, Central, Give Me Heaven" of that year – in terms of size and function. The cell or mobile phone – and its evolved cousin, the PDA – is a triumph of electronic instrumentation. Small enough to fit in a pocket or purse, these devices are multi-media wonders, making the twentieth century's most advanced personal computer a modern dinosaur.

Both instruments, however, share a common chronology. They became available and popular in the 1980s, although they had been considered long before. After World War Two, scientists and technicians sought ways to decrease the size and increase the range of personal communication systems. The mainframe computer and the two-way radio telephone were transformed into the personal computer and the cell phone, through such breakthroughs as the transistor and the silicon memory chip, as well as language systems like BASIC (Beginners All-Purpose Instructional Code). As early as 1960, a rather compact minicomputer, with the now traditional elements of keyboard and monitor, was introduced; but it was only in the 1970s that truly personal computers were sold – usually as kits.

The term "personal computer" was coined in 1975; in 1976 the Apple Computer Company was established and sold its successful Apple I. In 1981 IBM brought out its first PC, which reached 200,000 units in sales the following year. Computer hardware was developing at such a rate that *Time* magazine in its January 3, 1983 issue declared the computer the Machine of the Year for 1982. The previous American love affair with the automobile and the television set, the magazine said, "is now being transformed into a giddy passion for the personal computer." The laptop followed quickly. In 1986 IBM introduced its Convertible, considered to be the first real laptop and, shortly after, the Japanese firm Toshiba made a successful clone of the machine.

With the development of the internet, the computer became a global information device. One of the first scientists to speak of the communications value of the computer, J. C. R. Licklider, wrote in a seminal article coauthored with Robert Taylor, "The computer as a communication device," that "we are entering a technological age, in which we will be able to interact … in an ongoing process, bringing something to it with our interaction and not simply receiving something from it by our connection with it" (Licklider and Taylor 2003: 1). That sense of a boundless, global community of "netizens" was made possible with the subsequent development of the internet.

The first giant step was the establishment of ARPANET (Advanced Research Projects Agency Network) sponsored by the American Department of Defense and headed by Professor Licklider. This first time-sharing system uniting computers was complemented in 1982 by the TCP/IP (Transmission Control Protocol and Internet Protocol). By 1989, the number of hosts using the program had reached 100,000 and by 1992 the 1 million figure was reached. Moreover, in the year before, the British computer scientist who had developed the World Wide Web in 1989, Tim Berners-Lee, realized its success with the introduction of the first Web server. Through the now familiar HTML (hypertext mark-up language), the internet gained versatility by easy linkage and the addition of graphics.

The personal computer now became the window on the world for millions as it also became the back fence over which ideas and concerns could be expressed. However, it was predominantly an American instrument depending on a highly wired society. Elsewhere, particularly in Europe, Asia and Africa, the cell phone served that function. The mobile phone has become a personal accessory, or – as the acronym in which it is often referred, PDA, or personal digital assistant, implies – a multi-use tool to aid in navigating busy schedules amid a plethora of ever-changing information.

I-Mode (wireless internet access), popularized in Japan, made the cell phone a multi-media instrument. Games, news and music could be as easily handled as e-mail. In Japan the term "thumb culture" became a popular phrase to explain the dexterity with which the young used their thumb, while holding the cell-phone in the palm of their hands, to access the internet. In the Philippines, where the standard phone service was expensive, text messaging on the I-mode cell phone was a cheap way to communicate with family and friends. This short message service (SAS) is equally popular in China where the *People's Daily* reported on March 16, 2003 that one young woman received four messages and replied to them on her cell phone all within five minutes. The paper also reported that text messages had risen from one billion in 2000 to 90 billion in 2002; there were 206 million cell phone subscribers in the country. In 2011 there were 5.9 billion mobile phone subscribers globally, a number equaling 87% of the world's population. Moreover, the Chinese woman who received and sent four messages in five minutes in 2003 pales in comparison to American text messaging users in 2011, who send or received an average of 41.5 messages per day. Not surprisingly, young adults aged 18–29 sent and received 87.7 texts per day (websites "Global Mobile Statistics 2012" 2012; "Americans and Text Messaging" 2012). Globally, however, text messaging numbers leveled off in 2011, as the total number of texts was approximately seven trillion, meaning that roughly 200,000 messages were sent every second (website "More Than Seven Trillion SMS Messages Will Be Sent in 2011" 2012). Text messaging introduced a new linguistic format with its own argot in which words are greatly abbreviated, a series of letters serve as words and numbers substitute for prepositions. Among the most obvious are ATB (all the best), NE1 (anyone), B4N (Bye for now) and GR8! (Great!).

The popular appeal and versatility that the cell phone has now acquired was not imagined when the first such mobile phone was considered in 1947; it was not anticipated even when the first systems of transmission were set up in Japan and the United States in 1979. It was designed to be a mobile car-telephone, but the estimated one billion cell phones now in use worldwide are carried in pockets and purses and held in the hand in almost any imaginable situation. The number of mobile phone subscribers has grown exponentially. Worldwide there were 460 million in 2000, 643 million in 2001, 821 million in 2002, over one billion in 2003, and nearly seven billion in 2011.

The cell phone is an instrument of social change. Even more than the automobile, it has a democratizing effect in its application because it is restricted to no one economic group, age group, or specific location. For many it has a prosthetic effect, a synthetic appendage to the hand. In Japan, the "thumb culture" of the early twenty-first century led to speed typing contests on the cell phone, with e-mail and text transmission time included. Part of this thumb culture inspired the new category of *meru tomo* (friends only for e-mails), correspondents regularly contacted but never met.

Web blogging and the social network

Nothing has transformed the concept of "friend" like the web blog and its evolutionary offspring the social network. Blogs such as Open Diary and LiveJournal emerged in the late 1990s as sites where ordinary people could post personal and political commentary with content resembling that which graced the pages of the private diaries and journals of previous generations. American blog pioneer Jorn Barger edited one of the earliest sites, *Robot Wisdom*, a compilation of links and, in his words, "updates on the best of the [worldwide] web." Barger, whose blog is contemporarily active at www. robotwisdom.com, is a prolific writer whose work is entirely self-published, evoking the do-it-yourself (DIY) ethos central to North American Generation Xers and their generational descendants.

Blogs are most akin to fanzines (zines), which are roughly rendered and written, self-published and distributed hardcopy publications. Printed on standard copier paper, bound by staples at the fold, zines are an easily manageable 5.5 by 8.5 inch size. American, British, and Australian feminist zine writers of the 1990s are key progenitors of the contemporary blog form, as they wrote and self-published on issues that were relevant to their identities as women (reproductive rights, as well as the media's proliferation of the beauty myth, and ideal notions of femininity), often as rants, essays, and short stories. Like early bloggers, feminist – or riot grrrls, as they self-identified – zine writers (or zinesters) put forth feelings and ideas, using everyday language and appropriating images and essays from popular culture, often without concern for formal citation and writing style or proper grammar, spelling, and punctuation. And, similar to the virtual "communities" created by internet blogs and social network sites, zine creators developed global and national networks trading their publications through the mail and developing long distance friendships as pen pals.

The blogosphere expanded significantly in the first decade of the 2000s, with blogs dedicated to nearly every topic imaginable, including politics, parenting, fashion, sex, hunting, and gay/lesbian and feminist activism. The political blog was a crucial tool of the 2008 US presidential campaign between Barack Obama and John McCain, as little known political analysts published articles and op-eds at www.politico.com, www.huffingtonpost.com, and www.thedailybeast.com, shaping public opinion and shifting the dialogue and issues between candidates, at times on the hour. In their early form political blogs epitomized a democratic grassroots, "bottom up" ethos and these entrepreneurs compelled major television networks such as the BBC, ABC, and Al Jazeera, and printed news media such as *Newsweek, The Washington Post,* and *The London Times* to publish blogs of their own, featuring articles and op-eds written by some of their most feted journalists.

Yet the corporatization of blogs encompasses the personal, as well as the political. Blogs such as Open Diary spawned the spirit that draws, as of April 2012, 900 million people worldwide to Facebook, the social networking site founded in 2004 by Harvard University sophomore Mark Zuckerberg. Facebook, the platform for which Zuckerberg developed in his college dorm room in 2003, is (as of spring 2012) a $75 billion dollar corporation (website "Talks with Instagram Suggest a $104 Billion Valuation for Facebook" 2012). Facebook redefined time and space in unimaginable ways, reconnecting lost family members and friends, and – conversely – making the most intimate details of one's private life open for public discussion. Moreover, declarations such as "I'm about to be a bridesmaid again!" and "Work-induced headache ... so happy that today is Friday!" can be intermingled with more controversial and, in some cases, harmful posts.

In early 2010, for instance, 15-year-old Phoebe Prince committed suicide after being the victim of bullying at school and in cyberspace. Prince, an Irish immigrant whose family moved to Massachusetts in the summer of 2009, killed herself after incessant teasing in person and via text message and on Facebook. Experts studying bullying find that cyber-bullying is more insidious because it garners a larger audience beyond children's school and neighborhood environments. Herbert Nieberg, associate professor of criminal justice at Mitchell College in Connecticut and a psychologist specializing in adolescent behavior, asserts that, "In the old days kids would threaten to beat someone up, but now ... [k]ids go on to Facebook because they get a wider audience than in the hallway" (website "Cyber-Bullying a Factor in Suicide of Massachusetts Teen Irish Immigrant" 2012). Facebook brings to life the theory that Jean Baudrillard put forth in France in the late 1970s when he asserted that citizens of industrialized nations ultimately inhabit a realm of hyperreality. Those who traverse the hyperreal interact with the map, the image, or, in the case of Facebook, the digital platform, in lieu of a physical territory (website "The Precession of the Simulacra" 2012). Indeed, the social network is placeless and users "visit" and "interact" with one another through profile pages, which are built to project a branded version of individuality. The individual becomes a conglomeration of images, links, and comments where "friends" discuss and debate the mundane to the remarkable. Users may become "friends" with people that they have never met making the chance face-to-face meeting of Facebook acquaintances humorously awkward, as such meetings reveal the morphing definition of "friendship" in the internet age.

Twitter, founded in 2006 by Jack Dorsey, is a micro-blog, hosting (as of spring 2012) 140 million users who send and receive 140 character "tweets" through mobile devices and personal computers. Celebrities, politicos, and ordinary people tweet some 340 million messages daily, generating followers who themselves tweet. In 2010 the Library of Congress (LOC) acquired the Twitter archive, which contains every 140 character message since the micro-blog's inception; this acquisition makes the fleeting thoughts of millions of Americans available to future scholars and researchers interested in studying US cultural and political history of the early twenty-first century.

Longer and faster

The technological advances in transportation and communications have dramatically altered the dimensions of daily life. Space and time have become uncertain terms, without their former fixed relationships. The foot as a term of physical measurement is now archaic and obsolete in a culture in which walking is no longer the principal means by which to get around. The expression "take your time" seems inappropriate when car performance is rated, among other ways, in the seconds it takes a vehicle to go from zero to 60 mph. Notice that a few new z-words in English have increased inordinately in popularity: zip, zap and zoom in a rather onomatopoeic way express our current attitude toward mobility.

Travel has become a function of time, and time – as someone has said – is not now saved but frantically spent. Lewis Carroll sensed this quality of modernity in a chapter in *Through the Looking Glass* (first published 1856) as Alice and the Red Queen are running, although Alice cannot remember why. The queen commands "Faster!" and "Faster!" until Alice becomes exhausted and asks for a rest. As they stop, Alice remarks in surprise that they are at the very tree where they started. Indignantly, she says that in her country someone would get somewhere when running that fast. "A slow sort of country!" replies the Red Queen. "Now, *here*, you see, it takes all the running *you* can do, to keep in the same place. If you want to get somewhere else, you must run at least twice as fast as that!"

And so it seems today. Timing marks popular culture. Television quiz shows and advertising rates are meted out in seconds and minutes. On-demand delivery for parts in the automobile industry is complemented by 10:30 a.m. delivery for overnight air shipments. Sports events are exquisitely timed, as at the Olympics, and made more exciting by "overtime" when teams are tied. These and other such time-directed activities make up the kinetic quality of our era. This is one of the two qualities that Baudrillard said marked American culture. The other is the cinematic one, visions of things that – like the sugar plums in the poem *The Night Before Christmas* – dance in our heads. The 2005 advent of YouTube, the website that encourages ordinary people, celebrities, politicians, and everyone in between to "broadcast [themselves]," exemplifies the second quality. As of May 2012 pop icon Lady Gaga's video for "Born This Way" was viewed 93,856,492 times, and a video in the series "Nora: Practice Makes Purr-fect" of a piano playing cat was seen by 23,860,118 YouTube users.

Some individuals have argued that the image has triumphed over the written word. The printing press revolutionized the perception of the world and thereby degraded the visual; now the image is back in the ascendant.

Jack Johnson in the ring with James Jeffries (© Bettmann/CORBIS)

4   Picture this

A new world of images

Today, a picture is not necessarily worth a thousand words but it can be worth a substantial sum of money. Proof was supplied when the movie star Catherine Zeta-Jones won a suit alleging damages from unauthorized and unflattering photographs taken during her marriage ceremony to fellow movie celebrity Michael Douglas. The photographs appeared in one British magazine (*Hello!*) several days before the "official" photographs appeared in another (*OK!*). At the time, the bridal couple had arranged a million pound photo-op deal with *OK!* During the trial at the High Court in London, Ms. Zeta-Jones testified that the sum might have seemed high for some people, but "it was not that much for us" (O'Hanlon 2003: 1).

The "commerce in images" (Ewen 1988: 27) dates back to the late nineteenth century, when photography and printing were successfully joined. That commerce explains the complaint of the publishing director of *Hello!* that the Zeta-Jones suit was "not brought about privacy but about a commercial deal … " (O'Hanlon 2003: 2). There's no doubt that the making of images is now a major industry, and the visual in its myriad forms is the principal medium by which popular culture is expressed. The popularity of the visual is overwhelming, as statistics demonstrate. Consider the following:

380 billion photographs were taken in 2011, nearly 300 billion more than were shot in the year 2000 (website "How Many Photos Have Ever Been Taken?" 2012).

It has been estimated that over 1.4 billion televisions were in operation within the first decade of the new century.

An estimated 111.3 million individuals worldwide watching the 2012 Super Bowl (website "111.3 Million People Watched the Super Bowl" 2012)

Average annual feature film production in 2009 among the major film-producing countries was: India, 1,288; Nigeria, 987; the United States, 734 (website "Analysis of the 2010 UIS Survey on Film Statistics" 2012)

The *Motion Picture Poster Almanac* lists the prices of 500,000 movie posters. In 1997 the auction house Sotheby's sold a poster of the

1932 film *The Mummy* for £453,500 ($725,000), the highest price ever paid for a poster.

Ours has become a see-all culture in which it seems that little has been left to the imagination, and not much has been excluded from economic exploitation.

On the screen: movies and television

It was the screened visual experience that became the dominant one in the twentieth century and remains so in the early twenty-first. First the public movie theater and then the private television set made commonplace what had in earlier centuries been restricted and irregular, the theater of the well-placed and well-born. There is clear meaning in the frequent selection of names like Empire, Palace, Rex and Regal for movie theaters. Expressive of places and power once enjoyed by the few, these names now implied a socially transformative experience in which anyone with a little money might enter a world of splendor and delight. Interior decor often matched the theater's name as the baroque, once the architectural expression of grandeur, was carried to gaudy extremes. Outside, the main front display – the marquee in American idiom – became an electrical extravaganza as garish in form and color as the electrician's art would allow. The marquee was the visual antithesis of the dismal entrance to Dante's Hell over which appeared the words "Abandon all hope, you who enter!" Millions happily entered those palaces of distraction, the movie theaters (approximately 80 million weekly in the United States in 1938).

The supremacy of the movies was soon challenged after World War Two as television broadcasting swept around the world. In the 1950s, these two media competed for the viewing audience but in subsequent decades found the means to cooperate in increasing that audience. The history of this unsettled relationship began in the 1930s when television was first found feasible and when movies had become an established international industry. In the United States, Europe and Japan, experimentation with television equipment began in the 1920s. Actual broadcasting began in a limited way in the 1930s. On November 2, 1936, the BBC (British Broadcasting Company) aired the first high-resolution television program. Earlier in the same year, the Olympic Games were televised to a very limited audience in Berlin, while in 1939 President Franklin D. Roosevelt opened the New York World's Fair with television coverage that reached some 20 miles from Flushing Meadows, Long Island, to downtown New York. Yet only 2,000 television sets were owned in the United States before World War Two with about 10,000 in Great Britain.

Such irregular and limited beginnings were soon forgotten as television became widely accessible around the world. In 1950, 3,880,000 American households had television sets. That number jumped to 30,700,000 by 1955.

In Great Britain 2 million households had television in 1950. By the end of the decade the number had risen to 10 million. In China, the first television broadcasting began in Beijing in 1958. After a slow and restrictive growth, there was a remarkable increase in the number of television sets purchased and the size of audiences in the 1980s. Today, there are 115.9 million television sets in the country, with an average of 2.86 television sets for every 2.5 people. By the 1960s color television and 24-hour programming in many countries had made television a regular companion, one that, like the internet after it, enthralled the viewer into a loss of awareness of time. Average daily viewing increased to between three and four hours for all ages in the 1960s.

Technological changes in transmission occurred rapidly as well, with the overall effect of making the viewing experience both more convenient and more accessible. In 1965 the first feasible system for magnetic recording of television was introduced, and in the same year Early Bird, the first commercial communications satellite, was launched into a synchronous orbit. Ten years later, in 1975, Sony introduced its Betamax system for home television recording, only to find the system surpassed two years later by VHS (Video Home System), another Japanese invention, that not only made home recording simpler and longer – four hours a tape so that American football games could be recorded – but also gave birth in 1977 to the soon-profitable movie rental business.

Television became the all-encompassing medium, joining the advantages of the other major popular media (movies, radio and newspapers) into one, inexpensive domestic experience. Programs flowed as easily and regularly as tap water; and, ironically, flowed just as well where tap water was unavailable.

As television grew, the movie industry in the United States despaired. Attendance fell by nearly half by the end of the 1950s, forcing motion-picture companies to seek new means to regain some of their lost position. The first effort was enlargement of the movie theater screen. In 1952, Cinerama offered a new, curving movie panorama with three projectors locked in sequence focusing on a large concave screen. This was followed the next year with CinemaScope, a French projection invention of the 1920s that had never been commercialized. Using two lenses, the one fixed on the camera compressing the view and the one on the projector expanding it, the image size increased 100 percent. 20th Century Fox bought the patent and the existing lenses and introduced CinemaScope with a film version of the best seller biblical story, *The Robe* (1953).

The vastly expanded image now seen by the moviegoer led the French philosopher Roland Barthes to comment that he, as viewer, was now only separated from the movie image "by the arm's reach" to which he added parenthetically and in delight with the new cinematic relationship "God and painters always have outstretched arms" (Barthes 1999: 1). Then followed Todd-AO, a joint venture of the movie producer Mike Todd and the

American Optical Company that used 65 millimeter film projected as 70 millimeter, thus doubling the size of the traditional film. The 1955 production of the musical *Oklahoma* was done in this format.

The last and most spectacular development has been IMAX (Image Maximization). A Canadian development, it was first installed at EXPO '70 in Osaka, Japan, and has been refined since. A very expensive projection system requiring special housing (each film reel, of enormous proportions, weighs over half a ton), Imax is shown in theaters with limited seating and large wrap-around screens that give the viewer the illusion of being in the center of the action, a sensation furthered by the computer-controlled sound system. There are now more than 225 IMAX theatres in 30 countries around the world, the system supported by a film library of 180 films, most of which are scenic and action-filled.

The redemption of the movies came more from accommodation to television than through the search for new, competing ways of presentation. With the increasing technological ease by which movies could be aired on television and with television's omnivorous appetite for materials to present, movies became a standard and significant part of daily television presentation. Of equal importance, the extensive introduction of cable television in the 1970s, accompanied by the ending of state monopoly of television in European countries, encouraged the creation of pay cable television in which movie channels could be profitable. With that in mind, Ted Turner bought the movie studio MGM in 1986, primarily to acquire its film library of some 2,000 films and 1,000 cartoons. He then began a movie channel, Turner Classic Movies, which shows about 350 movies a month.

Today, there are about 50 premium movie cable channels in the United States, with some now selling their programming worldwide. Comparable cable movie channels soon appeared elsewhere. In Great Britain, Sky Television has 15 movie channels while Zone Vision, a British company, has created Le Cinema, a movie channel broadcasting to Eastern Europe; and Europa Europa does the same in Latin America. In Thailand, TrueVisions (formerly United Broadcasting Company) offers the 24-hour movie programming in Asia.

For Hollywood, however, one of the biggest financial boons came from the rentals and sales of DVDs of its films. Some of the sales have been tremendous. *The Lion King* (1994) has sold over 30 million videotapes. *Harry Potter and the Sorcerer's Stone* (2001) in the first three weeks of its release on videocassette and DVD made $400 million globally, and created sales records in both Japan and Great Britain (website "Harry Potter" 2002). The top grossing DVD of all time is *The Twilight Saga, Breaking Dawn, Part I*, which has sold over five million DVDs (website "The Numbers" 2012).

Growth of animation

With this proliferation of the means of viewing entertainment went a singular change in the form of content. Animation became something of a sub-industry. Although animation was used in the early days of filmmaking and became just another form of studio production, it underwent big changes in the late twentieth century. Walt Disney's team approach, soon followed by other animators, had led to regular short film features, of which Mickey Mouse and Donald Duck were the most famous characters. Then in 1937 Disney released the first full-length feature, *Snow White and the Seven Dwarfs*, a production that set the standards of art work and general subject matter now so familiar and so often criticized.

A major break in such style occurred with the Beatles' animated film, *Yellow Submarine* (1968). Not only was the color startling – a psychedelic experience of sorts, as some commented – but the animation also used a mixture of media that inspired what was later called the "blendo" style in which cels, cut-outs, clay figures – and more recently – computer graphics are blended (Cohen 1998: 1). By this date film animation was all but completely given over to full-length features, while television was doing the shorter features on both a weekly and daily basis.

Among the first to do animation for television were Bill Hanna and Joe Barbera. Already successful with their *Tom and Jerry* film series, for which they won five Oscars, they turned to television and a new approach. They introduced the family situation theme that has marched on through the years, right down to the current success of *The Simpsons*. In 1960 *The Flintstones* appeared, heavily indebted to *The Honeymooners,* the long-running Jackie Gleason comedy. Then in 1962 Hanna and Barbera took a great leap in time from the prehistoric to the postmodern with their future-set series *The Jetsons.* This double contribution of a new cartoon theme for a new medium has earned Hanna and Barbera a rightly deserved place among creative artists of contemporary visual culture. On May 20, 1986, CBS television broadcast a sixty-minute silver anniversary show of their work; and even today, British TV viewers can see both *The Flintstones* and *The Jetsons* regularly.

British television cartoon art also moved significantly forward on its own. The animation for *Yellow Submarine* was the work of TVC (TV Cartoons), a London firm. But it was cartoons directed at the younger television audience that were most successful. One of the most popular was *Postman Pat,* whose adventures as he delivered the mail were chronicled in simple drawings. Of wider appeal was *SuperTed*, the Welsh mini-hero who combined the dash of Superman and the cuddliness of the teddy bear. First featured on Welsh television in 1982, he became an overseas marketable product in the United States in 1989.

If, however, there was a new force in animation, it was seen through the huge eyes in the enormous heads of the characters in Japanese *anime*, or television animation. Initially derived from earlier American black-and-white cartoons, *anime* crossed the Pacific eastward in 1964 in the form of *AstroBoy*, the creation of Osamu Tezuka in 1963. Tezuka was a cartoonist virtuoso producing comic strips and comic books (*manga* in Japanese) before he was invited to try his hand at cartoons for television. Largely through his contention that cartoons could appeal to all age groups, Tezuka made cartoons for adults, and the rest of the Japanese cartoon industry soon followed (Patten 2002). In addition, violence and futurist themes prevailed; characters were zapped into oblivion, but often not before suffering, a condition usually avoided in American television cartoons. Today, Japanese cartoons are a major element in the export industry, dramatically shown by the wide success of *Pokémon*, in its various media forms. Further confirmation of this fact is found in a recent news report announcing that *AstroBoy* will now go global, with his voice dubbed in 60 languages (Seiler 2002: n.p.).

Meanwhile American technology was dramatically and drastically altering animation. The old "cel" procedure of painting single frames on celluloid made way for computer graphics, as in *Toy Story* (1995) and *Monsters Inc.* (2001). Computer generated images (CGI) have been used in any number of films, where such animation complements live action, as were the dinosaurs in *Jurassic Park* (1993) and the various shots of the *Titanic* at sea in the film of the same name (1997).

Computer artistry providing entertainment is one thing; but there has been serious concern over photographic alteration, which is easy and effective with digital photography. When the lips of President John F. Kennedy were computer-enhanced to match the words spoken by an actor imitating his voice, it provided an amusing aside in the film *Forrest Gump*. Commentators discussed the danger that such altered historical evidence could eventually escape detection. In comedic fashion Hollywood proved the point in *Wag the Dog* (1997), in which a president's re-election is jeopardized by sexual misconduct in the Oval Office of the White House. A digital film production of make-believe terrorism successfully provides an escape from the problem by appearing on the evening news as newly breaking evidence of a threat to American interests. As one of the characters in the film says, "War is entertainment."

Alteration and reproduction of visual objects

The equivalent of "object cloning" for still photographs is "retroscopy" for movie film. Both are visual alterations, easily done with digital equipment, that allow person and scene to be smoothly melded. Retroscopy creates a sequence where a person from one era can be segued into a situation filmed at another time. Among such hyperreal appearances, Humphrey Bogart has been employed, although long dead, to serve as an actor in a Diet Coke ad, while Fred Astaire, also over the great divide, has leaped back to dance around a new Royal vacuum cleaner. Reaction was severe when Ted Turner began to colorize the MGM film collection. Film buffs and critics objected in particular to the colorization of classic *films noirs* such as *The Maltese Falcon* and *Casablanca*.

Critics are particularly concerned because digitally altered photography leaves no evidence: there is no way to detect that such an alteration was made, let alone when. It is a matter of adding and deleting pixels. Digital cameras for personal use are being touted for their ability to remove unsightly objects like overhead wires from scenes of tourist interest or skin blemishes from the faces of family. The ideal conditions so seldom available in amateur photography can now be assured digitally.

This condition of altered reality causes another visual concern: how the easy reproduction of images has altered our ways of seeing art. The argument is this: the authentic now often seems less real than the reproduction. Postcards, posters and prints of art work, all readily available and affordable, tend to command our attention and indeed form our interpretation of what has not yet been seen *in situ*, where the original is located in real time and space. The current physical environment and previous locations of the original artwork provide what the critic Walter Benjamin calls the aura of a work of art. "The uniqueness of a work of art is inseparable from its being imbedded in the fabric of tradition." What surrounds the work of art, its aura, gives it special meaning.

This contention is part of Benjamin's extensive consideration of "Art in the age of mechanical reproduction" that appeared in his *Illuminations* (1950) and was one of the first serious statements about the effect of the reproduction on the original. Moreover, as Benjamin also pointed out, the work of art can now "meet" the viewer. It can enter the house, arriving by mail or, in our own time, by electronic transmission. And so Claude Monet's paintings of water lilies, in actual number fewer than two dozen, have multiplied into the millions as Monet's work has gained in popularity. Moreover, as a new example of mixed media, Monet's work can be downloaded to serve as a computer screensaver. Equally familiar is the enigmatic smile of the Mona Lisa. Would anyone dare estimate the number of images produced of Leonardo da Vinci's painting, arguably the most popular of all art works?

The matter is complicated by the workings of the marketplace. As never before in history, art has become a highly marketable commodity. On January 31, 2002, the well-known art auction house Sotheby's announced that it was joining the most successful on-line auction site, eBay, to auction fine art. Art collecting has been seen by many corporations, including the ill-fated Enron, as a form of sound investment, and Progressive Insurance boasts one of – if not the – largest corporate contemporary art collections in the world, which includes some 6,500 artworks. The collection, which is largely housed in the corporation's Cleveland-area offices, is not viewed as a capital investment, but rather as a spring board to inspire creativity and as a cultural asset among employees and visitors to the corporate headquarters (website "Progressive Corporate Art Department" 2012).

An interesting contemporary example of art in the marketplace is the impressive popularity of the populist painting done by the American Thomas Kinkade, self-styled "painter of light." Through the use of canvas lithography, he provides unusual reproductions that are then enhanced by hand-retouching to add something of the texture of the original. Currently there are 5,000 retail outlets selling these reproduced paintings and 350 signature galleries where the hand-retouching is done by on-site artists working on easels set up before the purchaser.

Kinkade has profited from a new expression of artistic endeavor, what might be called – perhaps disingenuously – production painting. All of Claude Monet's paintings of haystacks were individual interpretations of a commonplace scene. Even the lithographs of the posters of Toulouse-Lautrec were originally limited in number. The profusion of reproductions today – with a quality that may even make the original look inauthentic – both democratizes art and predisposes us to compare the original to the reproduction, not the other way round. Moreover, as the artwork frequently reproduced is for this very reason accorded the category of "the original," it is approached by the viewer with an attitude not reflective of the work's artistic worth but rather as an object of curiosity. It is seen in order to have been seen.

New inner and outer visions

Ways of seeing have always been culturally and artistically focused, but not until the appearance of modern optics – Galileo's telescope and Leeuwenhoek's microscope in the sixteenth century – did vision go beyond the range of the naked eye. By the early twentieth century, electricity charged new instruments that uncovered much more, the x-ray machine marking the beginning of that progress. Today, myriad electronic views of things large and small, but both beyond the power of the unaided eye, are converted into images measured in inches, not megabytes.

On a micro-scale, MRI (magnetic resonance imaging) systems exquisitely display the complicated activities of the body and the brain. On a macro-scale, the Hubble Space Telescope launched in 1990 has been the most spectacular of many telescopes, which have transmitted data from millions of light years away. These data have been digitally converted into awesome color photos of vast clouds of light. CRISP (an appropriate acronym for the Center for Remote Imaging, Sensing and Processing) at the National University of Singapore uses a space satellite to provide clear, detailed images of earthly occurrences: urban development, natural disasters, environmental changes (website "spaceimaging" 2001: 1).

These new revelations can delight, inspire and perplex our vision of ourselves and things around us. New techniques of surveillance that probe and pry may engender mixed feelings. The roving lens of the surveillance camera has examined and altered cityscapes the world over. It is estimated that there are one million surveillance cameras keeping watch for street and store crime in Great Britain alone. Moreover, security cameras will soon read the iris of the eye as a means of personal identification. In early 2002, news articles announced a finding by researchers at the Mayo Clinic that a high-resolution, thermal-imaging (heat-sensing) camera can detect faint blushing around the eyes indicating that the person was lying. This device will doubtless soon join the array of other instruments that allow police to determine guilt or innocence in crime detection. Such devices of detection now seem to beg for a metaphoric equivalent of the eye as the window to the soul.

Our daily encounter with images, both as sources of information and elements of entertainment, is inescapable. Contemporary popular culture is one of individual gazes and collective displays, one in which the dominant demand is expressed in three imperatives – "Show me," "Let me see" and "Let me be seen" – all subsumed under the familiar injunction "Picture this."

Image and imaging

The enormous increase in the number and accessibility of images, the wide display of images as elements of landscape and cityscape, the concern with corporate or personal image all are indications of the significance of imaging as one of the world's major industries. The contemporary world can be defined as one of carefully constructed appearances and exhibitions, which shape reality and define the person, and allow visual recording of dimensions scarcely imagined nearly two centuries ago when the first photographs were taken (1840s) and the first department-store display windows (1860s) were set up. Those visible signs of economic and social change announced the emergence of a "democracy of images" (Ewen 1988: 39).

The simple symbols of produce and product that preceded modern advertising techniques – say, the golden pretzel hanging over a shop in Salzburg, Austria that announced a bakery – were reworked into the high art of the advertising industry by the early twentieth century. Soon such images became a necessary condition of the success of the market economy. Advertising dazzled and compelled by contrived images that transformed the ordinary into the extraordinary. This transformation is clearly seen in the history of the bar of soap and its make-over, from a dull brown, hard rectangular bar used for washing, into a pastel-colored, scented, curvaceous object with a name like Caress or Dove, its name entreating the potential purchaser to consider soap as the means to intimate pleasure beyond clean ears. In the new world of industrially produced consumer products, usefulness was not enough to sell the item. And so advertising inspired industrial art, where shape and form seduced. In conjunction with appearance, advertising created a new literary genre, lyrical product poetry; and introduced a new art form that gave vibrancy to what was hitherto artistic still life.

This was not all. In this consumer environment, as it appeared in the late twentieth century, lifestyle shopping became a form of social interaction, recreational activity and improvisational entertainment, centered in the supermarket or shopping mall where "Just looking" became a standard response to the clerk's inquiry, "May I help you?" (Shields 1992). While this social effect of the modern form and practice of the market economy circled the world in the last two decades, the "sponsored life" also became a prominent condition of the citizens of the United States. "Virtually all of modern experience now has a sponsor, or at least a sponsored accessory, and there is no concern ... that cannot be reworked into a sales pitch" (Savan 1994: 3).

The silent sales pitch is now found everywhere in the form of product symbols and icons, like the universally recognizable Nike swoosh symbol (seen even on the rear window of a safari car in Tsavo, Kenya). It has also been made an architectural element, with the Golden Arches of McDonald's now more widely recognized than the Arc de Triomphe in Paris or the gateway arch in St Louis. What began in the 1930s, when the American restaurant chain Howard Johnson's identified itself with a standard pseudo-colonial architecture adorned with blue roof and orange trim, led to an advertising package that included architecture.

Signage also became a roadside feature until today, at the approach to any city, it offers a scene that rivals New England autumn foliage in its color and intensity. Robert Venturi, architect and critic, incisively remarked: "This architecture of styles and signs is antispatial; it is an architecture of communication over space; communication dominates space as an element in the architecture and the landscape" (Venturi et al. 2001: 8). Graphic, not geographic; pictorial, not picturesque; such signage is the contemporary world's equivalent of the old *civis romanus sum*, the comfort of familiarity and the assurance of common custom.

Pictorial communication has been seen to dominate social space in another way: the graphic has replaced the geographic as the defining element of the public domain, the place where citizens meet to air common concerns. The assertion rests on comparison: just as politics are no longer "of the populace" but of individuals chosen to represent that populace, so also are pictures today representative, with candidates facing the camera and engaging in pictorial exchanges (political advertisements) more often than engaging in direct debate (Hartley 1992: 35–36). What was once outdoor space, the Agora or Forum of antiquity, for instance, has become projected image. And here appearances also count. Since the first American televised presidential debates in 1960, the non-constitutional requirement for the presidency is quickness of wit and frequency of smile. Television, remarks one of its most severe critics (Postman 1985), is the medium formed in antithesis to print, the medium of analysis. It entertains, but does not entertain thought; it projects images, but does not allow reflection.

The result of this imaging is the emergence of a new popular reality, one in which public domain and world view are formed not on the street or out and about, as Tocqueville formed his ideas of the new United States in 1829–30, but in that small space of perhaps six or eight feet separating the viewer of today from the television screen. Tocqueville paused and inquired, and then passed judgment. The television viewer is briefly exposed, seldom for longer than 10 or 15 seconds, to projected images from places with names difficult to commit to memory. Insulated from the multitude, the faceless citizen enters the public domain as a viewer at home or strolling through the shopping mall or supermarket, or wandering about the theme park. It is not what is heard in debate or what is shared in openly expressed values, but what is seen, that defines this short-lived interest-group of spectators.

A recent modification of this condition is provided by the World Wide Web, described as an internet hypermedia system with a global outreach. The now familiar "www" allows textual and pictorial transmission by means of the computer, furthering the range of information and images accessible to the ordinary citizen. Art works in major museums, new car models, tourist facilities, real estate for sale, city scenes, entertainment and sports stars, pornography and the Eiffel Tower (among many other monuments) are there for the looking. Indeed, movies can now be seen by those viewers possessing fast modems while photographs of family and friends can be scanned and quickly sent in multiples to people near and far.

Through these electronic agents of image production, the individual personality – at least in its public persona – is also formed and deformed by images as it never was until the twentieth century. Of course, the effigies of rulers have appeared on coins for over two millennia; sculpture and portraiture also have defined the high and mighty in favorable attitudes. Indeed, nothing in the automobile age has come close to the glory of the equestrian statue as an expression of bold authority. What current images may lack in artistry, they more than make up for in frequency. Images are the currency of celebrity.

A new visual figure: the celebrity

The celebrity is a mid nineteenth-century creation. Celebrity is a status conferred by appearance, a multi-faceted illusion. The first person to study the subject seriously was the American historian Daniel Boorstin. In his book *The Image* he states that "the celebrity is a person known for his [or her] well-knownness" and places the statement in italics to assure the reader's awareness of the importance of this seeming tautology (Boorstin 1992: 67). The "well-knownness" has little if anything to do with individual attainment and everything to do with appearance. The image in magazine photographs, on television, in interviews and press conferences, is often arranged by a public relations manager who arranges to "insert" the individual in those scenes, such as ceremonies, parties and major sports events, certain to appear later as news items.

Celebrity status, like so much else in current popular culture, is a condition of numbers, of frequency of representation in the media. Boorstin quotes the authors of the "Celebrity Register" of 1959 as writing that, to judge a person as a celebrity, "all you have to do is weigh his press clippings" (Boorstin 1992: 58). To meet today's criteria, images would have to be added to that mass of newsprint. And so would websites, the 2000s equivalent of the 1930s movie fan clubs, but with global accessibility. In a way Woody Allen spoofed this idea in his film *Zelig* (1983), where the otherwise incidental character, Leonard Zelig, gains celebrity by being seen in the company of early twentieth-century figures like Charles Lindbergh and Adolf Hitler.

It has been suggested that the most photographed person at the start of the twentieth century was David R. Francis, president of the St. Louis World's Fair of 1904. In his desire to publicize the fair, Francis appeared in several hundred photographs taken with visiting dignitaries and at special events held on the fair grounds that year. It is safe to guess that Princess Diana was photographed tens of thousands of times and has been seen on thousands of feet of videotape. Appearing in public before large numbers at sporting events, rock concerts, galas introducing special concerts or fund raisers, the celebrity gives off a dazzling radiance in the light of myriad flash cameras recording the event. Moreover, the celebrity becomes image in the movies, in advertisements, on television news programs or when featured in one of the many personality magazines.

So seen, whether posed or caught unaware, the celebrity projects a familiarity of attitude and countenance that creates a bond and yet a sort of detached or no-contact intimacy between viewer and viewed. Psychologists have commented on the real grief felt by those thousands who lamented the death of Princess Diana in 1997 and the NASCAR racing hero Dale Earnhardt in 2001. So frequently seen in magazine photographs, on television and in public performances, these two celebrities, like many others as well, unconsciously entered the lives of their admirers. Television is a unique form of spatialization that brings some people close together even though in fact they are far apart. It also creates the pseudo-event.

However, the advent of YouTube in 2005 has reframed the idea of celebrity, giving credence to Andy Warhol's well-known 1960s assertion that in the future everyone would have 15 minutes of fame. YouTube, which, as previously discussed, gave ordinary people the chance to "broadcast [themselves]," made instant celebrities out of knowing and innocent parties. In 2010 Huntsville, Alabama resident Antoine Dodson became an instant celebrity when a local news interview with his response to the attempted rape of his sister went viral on YouTube. His comments were remixed into songs, most notably, "The Bed Intruder Song," by The Gregory Brothers, which led to Dodson creating his own line of t-shirts and a tour of numerous television/radio shows throughout the summer of 2010.

The pseudo-event or media event

The pseudo-event has the appearance of the real and the significant, according to Boorstin (who coined the term), but is intended and planned. It does not just occur: it is dramatically unfolded. The pseudo-event – sometimes called a "media event" – takes various forms, but is usually susceptible to television coverage in particular; the Oscar Awards ceremony is one obvious example. Purveyors of entertainment and news conspire to produce pseudo-events. As contestants are voted out of the CBS television show *Survivor*, they are often invited to appear next day on the news program *Good Morning America*, so as to get national attention for their imagined plight.

In this time of incessant image consumption, the photograph of the celebrity caught off guard, or the political figure revealing something of himself or herself, is also a pseudo-event. The term "paparazzi" was taken from Federico Fellini's *La Dolce Vita* (1960). One of the characters was an ever-active press photographer named Paparazzo. His professional progeny, who are armed with telephoto lenses and endowed with enormous patience, lurk and hide in order to catch the unsuspecting celebrity in a moment of indiscretion or awkwardness. Inconvenience turned into tragedy and the pseudo-event became the real event when paparazzi on motorcycles pursued Princess Diana and her boyfriend Dodi Fayed as they left a side entrance of the Hotel Ritz in Paris on the night of August 31, 1997. In an effort to elude the paparazzi, their driver raced through a road tunnel and crashed. And, thus, cruelly, Princess Di ended her life in a pseudo-event that turned eventful.

Both President Lyndon B. Johnson and George W. Bush created pseudo-events of their person: Johnson showed press photographers his scar from a recent abdominal operation; Bush showed press photographers the presidential seal he had had emblazoned on his Texas boots soon after his election. President Ronald Reagan made a media event of a carefully planned rehearsal of the greeting to be given to President Mikhail Gorbachev of the Soviet Union at the American Embassy in Switzerland on the occasion of an international conference. Most famous of all pseudo-events performed by the world's leaders was surely that of Soviet premier Nikita Krushchev. In protest against a statement made by a speaker during a session of the United Nations General Assembly in September 1959, he apparently took off one of his shoes and pounded it vigorously on the desk. Later, close examination of the event showed that Krushchev still had two shoes on his feet when he performed his little pseudo-event. The pounded shoe was a stage prop.

The examples are endless, from the compromised to the championed, from the tactless to the tasteless, as the price of celebrity requires the payment of privacy. The tenor Luciano Pavarotti, after the death of Princess Diana, pleaded for enactment of a law that would rein in the ever-roaming paparazzi as a means of preventing these unwanted appearances.

Product as appearance

The appearance of the product is the important element of contemporary advertising, a visual association of object and setting. The latter serves as trope for the former: rugged nature and versatile automobile, the Eiffel Tower and high-fashion clothing, construction site or sporting event and chilled soft drink or beer. The illusion becomes allusion, the visual means by which to qualify the virtues or benefits of the product.

One of the most successful campaigns to create a brand was the much-analyzed and praised one for Absolut Vodka in North America. As the Swedish company reached its centennial in 1979, its management sought to market the vodka abroad. The action took place in the United States: a new bottle was designed and a marketing campaign was built around it. The commercial-artist-turned-pop-star Andy Warhol was asked in 1985 to do a painting of the bottle. He suggested that other artists might be invited to interpret the bottle. Eventually over 300 artists were so employed and more than 1,300 different ads were run. The juxtaposition of the bottle with a well-known landmark, situation or object, gave the contents of the bottle an appeal to young, well-educated persons, who awaited the ads avidly. The simple tag line said it all: Absolut Athens, with the bottle appearing as a marble column on a site of classical ruins, Absolut New York, with the bottle forming the arches of the Brooklyn Bridge; and many more. Arguably the most appealing and discussed of them all was Absolut Rosebud, in which the sled made famous in Orson Welles' 1941 film *Citizen Kane* was reconfigured to appear as the Absolut Vodka bottle. Three popular books have been written on this advertising campaign, further testimony to the power and appeal of art advertising.

What is conspicuously consumed, purchased and used as a sign of status and wealth, is also what is conspicuous, made so through the power and intensity of advertising and, most recently, by the brand name seen in conspicuous places, whether at sport arenas or boldly on an object of clothing. Logos and emblems have acquired a significance only matched in the past by religious and national signs. Graphics now prevail, the arresting sign, bold in color and sharp in design, necessary because competing with so many others that crowd for space. Times Square in New York, the Ginza in Tokyo and Nathan Road in Hong Kong are nightly swarms of illuminated signs demanding attention. All American motorists know something of such visual effects upon approaching any city or any commercial strip that leads off from a highway. It has been said that each American sees anywhere from 5,000 to 16,000 advertisements every day, depending on how many he or she considers (Savan 1994: 1; website "Ad Exposures" 2012).

Products have been hyped as personality-defining – and personally enhancing – allowing the user to become more than he or she could be without use of the item or assuring the user entrance into a small cohort group distinguished by the product. In her critical study of the use of modern logos, *No Logo*, the journalist Naomi Klein argues that many corporations now market their name and logo, not their product. Companies like Nike, Apple and Calvin Klein are major examples. "Logos have been burned into our brains by the finest image campaigns money can buy," she asserts (Klein 2001: 346). The television ads of Michael Jordan performing as Air Jordan in Nike athletic shoes combined entertainment with advertisement, making man and product a very appealing combination.

The most significant development according to Klein is the loss of "unmarketed space" (Klein 2001: 58). A few years ago a large canvas with a huge photograph of the Apple Computer Company logo and the campaign slogan "Think Different" appeared strung across the road outside the Louvre Museum in Paris and featured a large portrait of Gustave Eiffel. In 2000 one of the traffic islands in Mombasa, Kenya, had a large Coca-Cola bottle standing in the center of a fountain. Aggressive marketing, with the targeting of new locations and new age groups, has become a major activity that has also evoked criticism. Not only are sports arenas and automobile races named after sponsoring brands, but even public institutions. The city of Huntington Beach, California, has made Coca-Cola its official sponsor. In return for awarding them the privilege of bedecking city property from beach chairs to fire stations with Coke signs, the city received an annual payment of $300,000 over the ten-year arrangement.

Tommy Hilfiger, the clothing manufacturer, has made a fortune from sportswear featuring his name in large letters, to the point that his clothing and footwear are simply known as "Tommys." What he has done is both followed and inspired further unpaid advertising as brand names define the clothed human body: underwear, belts, trouser linings, pockets and pocketbooks all say something about the wearer.

The identification of the brand with a lifestyle, not simply a product, has an extended history reaching before many of the examples presented in Klein's book. For instance, a series of ads begun in 1944 and continuing triumphantly for twenty years implied the delights of female fantasy guaranteed to those women who wore the Maidenform bra. In each a young woman was shown wearing only a brassière on her upper torso. The advertising line was the same: "I dreamed I was [in some unlikely social situation] in my Maidenform Bra." And so the model was seen as a toreador, a fireman, an aviator – in short, someone she would never be, or even think of being, without the confidence provided by Maidenform.

At the time Maidenform was uplifting women, a distinguished man with a black patch over one eye, immaculately outfitted, and described as The Hathaway Man, stood confidently for camera portraits, and thus intimated that others properly shirted up would do so as well. His outdoor, rugged counterpart was, of course, The Marlboro Man (the model doing the ad succumbing later to throat cancer). "Clothes make the man" is an old adage and one that was given a new and not flattering interpretation in Sloan Wilson's novel, *The Man in the Grey Flannel Suit* (first published in 1955). In the novel the young hero Tom Rath, in order to satisfy his wife who wishes to move into a better house in a better neighborhood, takes a new job that makes severe demands on his time and his allegiance. As he looks around this business environment, which he had entered after military service in World War Two, Rath says that "all I could see was a lot of bright young men in grey flannel suits rushing around New York in a frantic parade to nowhere." He realized he was one of them, more straitjacketed than comfortably attired. Only several decades later was the now popular custom of casual-wear Fridays adopted in much of the Western world, at which time corporate types could appear in jeans and with open shirt collars. In between, the young asserted their own ideas about attire and attitudes.

The appearances of youth culture

Complacency about social condition, and the smug determination of income as the measure of success by their middle-class elders, had been targeted for opposition by the young after World War Two. Two telling and widely appreciated examples of this protest appeared in dramas produced at this time. James Dean in his youth cult film, *Rebel Without a Cause* (1955), expressed by his body language his sense of dissatisfaction with the hypocrisy he saw around him, with the loneliness and alienation he felt, and with his despair of escaping the affection-stifling but loveless environment that was his home. It was in his souped-up car and in a drag race that he found comforting isolation and purpose. Dean himself was a pained individual who seemed to find his outlet – or himself – in the film roles he played.

A year after the release of *Rebel Without a Cause*, John Osborne staged his *Look Back in Anger*, a play that "forever changed the face of London theater," wrote the author of Osborne's obituary in *Time* in 1995 (Corliss 1995: n.p.). The play was semi-autobiographical, an outburst of disgust and frustration with the existing order of things. Language and gesture were no longer bound by theatrical convention, and artistic expression henceforth could stridently describe raw emotion. A review of the play in *Punch* commented that Osborne "draws liberally on the vocabulary of the intestines ... " (Bond 1999: 1).

The counter-culture then emerging with force was an expression of youth, of the teenager and the disaffected young adult, whose appearance and attitude, whose dress and language, whose pose, defied the standards of the day. The generation of the 1960s attacked the comfortable meaninglessness, insensitivity to social injustice and studied manners that they saw as the constituents of bourgeois culture. Youths pouted and mumbled, hunched their shoulders, raised their hands and arms in defiance. The young Marlon Brando expressed that mood in his early films, *The Wild One* (1953) and *On the Waterfront* (1954). Elvis Presley assumed a surly air, curled his lips and even swiveled his hips in defiance of accepted masculine custom. Later, as his career peaked, Presley appeared bespangled and coiffed, set out in white jump suit, high collar and cape. Elvis the Pelvis, as he was nicknamed, was a spectacular performer even before the stylized garb. He became a cult figure in his time and has so remained.

Although he died in 1977, Elvis Presley maintains a life of sorts as his image is daily projected by one or more of the now estimated 35,000 impersonators who can be found in Brazil, China and Korea as well as in the official Elvis clubs that gather in Memphis, Tennessee, annually to celebrate "The

King's" birthday. (He was born on January 8, 1935.) In 2002, 350 club presidents gathered for lunch on January 5, the first of the three-day celebration. No other popular artist in the last century has had such enduring levels of enthusiasm, nor such a familiar appearance. Elvis sightings are still reported, perhaps in his familiar outfit, the white color easily allowing ethereal visions to the faithful. Moreover, it is not unusual to see on vacant lots near busy streets the improvised, outdoor art galleries displaying brightly colored paintings of Elvis on velvet cloth. Elvis certainly was one of the twentieth century's major popular-culture icons.

As Elvis dressed up, hippies dressed down. Their uniform was not uniformed but it featured army-surplus clothing, such as military greatcoats with army insignia still in place, over T-shirts and jeans. In striking contrast were the teddy boys of Great Britain who dressed up. Primarily from working-class backgrounds, these young men wore Edwardian-style clothing that became briefly popular in postwar Britain. In a style of drape-shouldered jackets and stovepipe trouser legs and, often, suede shoes with crepe soles, they formed in small groups and gangs who bothered and often attacked others. At their worst they carried chains and knives and harassed the new immigrants from the Caribbean or Pakistan.

There was one other image that appeared threatening to the Establishment, a popular term by which to describe the power, authority and social indifference of the older generation. This was the appearance of members of a counterculture, the generation of the 1960s who were on one side of the "generation gap." On the other side were all those over 30 years of age, supposedly beyond the age of trust and candor. The appearance and attitude of the disaffected young was vividly described by a British journalist, commenting on the events of May 10, 1968, the high moment of the French student revolt: "This is a young revolution and most of the work is done at night. The best speech I heard was at two in the morning. ... It was given by a typical young *révolutionnaire*: black pullover, black trousers, long untidy hair, eyes gleaming with fatigue and lack of food ... " (Ali and Watkins 1998: 100).

The dramatic scene was part of the culmination of youthful protest, the student revolts that swept around the world, as no protest of the young had ever done before. Student agitation resulted from an unsettled – and unsettling – combination: dissatisfaction with the perceived smug bourgeois existence of the older generation (the parents of the protesting young); anger at persistent racism in the United States, and a decaying but still persistent colonialism in Algeria; outrage at American military intervention in Vietnam and at class differences still evident in Europe; and widespread disaffection with the Stalinist regime in the Soviet Union. Two events aroused particular concern. The first was the January 1969 Tet Offensive in Vietnam which suggested the ability to resist the American superpower. The second was the Prague Spring of 1968 when liberal governmental reform was briefly initiated but soon checked by intervention of the Soviet Union. Both military activities were to show the vulnerability of Soviet domination and the limitations of American military force.

This discontent with the existing order took shape in 1961, now seen as the initial year of popular discontent. The sit-in undertaken by four African-American college students in a Woolworth store lunch counter in Green-borough, North Carolina, was the act in which "the modern American student movement made its first mark on history" (Fraser 1988: 39). Soon similar sit-ins at universities and marches of protest followed in Britain and Germany, then in France and Japan, in the Philippines and Belgium.

Here was a truly global phenomenon, expressed differently in each country but with common ties and interests. In effect, there was a common vision of what was wrong with modern urban society and politics. That vision was sharply shaped by published photographs and television coverage of the major contemporary events that distressed the increasingly militant young. The visual contrast between Martin Luther King Jr. and Lyndon B. Johnson, the one standing high in confidence of his cause, the other stooped in uncertainty, was of major iconographic significance. So also was the dramatic setting and eloquent execution of King's "I have a dream" speech before the Lincoln Memorial and its contrast, the bitterly mocking chant of American college students as heard frequently on nightly television news: "Hey, hey, LBJ, how many kids did you kill today?"

If Vietnam was the first television war, the student revolutions of 1968 were the first youth movements to get television coverage (Arlen 1969; Fink et al. 1998: 9–13). In 1967 and 1968 the student movement reached its high point with confrontations on a global scale. The assassinations of Martin Luther King Jr. and Bobby Kennedy precipitated widespread protest marches and sit-ins. May 1968 was the month of the most intense activity. Perhaps its most dramatic setting was that of Paris on May 10, a date that has entered history as the Night of the Barricades when the students blockaded the streets around the Sorbonne and members of the CRS (national police security units) brutally charged and routed the students.

This new generation, angry and disaffected, developed its own forms of sight and sound – or at least it accepted new ones provided for it. By clothes and music the young quickly defined themselves. Denim trousers and overalls, formerly the garb of farmers and factory workers, became the uniform of both young men and young women, and henceforth were called "blue jeans," celebrated in songs by musicians like Eric Clapton and David Bowie. Neil Diamond probably made the definitive statement in his 1979 hit "Forever in Blue Jeans." Diamond sings that money may talk but it does nothing else and so he'd rather be "forever in blue jeans."

Marketing youth culture

Blue jeans continue to have their appeal and still remain premium wear of young people and also of people of all ages. Even though the United

States and much of the Western world is settling into early middle age, youthfulness remains a desirable state and, more recently, a recognized distinctive market.

While bound together by a document over two hundred years old, the citizenry of the United States showed little interest in other forms of preservation until recent decades. Popular culture, however, continues to emphasize youthfulness more than any other quality. Certainly there are the elderly and not-so-young in the center ring of popular culture: music stars like Madonna and Bruce Springsteen, and sportsmen like golf professional Jack Nicklaus, and, in the world of the Hollywood film, Paul Newman and Anne Bancroft carried on until their deaths at 83 and 73, respectively, as did Katharine Hepburn as an octogenarian, living to be 96. Nonetheless, the field, the stage and the screen are really the inherited property of the young, heralded in the media as the "new generation" or the "up-and-coming" – not to mention the boy bands or the teenyboppers. Automobile and cosmetic advertisements regularly emphasize vibrancy and luster, sensuality and vigor. Theirs is the rhetoric of youth. Only the pharmaceutical companies paint the picture gray; but even then it is often to assure the elderly – rapidly becoming a major segment of the population – that they too, if properly medicated, can still join in youthful fun.

Soon after World War Two, American businesses recognized a potential youth market and began to design and produce for it. In the 1990s that market burgeoned and was greatly assisted by the growing economy. It has been estimated that teenagers account for about $500 billion of the annual purchase of consumer goods in the United States, either through their own income or through an allowance, the latter now at a $50 weekly median. The rest of the market-driven economies of the world are now tapping into this growing market, most noticeably in Western Europe, Japan and Southeastern Asia.

It is interesting to note that the Dutch-based World Association of Research Professionals held a Worldwide Youth Marketing Research Conference in Beijing, China in 1999 to address the question: "Youth power: how to connect?" Representatives from Argentina, the United Kingdom, Indonesia, Poland and the United Arab Emirates, among others, read papers concerning the nature, growth and economic potential of the youth market. An editorial comment accompanying the paper abstracts stated the condition clearly: "Marketing to children, teens and Xers is a huge opportunity" (website "Youth power" 1999: 7). While a huge opportunity, it was not a simple endeavor.

The paperback *Generation X* (1964) – interviews with British mods and rockers – lent its title to a punk rock band (1976); in the late 1980s a Canadian psephologist used it for the generation born from 1964 onward, a meaning popularized in Douglas Coupland's comic strip (and 1991 novel) of the same name. Generation X may be much smaller than that of the Baby Boomers, but it has a lot more disposable income. Likewise, it is the first generation born with television fully rooted in the home, and with the emergence of cable television and VCRs, both of which became readily available in the mid-1970s. Likewise, Atari game systems (the first of which was the 2600, available for purchase in 1977) were a standard form of entertainment in middle class homes. Unlike their Baby Boomer predecessors, they actively controlled their media, changing channels with remote controls, muting commercials, recording their favorite TV shows, watching feature films multiple times via VCR, or forgoing the watching altogether, opting instead for blasting monsters or asteroids with the turn of a joystick and the push of a button.

In the early nineties as GenXers came of age as young adults, marketers began to explore ways to reach the diverse, media savvy demographic. Initially, advertisers co-opted an archetype that had been appearing in popular culture – the slacker, a one-dimensional character that initially stood for Generation X and was imagined by Richard Linklater in his 1991 film *Slacker*. Linklater's characters, an array of young people living in Austin, Texas, were alienated, cynical, angst-ridden people in their twenties with little or no interest in pursuing the ambitions and American dreams of others from the generations living during and after World War II. Generally, the slacker was imagined as white, male, and often angry and lacking in self-confidence (Bly 2010: 135). Paradoxically, however, Madison Avenue advertising executives knew that the demographic that they sought to reach was much more complex than this. Karen Ritchie, group media director for General Motors Worldwide, told colleagues at the Magazine Publishers Association annual meeting in October of 1992 that Generation X is "a fragmented generation in just about every way. To start with, it is racially and ethnically diverse. In its prime, [it] will be a generation of four minorities: [African]-Americans, Hispanic Americans, Asian Americans and whites. Minority marketing will have little relevance to these people, because all marketing will be minority marketing" (Ritchie 1992: 21). Generation X ushered in a new era of niche marketing and an end to clear-cut generational identities and market segments. It compelled marketing executives to co-opt more transgressive articulations of popular culture to sell products. Subaru's early nineties "What to Drive" ad campaign for its Impreza epitomized this, as it featured "Kid," a white, "hyperkinetic, 20ish punkster, who [was] almost incoherent as he prattled over the Impreza's relevance, comparing the car to punk rock" (Strauss 1993: 1B). The defiant nature of the music of GenX rebellion was being used to sell cars. Roland Barthes once said that the image always gets the last word. This quote is particularly apropos to this period in the history of American marketing, where a once rebellious youth subculture could be diluted in an ad campaign to sell cars.

Quite exposed and carefully posed

Casual in appearance and committed to social change 50 years before such marketing strategy aimed at youth, the young, particularly in the United

States, found in the 1940s newly liberated territory at the seashore. Always a transition zone between the known and the unknown, the measured and the measureless, the shore now became the beach, the bright sandy strip where the inhibitions of civilization were cast aside. Both custom and costume were there stripped down in the postwar era and it was a style event that announced this change.

The bikini, named after the tiny Pacific atoll on which atomic testing was taking place, was an abbreviated challenge to modesty and an assertion of physical wellbeing, which made its appearance in the summer of 1946. It was then that a French clothing designer Louis Reard, formerly an automobile engineer, designed this two-piece bathing suit and convinced a fashion model to strut it out at a popular Parisian swimming pool. Far removed from the two-piece costumes seen just before World War Two, the fashion was soon happily embraced by the young, svelte and happily liberated (as much from the agonies of the war as from the restrictions of high fashion). For centuries some men had enjoyed the privilege of the "male gaze" – as attentive spectators of all that artists deemed feminine and alluring – but here was the female nude – or near-nude, at least – in real time. And before long it was seen in feature-films too. The French film star Brigitte Bardot consented, at age 21, to be costumed in a bikini for the 1956 film *And God Created Woman.*

Taboos on nudity had lingered on since the time a Renaissance pope added fig leaves to the nude paintings then appearing. Both as a statement of personal freedom and a mild act of defiance, the bikini-wearers' little act of disclosure was expressive of a large change initiated by the young: the discarding of convention. With considerable rapidity, in less than two decades, people's appearances underwent striking change. From the carefully controlled, graceful movement of fashion models on the runways or catwalks at the annual shows of new couturier clothing in Paris to the wild and sweat-producing gyrations of rock groups like the Rolling Stones, the cultural attitudes of the 1960s and 1970s were sharply distinguished: managed poise opposed by youthful energy, the smooth prose of advertising in magazines and on television, in contrast to the verbal outbursts on the street and at the rock concert.

More than attitudes were discarded, however. The unfettered body was now not only celebrated but publicized as "cheesecake" and "beefcake." The curvaceous and the muscled had appeared in pictorial magazines since the 1950s, already strongly suggesting sexual prowess. On the screen that correlation had been made in *From Here to Eternity* (1953). Wrapped in intense embrace on the beach, as the waves lapped at their supine forms, Burt Lancaster, beefed up, and Deborah Kerr, toned down, opened the way for widespread viewing of the un-garbed human condition. That same year Hugh Hefner produced *Playboy,* a magazine that popularized – and even legitimized to a degree – the niche magazines referred to as "adult." As the centerfold of the very first issue, Hefner used one of the nude photographs he had purchased of a model named Norma Jean Baker, who would be brilliantly made over as Marilyn Monroe. Then, a photograph of an unclothed young woman became daily fare on page three of the British newspaper *The Sun*, first published in tabloid in 1969.

The female body has long been a malleable as well as a marketable object, adorned, configured and appreciated according to perceptions of beauty by the male gazer. A comparison of a Rubens nude (early seventeenth century) and a fully attired Gibson girl (late nineteenth century) will demonstrate what happened to the female waist and hips as art objects. The flat-breasted *gamin* of the 1920s gave way to the well-molded, long-legged young woman of American films of the 1930s and 1940s. Her height was further accentuated by British designer Mary Quant's introduction of the mini-skirt in the 1960s. Quant's chief model was nicknamed Twiggy, a choice metaphor for the long-legged, short-skirted woman who became fashionable at that time and so has remained.

Men pretended at least to craft their own bodies. As one of the earliest of the modern body-builders who made the sport popular and entertaining in the 1960s, Charles Gaines explained in *Pumping Iron* that "the body is an art medium: malleable, capable of being aesthetically dominated and formed the way clay is by a potter. A body builder in training is a kind of sculptor of himself" (Gaines and Butler 1981: 43). As if in confirmation of Gaines' argument, the Whitney Museum of Modern Art put on a brief show (brief in garb and duration) entitled "Articulate muscle: the body as art" in February 1976, with Arnold Schwarzenegger as its principal mobile sculpture.

Even though men were pumping iron around the world (the sport soon being globally popular in countries like France, Egypt, Iraq and Jamaica), bodybuilding was never as popular as working out, where both men and women exercised to tone their bodies, for the sake of both appearance and health. Regular and carefully programmed exercise was a sign of what was called fitness, the physical contribution to well-being, matched by concern with nutrition and psychological "stress management." In the 1970s, aerobic exercising became popular in the United States as did those imported mind–body regimes from China, Japan and Korea: karate, tae kwon do and tai chi.

Then the men flexed in response

Complementary to exercise grew personal grooming and the use of cosmetics. Of course, the adornment of face and body is a practice that reaches far back in time. Body piercing and tattooing – both now back in favor – are among the oldest such aesthetic modifications, along with eye and hair treatments. And men were not exempt, as the fashion for wigs in the seventeenth and eighteenth centuries amply proves. Ditto for beauty marks, face powder and rouge, particularly among the court aristocracy in France. In the early nineteenth century, dyeing the hair was also popular, as in Honoré de

Balzac's novel *Père Goriot,* in which old Goriot uses his wealth to assure his two daughters the means to high social status in Parisian society. After having sold all his earthly possessions in this endeavor and taken a small room in the boarding house where he had earlier been living in spacious comfort, he no longer can even afford hair dye, his last means of maintaining appearances.

The woman's use of cosmetics as a widespread practice in European countries and the United States became popular only at the end of the nineteenth century. Prior to this time, painting one's face was widely understood as the prostitute's advertisement of profession. As a result, cosmetics were rarely sold: women who wanted them had to make their own, using "kitchen chemistry" – just as they made medical treatments. By the turn of the century, attitudes had changed; cosmetics, primarily for face and hair, were being marketed. In the European Union of today, the cosmetics industry is a $55 billion industry. The term "make-up" grew in favor in the early twentieth century. It neutralized the connotations of "face paint" and helped cosmetics to be perceived as enhancing nature, not disguising women without the goodness that the unadorned face radiantly displayed, as many in mid-nineteenth century America and England thought. Moreover, enterprising women saw the opportunity for service and success by developing beauty salons and beauty products. Some were future product names like Elizabeth Arden and Helena Rubenstein, and African-American women like Annie Turnbo-Malone and Madam C. J. Walker offered products specifically to the African-American population in the United States (Peiss 1998: 61–96).

From this time forward, cosmetics grew in use, variety and success as a market item. Annually, the cosmetics industry grosses about $170 billion a year worldwide, the largest markets being in the United States, the European Union and Japan. However, products have been moving briskly into China by way of Hong Kong and are expanding into central and eastern Europe as well. In 2001 the IN-COSMETICS exhibition in Paris attracted 200 exhibitors and representatives from 75 countries. A growing segment of the European industry is that of male cosmetics, now boldly intended to enhance the allure of macho men. This trend follows the American and Japanese precedents, where male cosmetics are more than a niche market. In 2010, according to the *Global Cosmetic Industry,* global sales of men's grooming products was $27 billion. According to the same publication, the Japanese market for male cosmetics increased by 70 percent between the mid-1980s and the mid-1990s. Males aged between 16 to 25 were a new marketing target group, according to an article in the June 22, 1998 online publication *Trends in Japan.* Many young men now arm themselves with face wipes and deodorant sprays, and use depilatories to remove unwanted body hair. Most striking is the use of hair dyes, a shade of orange being very popular.

In America, critics have found a new rival to the Apollo Belvedere, once seen as the ideal male form. Now it is the bulked-up G.I. Joe dolls. The androgynous male rock-star ideal of the 1970s and the androgynous models of 1990s male cosmetic and underwear ads for clothing companies like Calvin Klein and Abercrombie and Fitch have given way to the take-command, rugged-and-right male of the moment. Critic Camille Paglia, commenting on the dedicated firefighters struggling to deal with the massed ruins of the World Trade Center Towers, remarked "how robustly masculine the faces of the firefighters are. ... They're not on Prozac or questioning their gender" (Goodman 2002: H2).

Only the internationally recognized abstract symbols for men and women that define the still respected zone of separation, the public lavatory, have maintained consistency of form. Throughout the late twentieth and early twentieth centuries, both men and women have "re-invented" themselves in much of the world. At the start of the new century, Sarah, Duchess of York, then icon of Weight Watchers advertisements, put it in a chapter heading in her book *Re-Inventing Yourself With the Duchess of York* (2001), one must begin by "deconstructing your self-concept."

What women had been and could be, how they were depicted and what roles they were required to play, were public concerns following World War Two. Gender roles were slowly altered in light of arguments made by women who would now be called "feminist" authors rather than "female" writers. No doubt the most significant, the pacesetter of this new movement, was the French philosophy professor and novelist Simone de Beauvoir. Her detailed assessment of womanhood, *The Second Sex*, first appeared in 1949, and was translated and published in an American edition in 1957. The work, hardly the first on the subject, gained eminence because of its detailed history and current assessment of women – the "second sex" – as culturally subordinate to men.

As she wrote, "males could not enjoy this privilege fully unless they believed it to be founded on the absolute and the eternal; they sought to make the fact of their supremacy into a right" (Beauvoir 1976: xxii). Yet even with legal changes and new opportunities for the independence that is derived from a career, the woman who eschews the traditional pattern of dependent domestic partner "remains dominated, surrounded by the male universe." Hers is an "immanent enterprise," directed to proving herself, not to being "passionately concerned with the content" of her occupation (Beauvoir 1976: 702). Moreover, Beauvoir's philosophical argument for subjectivity – "that the world ... can only be viewed from a particular point of view ... [through individuals'] relations with the world and other consciousnesses," was the foundational theoretical nugget of a generation of white, male French poststructuralist theorists who gained fame and notoriety in the 1970s and 80s (Fullbrook and Fullbrook 2008: 76). Presciently, in his review of the American edition of *The Second Sex*, the popular American essayist Philip Wylie wrote that Beauvoir's narrative "flows from a quality that men often deny to women: genius."

The reception of the book in the United States was profound and extensive among a new generation of women authors who took up the feminist cause.

Betty Friedan, who acknowledged the influence of Simone de Beauvoir, took the "woman problem" forward in an analysis of postwar life in the United States when, she argued, the dominant literature on the subject generated the "feminine mystique," the ideology that asserted female happiness was derived from women's "role ... to seek fulfillment as wives and mothers" (Friedan 1963: 15). To escape this condition, Friedan argued, the contemporary woman should "find herself ... as a person, by creative work of her own," not simply a job but "one that is equal to [her] actual capacity" (Friedan 1963: 344).

Changes in female status were accompanied by changes in appearance. The business suit and trousers de-pedestalized women and gave the impression, as intended, of women's growing partnership with men in the world of commerce and business. Gone were very visible purses or handbags hanging from the forearm (though still part of the Queen of England's body armor), as were white gloves and hats. It was Yves Saint-Laurent, widely acclaimed as the most significant couturier of the last century, who dramatically changed female fashion. He introduced the pants suit and redesigned the trench coat and the tuxedo for women. He also gave the male a whiff of good stuff with his Opium and Jazz line of male toiletries.

The blurring of outward appearance, the "ambiguation" that characterizes so much of contemporary popular culture, is captured in the term "unisex," seen on barber shops and styling salons where men and women sit and receive treatment both by women and men stylists. As visible and more pervasive among the young are the T-shirts and jeans that remain the clothing issue of preference for both sexes. Thorstein Veblen's notion of "conspicuous consumption" was based on a class-structured society in which only the rich and "comfortably situated" could be stylish or show the distinctiveness of their status. What has radically changed is its exclusivity. Appearances are now easily acquired by the majority: the mass production and distribution of clothing and beauty accessories, as well as the availability of domestic items, whether cutlery or cars, has blurred distinctions of consumption (Seabrook 2000: 161–75). The enabling agent of this consuming society is the gold or platinum credit card, the silent variant of the wish-granting genie but which comes out of the wallet and requires only a signature, by-passing the employment of the genie who comes out of a brass oil-lamp only when the sooty lamp is rubbed.

All of the obsession with appearances has led inevitably led to a contemporary search as intense as Ponce de Leon's famous quest for the fountain of youth. If youthful exuberance shook the starchy social attitudes of the distrusted over-30 generation as the twentieth century wound down, they also made youthful appearance a social imperative. Its most recent popular form is cosmetic surgery. Statistics are most informative: in 1998, 600,000 Americans had such surgery, 350,000 Argentines and 65,000 Britons. Cosmetic surgery centers are found in Canada and Yugoslavia, in Italy and Australia, in Sweden and Poland – to name just a few obvious countries. "This is true democracy at work," commented a Brazilian doctor. "Plastic surgery can be important for self-esteem for anyone and should be available" (Jones 2001: 2). More recently, however, cosmetic surgery has expanded in more ways than imagined just a decade ago. In 2011, 13.8 million procedures were conducted in the US and surgeons found new markets for niche procedures, including labiaplasty, the surgery to trim labia, and vaginoplasty, a procedure to tighten and "revitalize" the vagina. While statistics on the numbers of these procedures conducted annually remain ambiguous, feminist critics and scholars contend that the idealized vaginas in pornography have contributed to the popularity of the procedures. One feminist blogger quipped: "In a wonderful example of a Baudrillardian nightmare in which the virtual not the actual has come to define what is 'normal' … women and oftentimes their partners are taking … airbrushed [porn] models as guides to the way women's genitals should be. The mature genitalia with their wrinkly bits and pieces are now perceived as imperfect. We can, and some think we should, get our genitals surgically deconstructed and reconstructed to look like we looked when we were ten" (websites "138 Million Cosmetic Plastic Surgery Procedures Performed in 2011"; "Labiaplasty. Baudrillard. That is All" 2012).

Originally a sort of severe beauty treatment that only women spoke of undergoing, cosmetic surgery has become a "man thing" as well in the last few years. In a highly competitive environment for choice managerial positions, where – again – appearances count, the younger-looking man, it is avowed, has the advantage. The rather standard comment is that the contemporary American male is more interested in looking appealing in the boardroom than in the bedroom. According to statistics released by The American Society of Plastic Surgeons in 2010, men had 1.1 million procedures, the most common being facelifts and liposuction. Enthusiasm for Botox injections swept across the United States as the means to remove facial wrinkles and to give anyone who does not mind the inability to frown a bright outlook regardless of age (website "138 Million Cosmetic Plastic Surgery Procedures Performed in 2011" 2012).

Self-reflection

Just over a hundred years ago, Oscar Wilde wrote *The Portrait of Dorian Gray*, a short work concerning a dashingly handsome young man who avoided the road map of old age and debauchery through an ingenious trick: a portrait of himself which assumed all the effects of such biological and social wear and tear. The portrait was hidden away so that all Dorian Gray's friends saw in his person was ever-vibrant youth and unchallenged dissipation. (Eventually, Dorian destroys his own portrait, and the rest follows without need of further description.)

Such visions of ourselves, of course, reach far back before Oscar Wilde's time. Once, according to classical Greek legend, the handsome Greek youth Narcissus fell in love with his own appearance as reflected in water (into which he, a non-swimmer, fell). Then there was the wicked queen, "fairest of them all" until Snow White came along. Across the span of civilization, the high and the mighty, the majestic and the heroic have assumed attitudes and struck poses and enjoyed the adulation of their peers. Occasionally a frog turned into a prince and a step-sister quit washing stone floors when the shoe fit and thereafter danced on as queen happily ever after. But only in the twentieth century did the possibility of democratically distributed beauty and strength occur through the market and by modern technological means. This manufacture of appearances, with a global stretch that has touched every culture, is a major part of the postmodern technology.

Popular culture offers evidence of its far-spread existence by images and appearances in an incessant flow. At no other time than now has the several-centuries-old expression for understanding, "I see what you mean," been so appropriate.

Sound and fury: NYC music scene 1994–2000 (© Teru Kuwayama/CORBIS)

5   All the world's a stage

Contemporary entertainment in its many forms

On June 23, 2001 about 3 billion television viewers saw and heard a concert presented by "the Three Tenors" (Luciano Pavarotti, Placido Domingo, and José Carreras) in the Forbidden City of Beijing, where a live audience of some 30,000 filled the vast courtyard of the Meridian Gate before the imperial palace. It was the grandest media event the Communist regime had ever organized. Against a palatial backdrop glistening with the lacquer-like brilliance of traditional Chinese gold and red, the three aging singers reached high and low as they sang in Italian, English, French and Spanish, ranging in selection from grand opera to American musical. It was far-reaching entertainment, global culture, a theater in the earthly round.

And yet, though spectacular, it was also, as Yogi Berra is famous for having said, "*déjà vu* all over again." The three tenors had been doing this for over ten years and their thirty concerts had all been staged in improbable locations. Pop culture gives such places cachet by using the word "venue." The threesome began in Rome in 1990, singing at the Baths of Caracalla as part of the celebration attending the World Cup (soccer) finals. Next they gathered under the Eiffel Tower in Paris. Then they came together in the luminescent opulence of Las Vegas. At the Rome concert, Domingo said that "Music and sport are the most universal things in the world." Ten years later in Las Vegas, he speculated that some people came to the concerts because they liked classical music and others came "because of the event." (An "event" – which one historian described as an eruption, a bursting forth as a tear in the otherwise only wrinkled cloth of the past – changes things. Domingo's event was, however, like a bright artifice, theater at its best.)

These performances by the three tenors exemplify a contemporary condition, a postmodern truth: we sit before a world stage. Whether in a vast audience outdoors or as an audience of one of the television set indoors, we now open our eyes to the world. This is the age of the spectacle and the spectacular. The old adage "Seeing is believing" is still taken for granted but now "Seeing is enjoying" too. Analysts use the term "spectacularization" for the way activities and places are set up or rearranged to assure entertainment at its most dazzling: political conventions, theme parks, the opening of major sports events, "native" performances for tourists, rock music concerts, the interior decor of cruise ships – and the global 24-hour celebration of the new millennium, topped off by the fireworks display for which the Eiffel Tower was both the frame and the symbol.

Long before this particular display of Gallic verve, however, outdoor displays bore the French signature. In 1947, the first of the now globally popular *son et lumière* shows was produced. Attractive artifices, these light-and-sound productions recount the history of major monuments and edifices, using a varying display of lights to illuminate features of the building that figured in history, all enacted before an audience sitting on the grass or on chairs under a canopy of stars. It made relaxing nighttime entertainment, a welcome relief from the wearying tourist strolls of the daytime. It was new expression of docudrama that illuminated and vividly described what the structure stood for historically, and what its occupants lived or died for.

The châteaux of the Loire Valley were among the first grand piles of stones that lent their magnificence to *son et lumière*. The concept soon crossed the Channel to England where in 1969 it came to Blenheim Palace, family home of the Churchills, a stately eighteenth-century structure now further ennobled by the rich voice of Richard Burton providing the narrative, accompanied by the changing light effects. Seemingly always in the forefront of global trends, the United States had its first *son et lumière* show in San Francisco in 1959. More recently, the Pyramids of Egypt have been bathed in light and rhetoric, with the once silent Sphinx speaking "of the 5,000 years I have seen all the suns man can remember come up in the sky" (website "*Son et lumière: Giza*" 2001: n.p.). The French government gave a *son et lumière* show to Mount Vernon, George Washington's home, on the occasion of the bicentenary of the American Declaration of Independence. By the end of the century, such shows recounted the history of the Acropolis in Athens, the cities of Delhi in India and Mombasa in Kenya, and the battle of Ladysmith as part of the centenary (2000) of the Anglo-Boer War in South Africa. In such manner, the historical site became the historical stage.

Even as Europe was still burdened by the destruction of World War Two, the *son et lumière* shows illuminated the fact that entertainment was becoming an industry marked by technological enhancement, geographical extension and cultural diversification. In effect, the theaters of war were replaced by the theaters of distraction. Instead of the horror of firebombs, fireworks burst forth in celebration of uneventful things, like the nightly closing of an amusement park. The cities blacked out during the war soon were ablaze in light. Wartime searchlights were replaced by floodlights and laser beams (and light pollution became a new atmospheric problem). Even Adolf Hitler's briefly contemplated construction of a 100,000-ton battleship has its peacetime counterparts in tonnage, but freighted with different purpose. Several cruise ships are now of that size but move only to assure maximum entertainment.

The Berlin Wall

Were one example to be singled out to demonstrate the influence of entertainment in the contemporary world, it would be the celebration of arguably the most powerfully symbolic act since World War Two: the dismantling – better, the tearing-down – of the Berlin Wall. Hastily erected between East and West Berlin in 1961 as a means to restrict the egress of Germans from the Communist regime in East Germany (though ostensibly put up for the opposite purpose), the Berlin Wall was 96 miles long. It stood for the front line between the world's two armed camps – the one championed by the Soviet Union, the other by the United States – in the Cold War.

With the Soviet Union in a state of collapse, the Berlin Wall was opened on November 9, 1989 and soon pulled down by joyful Berliners. Within months, Roger Waters, a former member of the rock band Pink Floyd, made another kind of history of this momentous event. Famous for its electronic showmanship, Pink Floyd was perhaps best known for its 1979 album *The Wall*. It was originally staged by Waters, who was asked in 1989 to do another version to aid a relief fund. He agreed, and considered locations as far apart as the Grand Canyon and Wall Street. But he was seized by the fall of the Berlin Wall as the exceptional and appropriate site and occasion. He later described the concert as "a liberating of the human spirit."

The preparation of the site on Potsdamer Platz and the difficulties of both organizing and staging the concert have a drama of their own. In brief compass, here's the story: construction of a wall 82 feet high and 591 feet long, of polystyrene bricks; gathering together musical performers including the East Berlin Radio Symphony Orchestra and Choir, the Marching Bands of the Combined Soviet Forces in Berlin and pop singers like Cyndi Lauper, Bryan Adams and Van Morrison; arranging lighting and sets of enormous proportions (including a five-story-high inflated pig's head designed by Gerald Scarfe). The concert took place on July 21, 1990, before an on-site audience of 250,000 and a viewing audience of 500 million in 35 countries where the concert was broadcast live.

Not even the $13 million, one-hour-long fireworks extravaganza put on by the Chinese government during the handing-over ceremonies when Great Britain gave up control of Hong Kong on June 24, 1997 could compare to the Pink Floyd's "Live Wall." At moments of significant change, these two performances treated commemoration as great entertainment, not as solemn ceremony. (Winston Churchill had planned the greatest victory parade ever in London in honor of Franklin D. Roosevelt who, however, died just months before World War Two ended in Europe.)

Busy leisure

Like wild flowers in the summer, entertainment flourishes, even runs riot, in our global climate where the season of leisure is longer than ever before.

Entertainment is the time-filler of all those liberated from labor, once required from sunup to sundown. All entertainment is expressed as non-work, even when it takes considerable effort. The physical exhaustion of a marathon run, the anxiety of a bungee jump, the painstaking effort to hand-turn a piece of pottery – all are entertaining, amusing or inspiring diversions from routine. Almost all are "products" prepared and delivered along industrial lines with their own unit costs (entrance fees for marathon races, set rates for individual bungee jumps and, of course, ticket purchases).

None of such activity is necessary, required or pre-ordained. It is a matter of choice, whether enthusiastically or indifferently made, by those who have the money and the time to seek self-fulfillment or to enjoy self-indulgence. It may mean working at or toward or for something, but it does not mean working. Without any qualifying preposition (think of "work out," for instance), work often meant drudgery and monotony and the lack of individual purpose beyond simple survival.

The concept of leisure was until recently known only to the few, those now called the leisured classes: the idle nobles at a royal court of seventeenth-century Europe, the sons and daughters of self-made men and "robber barons" of late nineteenth-century America, for instance. These privileged ones are seen in their delicate beauty as the fair maidens and elegantly prettied-up young men in the paintings of Watteau and Gainsborough. They appear later, in different pose and costume, in the boulevard comedies so prominent in Europe at the turn of the twentieth century and, a couple of decades later, in the novels of F. Scott Fitzgerald or the mysteries of Agatha Christie. And they swirl around, dressed in evening clothes in vastly proportioned interiors, as the subjects of Hollywood musicals of the 1930s.

Leisure as an industrial product

Leisure time, as distinct from the existence of the leisured classes, was an industrial product. Before the middle of the nineteenth century, there were few entertainments for the common folk. Morality plays before the cathedral entrance in the Middle Ages, wedding feasts and country fairs of the early modern period were chief among them. Leisure activities feature in the paintings of Pieter Brueghel in the sixteenth century, notably children's games, which anyone growing up before the availability of AA batteries can look at with some sense of nostalgia.

At one time quite localized, infrequent and primarily a condition of the wealthy, leisure time has been converted into a viable oxymoron: the leisure industry. Entertainment thus becomes a new commodity, a new consumer activity. A major part of the service sector of the economy, the leisure indus-try and the entertainment industry form a sort of yin and yang of pleasurable diversion for the tourist, the amateur sportsperson, the spectator, the member of the audience – any and all of those stepping back from their daily routine.

Diversion is assured, of course, by hotel maid, tour guide, bar tender, chorus line and waiter – the *lumpenproletariat* of the service sector.

At its other or top end are found the crowd-pleasing entertainers, in film and sports and on television. The salaries of movie stars are, as befits their title, astronomical. At the apex was Jim Carrey's $20 million for his role in *The Cable Guy* (1990). Television news, regularly described as entertainment, is as dependent on personality and wit as it is on informed analysis. This condition made news itself when Katie Couric negotiated a $15 million annual salary contract with CBS in 2006 when she took the helm as evening news anchor, a position she held for five years. (She also has a fan website, not of her own making, however.)

Barry Bonds, the San Francisco Giants outfielder, negotiated a ten-year $80 million contract in early 2002. It included a personal service contract that will guarantee an annual $1 million donation to the Bonds Family Foundation for ten years after Bonds takes off his uniform. Not so grandiose but wildly expansive have been the salary incomes of the English footballer, David Beckham. His salary at Real Madrid came to a yearly £24.6 million ($40 million) over a four-year contract. Beckham was greeted in Tokyo in December 2002 with a 10-foot-high statue made of chocolate, in celebration of his two-year chocolate and cosmetics advertising contract of $3 million annually.

Clearly, entertainment pays. The industrial process, originally steam-motivated and given to turning out tangible products, today provides the vocabulary and the pattern by which entertainment is mass produced, and it does so primarily through the agency of electricity, as the amplification and television broadcast of the Three Tenors concert in Beijing so clearly demonstrated. Vacations, for instance, are "packaged," and "tourism product" is a familiar term by which to describe what tourists see and how they are accommodated.

Vacations and leisure time

Now universally accepted as a desirable condition, vacations were early in the nineteenth century an indication of middle-class status in the United States (Aron 1999: 5). They were likewise in Europe, where earlier those who frequented casinos and took the waters at spas were either nobles or wealthy. The seashore, seen as foreboding and uninviting in previous centuries, became a major recreational site by the middle of the century, access made easy by train. A revolutionary change in "vacationing," a term introduced in the 1850s (Aron 1999: 32), occurred in the twentieth century with the widespread introduction of paid vacations. In 1936, for instance, the French government made a paid, two-week vacation in August mandatory for all employees. By the late twentieth century, this had risen to five weeks, as it had in other European countries like Finland, Sweden and Austria.

And yet an anomaly in this development has recently appeared, particularly in the United States. As corporations have been downsizing to enhance profits and thus assure stock price gains pleasing to their investors, the workforce has diminished. The dual result has been that overtime work has increased for those still employed, and dual-spouse employment has also increased. In addition, the work-and-spend syndrome has developed, wherein consumption absorbs much of what is gained by working. Although described as "an affliction of affluent, mostly white, Americans" (Schorr 1991: 112), it is evident in other parts of the world as well.

Leisure therefore comes at a price; indeed more and more of it is sold as a commodity. If buying – personal consumption of non-essentials – is factored in as a form of leisure and entertainment, as many writers on the subject have suggested, then one can argue that free time is costly. And, should one wish to "get away," the traditional walk in the woods has been replaced by the giant steps of modern transportation.

Transported ecstatically

The industrial process produced not only consumer goods but also new forms of transportation that did not rely on animal muscles or wind or fast-flowing streams. It was the railroad whose locomotives were powered by steam that first allowed for easy, long-distance travel on land. Steamers – ferries, river boats and ocean liners – transformed journeys on water. Less than a century later the automobile emerged, personalizing the traveling experience; and then came the airplane, the most successful long-distance form of mass transportation. As time for diversion expanded, so did the space over which it could be expended. Jules Verne's famous novel *Around the World in Eighty Days* (1873) introduced the idea of "globe-trotting" and did so as an idle wager of wealthy British club men. As we know, Phileas Fogg won the wager and set the pace.

Fogg's may have been one of the first examples of "adventure tourism," of taking a chance for the thrill of it. Hair-raising recreation like paragliding and white-water rafting were not known to Fogg, though he was nimble-footed and risk-prone. But he expanded the geography of travel and changed its very nature, if only in fiction. Tourism, speedy travel afar and for short spurts of time, now entered the vocabulary just as it soon became a major industry. About two decades after Fogg left the comforts of London, critics were complaining of crowds of tourists. The *Edinburgh Review* in 1898 declared the route to the French Alpine resort of Chamonix to be "tourist-mobbed."

If France became one of the major tourist destinations at that time – and so it has remained down to our own time – other parts of the world were soon so visited, even "mobbed." Resorts now accommodated members of the laboring class with leisure time as well as members of the traditional leisure class. The "day trippers," on a one-day round-trip rail excursion, left London for Brighton, Jersey City for Asbury Park, Paris for Deauville. In the interwar period, places like Hawaii and Nice, Algeria and Bermuda attracted a larger and more varied clientele than ever before. The 1933 musical film *Flying Down to Rio*, featuring Fred Astaire and Ginger Rogers with a chorus line dancing on the wings of an airplane, gave a whimsical glimpse of the future on wings.

The aircraft and tourist industries generated what is now called "synergy": each gave a big boost to the other in the decades following World War Two. The World Tourism Organization reports that "in spite of occasional shocks, international tourist arrivals have shown ... uninterrupted growth: from 25 million in 1950, to 277 million in 1980, to 435 million in 1990, to 675 million in 2000. By the early twenty-first century, international tourism is a billion dollar business; in 2010, receipts are estimated to have reached $919 billion (the equivalent of 693 billion euros), a 4.7 percent increase even amid a global economic downturn" (website "Facts and Figures: Information, Analysis, and Know-How" 2012). Not included in these figures are college and university students studying abroad, business people on assignment in countries other than their own in corporations that are becoming international and global in scope, or family members visiting relatives. The rapid ascent of air travel, however, took a nose dive after the 9/11 terrorist attacks by two hijacked commercial airliners used as guided missiles, on the towers of the World Trade Center on September 11, 2001.

Tourism

Most of those transported abroad in a few hours were tourists, either seeking glimpses of other worlds with cultures seemingly steeped in other times or seeking momentary escape from the rigid forms of a highly urbanized culture in which time was declared to be money. The easily appreciated icons of each intended destination were widely displayed in tourist agency brochure and magazine advertisement: the Parthenon and a Parisian café, the Taj Mahal and a *luau* in Hawaii.

Tourism has long offered as its principal products the antique and the exotic, the long-gone and the far-away. Its appeal is of the seemingly different. That desired condition of show-and-tell arouses the concern of cultural critics, and for a simple reason. The antique and the exotic imply stasis, a condition of non-change, the one suggesting the ageless, the other the unhurried. "Imagine walking in the footsteps of Alexander the Great," reads a tourist ad for Turkey. "Find a vacant hammock and remember how to dream," reads the caption for a seaside scene in an advertisement for the Cayman Islands.

In terms of culture contact – and possible conflict – the dynamism and super-modernity of the West are thereby contrasted with the perceived and desired slow pace, the assumed quaint and unspoiled nature of those culture areas made to serve as theaters of delight. Whether to sense something of the ancient or the exotic, "experiencing heritage" thus becomes a major reason for tourist travel and results "in a commodification of the past" (Waitt 2000: 838). Unintentionally offering evidence in favor of this argument, a report of the Egyptian tourist minister Mamdouh el-Beltagui warned against those who wished to slow down or halt Egyptian tourist development. "We have to get our share of the world tourism traffic," he argued, "in order to assure more jobs and greater access to hard currency ... " (Attia 1998: 6).

To some of its critics, tourism is seen as cultural and economic imperialism or a form of exploitation that subjects institutions and populations to service in the host country that satisfies the desires and fantasies of the well-off outsider. Cultural or heritage tourism certainly is one major component of the global tourism industry, but much of that heritage, so widely advertised in enticing photographs and text, is arranged for Western eyes. "Tourism, in many ways, is a form of neo-colonialism" (Boniface and Fowler 1993: 19). The former colonial relationship of dominator to dominated continues in tourist-led representations of the "way things were." Historic sites, even historic land in the form of national parks, are constant rehearsals of the white, Western world view, it has been asserted.

That statement is given credence by the Singapore Tourist Promotion Board which in a 1986 report placed the "exotic east" and the "colonial heritage" as two of the five categories designed to attract tourists to stay longer than the average 3.5 days (Khan 1999: 76). The decried preponderance of the West in tourism is statistically stated by the World Tourist Organization's report that in 1995 found that 81.8 percent of all tourists came from the United States, Canada, Western Europe and Japan. Yet, even in the United States, the most avid globe-trotting tourist nation, tourism is the third largest national industry.

As a postmodernist development everywhere, extensive tourism is an indication of more widely distributed disposable income, more convenient means of travel and higher levels of literacy and education. More recent assessments of tourism have provided a more beneficial side and the idea of the "destination community," a locale of interactivity by both hosts and visitors, in which change is mutually initiated and mutually regulated. "Cultural tourism has achieved great success in terms of economic profit and social reward," Zhang Xiqin, Vice-Director of the China National Tourism Administration, stated in a terse summary statement of current, widely held opinion (website "Theme parks" 2001: 1).

Cultural tourism has also added a new dimension to theatrical entertainment. Craft industries have been revitalized in every region and culture of the world. The tourist is invited to wander leisurely around and to peer into the workshops that now comprise artisan villages, making wooden giraffes in Mombasa, Kenya, or weaving tapestries in Tunis, Tunisia. Anyone who has gone to Turkey or India and visited a rug showroom has enjoyed the theatricality with which rolled rugs are snapped open and flipped smartly to the floor. Among the contemporary examples of improvised handicraft, none is perhaps more clever than the toy cars and airplanes, made of empty cans of Sprite and Coca Cola and found hanging brightly from street-corner kiosks in Ho Chi Minh City. Even the famous Augarten porcelain workshop in Vienna, founded by the Empress Maria Theresa in the eighteenth century and re-founded after World War Two, has special tours, which end in the gift shop. In sum, tourism has re-energized the world's craft industries and has returned craftsmanship to the state of a profitable art in many parts of the world.

Such developments suggest that tourism has moved on since the 1969 film parody, *If It's Tuesday, This Must be Belgium*. The assumption of "golden hordes" invading, desecrating and looting the cultural riches of other people is surely obsolete. People still travel to see the antique or the exotic, but new kinds of tourism have sprung up since the 1960s. The qualifying terms of such particularized tourism are many: sports tourism, adventure tourism, fantasy tourism, ecotourism and even sex tourism. Relatively frequent and inexpensive air travel has allowed relatively easy movement to most any part of the world where fancy and desire may be played out.

In 1966, the documentary film *The Endless Summer* followed two California surfboarders as they went around the world seeking the best beaches on which to practice their popular sport. Golf tourism is also avidly and widely supported, with the current king of Morocco holding an annual tournament, to which he invites (and often pays) well-known golfers. Foot races like the now famous Boston Marathon (26,895 participants in 2011) and the intensely crowded Chicago Marathon (37,670 participants in 2011) attract huge numbers from around the United States and the world. And for a few participants they are also profitable: Haile Gebrselassie, an Olympic runner from Ethiopia, was offered an estimated $500,000 to appear in the 2002 London marathon.

Re-enactors engage in their own fantasy roles and provide the spectator excitement as medieval knights and American Civil War soldiers at annual festivals serving as outdoor theaters of the softly scrimmed past. Those individuals daydreaming of hitherto unattainable achievements can go to fantasy camps, where, as at Lake Placid in New York, they can win their own "Olympic gold" as a skater and rejoice in the cheers of other participants. They can do much the same at different locations with baseball, football and professional wrestling. Unlike Miniver Cheevy in Edwin Arlington Robinson's 1910 poem, who regretted the day he was born because he yearned to be a knight of yore, the contemporary dreamer need not sigh, if he or she has the money to act out fantasy or daydream with a supporting cast provided by the tourist center. Other opportunities of a deleterious nature also exist. The sex tourism now so prevalent in Thailand brings Europeans principally to that country where they find and grossly exploit a readily available population of young – of very young – people, often sent out on the streets by their parents desperate for money. Tourist guides to Amsterdam provide information on that city's gay zones.

Niche tourism: ecotourism, adventure tourism and the "pilgrimage"

Of the many forms of niche tourism that have recently emerged, none has been more popular and seemingly beneficial than ecotourism. Praised as both environmentally sound and environmentally supportive, as the means for greater appreciation of the varied climate zones in which we live and assurance of their respect and maintenance, ecotourism has been particularly developed in Central and South America, notably in Costa Rica, Panama and Ecuador. The most popular site has been the Galapagos Islands, made famous a century-and-a-half ago when Charles Darwin first posited his theory of evolution as a result of his examination of animal life there. Now widely sought for their unique, isolated habitats where the only visible sign of human intrusion is the footprint of the ecotourist, and where access is provided only briefly by ship, the islands entertain and instruct by presenting a natural environment, isolated from human domain and dominion.

A forerunner of ecotourism was – and is – the photo safari now so popular in Kenya, Uganda and South Africa. Led by Kenya, the photo safari quickly became an exotic tourist activity in the 1960s in those African countries that established vast reserves guarded by soldiers to prevent poaching. In 1978 Kenya abolished the big-game hunting of the likes of Teddy Roosevelt and Ernest Hemingway. In effect, the reserves have become large-scale zoos where the visitor sees the wild life from the open top of a Safari van which makes stops whenever such wild life is spotted. The countryside criss-crossed by tires is proof of the constant presence of this form of tourism

Adventure tourism is primarily an outdoors, off-the-beaten-path activity that has caught the enthusiasm of the young. It includes a variety of newly popular sports such as hang gliding, rock climbing, white-water rafting and helicopter skiing (whereby the skier is lifted by helicopter to otherwise inaccessible places). Perhaps the most sensational, daring and stomach-turning of these activities is bungee (also spelled bungy) jumping, begun commercially by an enterprising New Zealander, A. J. Hackett, whose elaborate and entertaining website (www.ajhackett.com) provides the story. Fascinated by the people of Pentecost Island, Vanuatu (New Hebrides) who jumped from towers with rope attached to their ankles, Hackett began experimenting with elastic tethers that, yo-yo like, would spring back as the jumper reached near to the ground.

Like experimenters of other things before him, he jumped off the first level of the Eiffel Tower in 1987, thus gaining notoriety for himself and publicity for his sport. He now offers a variety of jumping-off places in the Remarkables, the mountain chain around Queenstown, New Zealand. The highest jump area is from a gondola suspended by wires at a height of 440 feet over the Nevus River. As one participant said of his experience, reported on the Hackett website, "I'm gone. Aagh!! It's such a long way down, 8 seconds falling. What a rush!" Others, precipitating themselves from heights of varying length, have said much the same as they jump from the New River Bridge in West Virginia on an annual "Bridge Day" or over the Zambezi River, amidst the mist from Victoria Falls, in the 333 foot descent.

It has been reported that 50,000 individuals have taken the dive from one of A. J. Hackett's jumps. Granted this is a small number in terms of global tourism, it is considerable for New Zealand, with a total population of only 3.5 million.

Tourism as spiritual awakening is a phenomenon put forth in Elizabeth Gilbert's 2006 *New York Times* bestseller, *Eat Pray Love*. The memoir charts her evolution as a white upper middle class American who abandons the trappings of Western affluence to "find" herself in the "exoticism" of Bali and India. Gilbert's journey reflects a broader historical trend among Westerners who look to the East for a more "primitive" human experience on which to model their spiritual practices and awakenings. Like French artists Paul Gauguin, who lived with and coupled with – some art historians say "colonized" the bodies of – Tahitian women, or Pablo Picasso, who looked to African art for inspiration for its "essentially" "primitive" artistic "truths," Gilbert's text, and often the tourism that it inspires, assumes that Easterners are somehow more connected to the earth, and that their realities as "Third World" subjects connect them to a higher spiritual plane.

The cruise as entertainment

No form of entertainment in motion, however, comes close to rivaling the cruise ship. Both as an industrial structure and as a cultural phenomenon, the cruise ship first made its big splash in the 1960s. (The *Queen of Bermuda*, an elegant white-hulled ship, made weekly tourist departures from New York in the 1930s.) The Caribbean quickly became the cruise-ship favorite, where sea travel could be achieved in small increments, thus raising profits by relatively quick turn-arounds (four days the usual) and reducing the inconvenience of seasickness. This form of exotic vacation, where desires could be pampered and gourmet dining could quickly turn into gourmand eating, was popularized by the American television series, *Love Boat*, essentially a romantic comedy filmed on board the Princess Lines' vessels *Pacific Princess* and *Island Princess* and shown weekly between 1977 and 1986. This television comedy gave a major boost to the cruise industry, one form of contrived reality helping to define another.

As this form of tourism grew, the major cruise lines built ever-larger ships with more features. The *Grand Princess* (placed in service in 1999) and the *Voyager of the Seas* (in service in 2000) became statistical wonders of size, tonnage, supplies carried, fuel consumed and entertainment provided. Here are the publicized features of the *Voyager of the Seas*: 1,020 feet long, 142,000 tons, 1,557 cabins for 3,844 passengers, 35 bars and lounges, 14 elevators, a Royal Promenade – serving as a grand shopping mall and food court – four decks high and nearly 400 feet long, a climbing wall, a nine-hole miniature golf course, a skating rink, a 900-seat theater and a full-scale basketball court.

As the new millennium began, there were 145 large cruise ships afloat, catering to nearly 7 million passengers annually. Moreover, the average age and average income of passengers both declined in the last decade, with many people in their twenties, with incomes of $25,000–$35,000, setting sail. Aboard all the large ships, entertainment has been a major factor, the Carnival Cruise Line advertising itself as having the "fun ships." The intended result is to assure that the ship serves as a floating resort. As more than one critic has argued, the destination of the cruise has become the ship itself. A 1998 advertisement for Crystal Cruises, one of the most luxurious, stated: "As soon as you set sail aboard Crystal, you have already reached Utopia" – which, as most university students know, was Thomas More's coined word for "no place," a non-existent, perfectly organized society. The seaborne cruise promises to approximate that condition. The cruise industry experienced a public relations setback in early 2012 when, evoking the *Titanic* disaster, the *Costa Concordia* struck rocks off the coast of Tuscany, Italy and sank. While most of the 4,234 passengers survived, at least 32 bodies were found and two remain (as of May 2012) missing, and passengers recounted stories of chaos and mayhem as they tried to board rescue rafts and jump to safety (website "Cruise Ship Wreck Search Suspended" 2012).

With television in every room, Broadway shows nightly in the theater, round-the-clock food and beverage service and the ship's daily newspaper, the cruise ship offers a self-contained, efficiently regulated and spotless environment with every indulgence, every entertainment that money can buy – and that can be compressed into four or seven days of travel. "Pamper yourself!" is the cruise ships' imperative.

Individual entertainment

Just as travel has grown in range, frequency and numbers, entertainment is increasingly found just a few feet from the armchair in the home. While 30,000 sat in the open air to hear the Three Tenors Concert in Beijing, the estimated 3 billion others saw it alone or in small groups of two or three on a television screen somewhere in the place they call home. This respatialization of entertainment – its special miniaturization on a global scale – is the result of obvious technological innovation: first, television, then the computer and the World Wide Web.

Certainly, indoor, individualized entertainment was there for the literate folk of the nineteenth century who could read: romantic novels, "penny dreadfuls" and newspapers occupied leisure time and provided distraction. Before portable DVD players and Smartphones, there were the British "train novels," identified by their blue backings and sold by WHSmith at railroad station bookstalls for those interested in whiling the time away. (The publishing house whose imprimatur appears on this book got its start producing such distinctively yellow paperback editions: George Routledge's Railway Library that included Harriet Beecher Stowe's *Uncle Tom's Cabin* as one of its early offerings.) Radio and phonograph offered additional indoor entertainment. The soap opera and the comedy hour were American entertainment innovations in the early years of radio.

A handful of games

Offering the entertaining in truly miniature form are the computer games that have been enthusiastically seized on by the young. (In one small survey, the National Institute of Media and the Family found in 1996 that 84 percent of all teens play video games.) With sports, adventure, mystery and history as the subjects of the games, the player becomes an actor in small-scale electronic theater.

Developed first by the Japanese and Americans in the 1970s, electronic games were played on large-format machines in game arcades, and then on television sets. Soon they became standard computer fare but were revolutionized by miniaturization when the Japanese firm Nintendo introduced its Game Boy, a hand-held computer-based platform that allowed the interchange of game cartridges. In 1998 the company added its immensely popular Pokémon card game to the Game Boy cartridges.

Nintendo has had an extended and rather romantic history. It started in 1889 as a playing-card company in Kyoto, with cards turned out by hand. It later made American-style playing cards and negotiated with Disney to use that company's cartoon characters on the face of the cards. However, the company's fortunes changed dramatically when it moved into the manufacture of games and toys in 1963. Today, Nintendo and Sony dominate the games industry but were joined in 2001 by the software giant, Microsoft, which began producing its own game platform. The global sales of video games in 2011 were estimated at $74.5 billion, with estimates for 2013 $97 billion in sales (website "Spending on Gaming to Exceed $74 Billion in 2011" 2012).

Continuing global entertainment: the movies

It was the movies, however, that revolutionized the interior form of entertainment and did so on a grand scale. In the 1950s, the decade before television made its commanding appearance worldwide, movie theaters were dominant urban features. France, with the largest number of any nation in Europe, counted 4,000. Japan had 7,500, while the United States had 25,000. Slowest among the major nations of the world to acquire television because of the Communist regime's fear of lack of control of it, China was peppered with 140,000 movie theaters.

Ubiquitous as it was at mid-century, the movie theater created its own psychology of space. In the darkness of the theater, before the large silver screen, the moviegoer felt a special intimacy, a close and direct affinity to the large two-dimensional apparitions that appeared on the screen. Unlike any other previous art medium, the film could appear very realistic, detailed in accuracy of scene and setting, and able to shift from one place to another, as only the words on a printed page were able to do before it. The film was also a means to project fantasy, to make "make-believe" vividly apparent. In sum, what could be imagined could be made real, if only in two dimensions, by the movie camera and projector.

As an industrial product, easily distributed but expensive to produce, as an art form therefore directed to a large public, movies were first and foremost entertaining, never as enlightening as some early critics had hoped they might be. However, in the hands of a super-director as indeed was the Japanese Akira Kurosawa, fine cinematic art and rip-roaring excitement were masterfully combined. His *Seven Samurai* (1954), an action film in the manner of a transposed Hollywood western but with a more subtle storyline and landscapes of haunting beauty, was also one of Japan's top box-office draws. Its range of appreciation is measured by the American remake, *The Magnificent Seven* (1960). Although *Ran* (1985), Kurosawa's praised classic, was a grand and spectacular rereading in Japanese context of Shakespeare's *King Lear,* his earlier film *Yojunbo* (The Bodyguard, 1961) was remade as a spaghetti western titled *A Fistful of Dollars* (1964).

Spaghetti westerns – as the term implies – were (originally) Italian films, primarily made under the direction of Sergio Leone and giving Clint Eastwood his first ascent to stardom. While they can hardly be called well-crafted, they were popular in large measure because they were formulaic, what in Hollywood idiom has been called "shoot-'em-ups." Such formulaic approaches also characterize Indian and Hong Kong film production. Indian filmmakers have specialized in love stories, paced by an operatic treatment known as *gana,* a duet sung between the two lovers, an approach very popular with audiences. Unique unto themselves are the martial-arts films, the Kung Fu series, made famous by Bruce Lee and Jackie Chan, that have made Hong Kong a major film site. The action techniques developed as a mainstay of this film genre have been imported into Hollywood and have enriched recent films like *The Matrix* (1999), *Charlie's Angels* (2000) and *Rush Hour* (1998) in which Chan co-starred.

The Matrix was filmed in Sydney, Australia, an example of the widespread use of far-flung sites for films and a further element in the global reach of films. In order to utilize outdoor settings more resembling the American West than did locations in Italy – and also to keep production costs low – the spaghetti westerns were primarily filmed in Spain. Although the ship *Titanic* never even completed its maiden voyage, the film *Titanic*, also expected to take a dive, profitably made a vast global circuit. By the end of 1999, the film had reached $3.2 billion in global sales. Of this figure, $1 billion came from video sales, a total of 56 million units, with 32 million sold abroad.

As movie-house ticket sales have generally declined, videotape production and now DVD issues have more than taken up the slack. First introduced in 1956 videotaping gained in popularity after 1971 when the VCR became part of what is now called home entertainment. At the turn of the twentieth century, it was estimated that the average American household now had four video cassette players. DVD eclipsed videotape by 2003; according to a report posted on August 8, 2003 by the British Video Association, 66 percent of video sales in Great Britain were of DVDs, compared with 47 percent the previous year. Today people watch films and television shows through streaming video DVD mail services such as Netflix, which, in 2011 had 24 million users. Films are also available (legally and illegally) on YouTube, Google Video, and Hulu, which in 2012, added Hulu Plus, where viewers could access visual media for (like Netflix) a flat monthly rate.

Television

Even though movies have become an important part of television programming and even though they have inspired the creation of several movie channels, the television experience remains a unique one. While the most versatile of the media, with an electronic eye on all human activity and the images it projects found on screens in all sorts of private and public places, it has succeeded mainly as entertainment. It does so because closure, more than disclosure, governs time and space as they are rectangularized on the television screen. Television's popularity derives in some measure from its time-bound format. An hour is usually the maximum allocated for a "show," whether news or drama. And even that is something of a fiction in the United States where a large chunk of that time, about 15 minutes, is taken up with advertising. The unfolding – or disclosure – found in the novel, the play or even the feature film (some of which now run for three hours) is replaced by the neatly packaged segment – or closure – in which commentary and narrative allow little pause for reflection or consideration.

The theatrical has largely replaced the dramatic. Even news broadcasts have sets. And the content of such shows is in some measure selected and presented according to its visual appeal. Disaster and destruction, not deliberation and debate, are successful news items, as are the unseemly but avidly watched reportage of crime and scandal.

What is exaggerated and intense in the United States is not uncommon elsewhere. The format of television, wherever it appears, is invariably one of news and entertainment, with sitcoms and variety shows of great popularity. Shorter and more intense have been the mini-series, usually movies produced for television and appearing in four or six episodes. One of the most successful and dramatic was *The Singing Detective*, a 1986 British production, written by Dennis Potter, considered by many critics to have been one of the very best writers for television. Far more elaborate in production was *The Jewel in the Crown*, a 13-episode production aired in 1984, filmed in India, depicting the last days of the Raj, British imperial control of India. A long-time favorite, *The Count of Monte Cristo*, was produced once again in 1998 with the well-known actor Gérard Depardieu in the lead. Presented as a French television mini-series, the production was reprised with subtitles on American television (Bravo) in 1999. Such productions were made with the television screen in mind, not the movie screen, determining the shots to be taken.

Perhaps the most interesting development of a dramatic form on television is the soap opera, now an international phenomenon. Australia, Brazil, Japan, Canada and, most recently, China, join the United States and Great Britain as producers. In an entertainment medium in which popularity fades in a matter of a few years, the soap opera has incredible endurance. *The Guiding Light* began as an American radio soap opera in 1937, converted to television in 1953 and ran until 2009, but with the article dropped so that the title reads: *Guiding Light*. The English soap opera *Coronation Street,* centered on the problems and difficulties of working-class people, is now forty years old. Its Australian counterpart *Number 96*, about a group of people living in a Sydney apartment, ran through 1,000 episodes between 1972 and 1977. In 2000 the Chinese took the millennial step and allowed the introduction of a soap opera, *Joy Luck Street*. A representative of Granada Television of Great Britain – the producer of *Coronation Street* and an investor in the Chinese show – declared, "I would be amazed if this country doesn't get addicted to soaps" (Saywell 2000: 1).

If there is a current addiction, China excluded, it is with the reality show. Considered by some to be a mix between soap opera and docudrama, it invites the viewer to become a voyeur. The unscripted action, often banal and mean-spirited, which in other times would have raised eyebrows, in our time raises the hope among the participants of reaching celebrity status and/or gaining a cash prize. Whatever the stage set or the location in which these shows are played out, each depends on a Hobbesian dynamic: a theatrical environment in which life appears to be nasty, brutish and short. The basic rule of the reality show is either elimination of contestants in a high-handed or low-minded procedure; or revelation by a spontaneous uncovering of their flaws, conceits or pettiness.

The first and one of the most enduring of these shows is MTV's *Real World*, begun in 1992 and modeled after the 1973 series *An American Family,* a PBS documentary that captured the "real" lives of the Loud family from December to May 1971. One series of 23 episodes of the *Real World* has been produced annually, in which six or seven young people live together in one place in an urban environment – Honolulu, London and Chicago are among those that were chosen – and act out their camera-ready social encounters. The MTV success *The Osbournes* (2001) allows the viewer to gaze in wonder or delight at a truly dysfunctional family, headed by the British rock star, Ozzy Osbourne, a personality whose on-stage behavior has been labeled bizarre and whose working vocabulary on the television show is punctuated by an unusual number of bleeps.

Unlike *The Osbournes*, many of the reality television shows are American imports. A European phenomenon, generated principally in Great Britain, Sweden and the Netherlands, but exaggerated in the United States, the reality show adheres to an unvarying format: a challenge and test in which ordinary people are subjected to stress situations that ultimately pay off for the winning group or team. Swedish television producers reworked the old desert island theme into an out-sourced show called *Survivor*, arguably the most successful of the reality shows. Remanufactured under license in the United States, the show engages teams that are challenged by pseudo-primitive conditions (television cameras and medical help always on hand, as well as the genial moderator) in places like the Marquesas Islands, the Australian Outback and the African savannah. From the Netherlands came *Big Brother*, a show in which well-placed television cameras recorded the contestants housed together and performing without privacy those diurnal acts of no significance but perhaps of scatological effect, along with the petty grievances and tense situations that years ago the French author Jean-Paul Sartre described in his play *Huit Clos* "Behind Closed Doors" as the abiding horror of hell. Recent iterations of the reality show include American cable channel's *Toddlers & Tiaras,* which charts the often disturbing lengths to which parents go to have their very young children (most often daughters) win beauty pageants.

In tandem with these reality shows was a renaissance of the quiz shows that had first appeared on American television in the 1960s. The most popular and widespread was *Who Wants to Be a Millionaire*, a British contribution to popular culture. The show first aired on ITV in Great Britain on September 4, 1998. Over the next two years, it made its way around the globe, eventually appearing in 34 countries, ranging from Finland to Australia, by way of Egypt and India. Globally in the early 2000s the show was exceptionally popular, gaining about one-third of the viewing audience in most countries but reaching up to 72 percent in Great Britain and, at top, 80 percent in Norway. Its popularity was at the center of the 2008 Academy Awarding-winning film *Slumdog Millionaire,* a British film centered on a young man from the Dharavi slums of India who becomes a contestant on the game show.

An effort to combine some of the contrived nastiness of the reality show, where participants are voted out by other members of the group, and the tension of the quiz show, was made in the form of *The Weakest Link*, a BBC show that began in 2000 and made the international rounds from Russia to Thailand, but with popular criticisms of it in the latter country. According to *BBC News*, the Thai National Youth Bureau protested that the show promoted "fierce competition and selfishness among participants," attitudes not according with traditional Thai generosity (*BBC News* February 19, 2002: n.p.). That concern derives from the show's format in which eight contestants vote out in each round the "weakest link," the person they consider least successful in answering questions. As with the reality shows the purse goes to the remaining combatant, with all others joining the ranks of losers.

Sports as visual entertainment

For all their appeal, all such shows as those just described remain anemic when compared with sports broadcasting. "Television and globalization are consolidating the global football market," said José Angel Sanchez, the head of marketing for the Spanish football team Real Madrid (*The Economist* June 8–15, 2002: 9). His statement can be extrapolated to refer to most sports. In less than a year after it had offered the world's first high-definition television service, the BBC on June 21, 1937 broadcast the Wimbledon tennis championship. Across the Atlantic, in 1939, the first American National Football League game was televised. In 1947, a St. Louis television station broadcast the first United States Open Golf championship. Spectator sports were a television natural, and the symbiotic relationship between the two was enhanced in 1970, when *Monday Night Football* became a regular feature on American television. Between 1989 and 2001 it was regularly one of the top ten primetime network television shows.

By increasing the number of commentators and moving coverage from four to nine cameras, *Monday Night Football* gave the viewer a visual presence denied to even the best-seated stadium viewer. That condition was soon improved to near omnipresence as the art and management of television sports coverage became even more impressive. According to an article in the *Chicago Tribune* of July 14, 1996, NBC coverage of the 1996 Summer Olympics in Atlanta, Georgia, required 97 television cameras, 14 mobile units and 250 staff personnel. An editing unit, 33 individuals strong, immediately edited all of the televised material and then distributed it by satellite. At many sports events, and the Sydney Summer Olympics of 2000, blimps with gyro-stabilized camera equipment have provided aerial views as well. Not even the gods on Mount Olympus had a better view of the ancient Olympic Games than does the contemporary television audience.

And, although the Greeks ran, wrestled and threw the discus for the honor of an olive wreath, they were also assured comfortable subsistence if they won. And so with contemporary sports. As José Angel Sanchez (quoted above) said, there is a "global football market." Professional sports, as spectator sports, now dominate. Perhaps English football established the condition in 1885 when professionalism was first allowed. American baseball, by this time, was also a paying profession, as was boxing. Although FIFA (Fédération Internationale de Football Association) was established in 1904, it remained subservient to the Olympics, where the international football matches were held. By the 1920s, however, professionalism had become dominant in football, thereby disqualifying some of the best athletes from Olympic competition because they were not amateurs, the Olympic ideal. The leadership of FIFA therefore decided in 1928 to hold a quadrennial international competition, the first event taking place in Uruguay in 1930. Thus the World Cup was effectively institutionalized, and professionalism has reigned since. Even the Olympics, conceived by Baron Pierre de Coubertin to represent amateurism at its best, went "pro" in 1988 when amateurism was no longer deemed a condition of participation.

What has been called "shamateurism" crept into sports at an early date. Athletic scholarships, so prevalent in the United States, team sponsorship by corporations, privileges and training facilities given by Communist governments, like that of East Germany, and pots of gold, now found just beyond the eighteenth hole of most golf tournaments, have all proved more potent rewards than cheering crowds. Sports are big business and a big part of the entertainment industry. That is why they are as expensive to produce as they are bountiful to their outstanding competitors. The German entertainment media KirchGruppe paid $2 billion for the television rights to the 2002 and 2006 World Cups.

The global nature of television and sport has been most dramatically joined in the World Cup. The statistics are overwhelming. At the 1998 World Cup, the television audience for all 64 games was estimated to be 37 billion viewers; the final play-off was seen on television by 2 billion viewers. Such has the range and intensity of viewer interest grown since the first televised world cup final at Wembley Stadium, London in 1966. What American professional football and world football (or soccer) have demonstrated is the tremendous growth in television viewership of spectator sports. Some critics see that growth peaking, but golf – traditionally not a spectator sport – began to grow on television, in large measure due to the compelling skill, personality of Tiger Woods, perhaps proof of the old adage that everybody loves a winner – until, of course, they no longer win. However, the spectacle knows no bounds and when Woods crashed his vehicle outside of his house in November 2009, and details of his affairs and failing marriage with Elin Nordegren became public, the fledgling gold star again made front page news.

A natural alliance: sight and sound

Television, even more than the movies, has changed the way we see the world. Both media, however, have also attuned our sense of hearing. It has been said more than once that there was seldom silence in a movie theater even in the age of silent films. Musical accompaniment on the piano or, grandly, on the theater organ, helped establish mood and aroused emotion.

Perfectly appropriate, the first "talking picture" had a musical theme. This was Al Jolson's *The Jazz Singer* (1927). Soon studio orchestras and studio composers enveloped the film in music. The Oscar ceremonies soon responded to the sound of music. Awards for the best musical score and the best original score were introduced in 1934 and 1938 respectively. Among the best known compositions for film – and Oscar winners both – are Maurice Jarre's music, notably "Lara's Theme," from David Lean's *Dr. Zhivago* (1965) and John Williams' brassy theme music for George Lucas' *Star Wars* (1977).

As for wide-ranging influence, no piece of music attained the success of Bill Haley's 1954 recording of *Rock around the Clock* that served as background music to the credits for *Blackboard Jungle* (1955). The song has been credited with making rock-and-roll an international musical success. Rock-and-roll was as much a visible as a musical phenomenon. It reached out to young audiences in the various films that served as musical vehicles, of which the beach movies were the most famous, such as *Gidget* (1959) and *Beach Party* (1963). More direct was Paramount's *Let's Twist* (1961) which helped create the dance epidemic so closely related to rock-and-roll. Then came the T.A.M.I. (Teen Age Music International) show of 1964, a rock festival several days long held in the Santa Monica Civic Auditorium, California. Some fifty live performances were both televised and filmed, with appearances by James Brown, the Supremes, Gerry and the Pacemakers, and Mick Jagger and the Rolling Stones.

What the cable channel MTV (Music Television) did in the 1980s was to regularize and intensify this new recording arrangement: the visual supporting and enhancing the single song. This combination, soon to triumph on MTV, had already been tried with limited success in France in the early 1960s. Called Scopitone, a combination of record and 16mm-color film, the system was a jukebox surmounted by a screen. Some 300 songs were so recorded and played on this jukebox, but the visual quality was poor, and the music was not top pop. Although initially well-received in West Germany and Britain, Scopitone quickly failed in the United States, particularly with the advent of color television.

MTV was launched in 1981; since then it has evolved from being an inexpensive cable programming format to an international cultural phenomenon seen in 140 countries by some 350 million viewers and offered in local variations in Japan, Brazil, Australia and India, among others. It has made or enhanced the reputations of stars like Billy Joel, Michael Jackson and Madonna. It also became a major source for the popularization of rap music.

Perhaps its most significant cultural impact occurred on July 13, 1985, when it provided 16 hours of television coverage of Irish rocker Bob Geldof's effectively organized "Live Aid Concert," performed in London and Philadelphia. Seen in 150 countries and raising $150 million for famine relief in Africa, this truly historic event demonstrated a global fact acknowledged by many as well as by Geldof: "The notion was that the planet has one language – pop music." And, equally obviously, the medium by which that language was communicated was television, a contemporary condition recognized and exploited by MTV.

To celebrate MTV's twentieth anniversary, the photo-enhanced celebrity magazine *People* put out an extra, declared to be a "collector's edition," dated Summer 2001. The edition, from which most of the information above was derived, suggested the cross-over effect of the visual media and the varying modes of staging contemporary entertainment. In a recent and unusual variation of such relationships, the Houston Opera Company in 1999 offered first in Houston and then in Philadelphia a production of Bizet's *Carmen* that has been described as a "multi-media" production. With extensive use of lighting as part of the stage architecture, the opera company also arranged television cameras on the stage and large television screens above the stage so that the audience could see what was seldom seen before, close-ups of the singers. "Visceral impact equal to that of a rock concert," exclaimed the opera company brochure.

The electronic concert scene

A combination of circus and fireworks display, a light show as dazzling, if not as blinding as the music is ear-smashing, the rock concert is contemporary entertainment at its technological extreme. According to the British lighting designer Kevin Shaw, the shift from traditional theater or vaudeville lighting to that which has become the hallmark of rock performance is difficult to date. But by the early 1970s, technological improvements in lighting projectors, dimmers and lamps, as well as materials and equipment for on-site construction, allowed for a great variety of lighting techniques with rapid change to accommodate one-night performances.

Rock music, electronic enhancement and theatricality have had a long, collaborative history. The term "rock 'n' roll" was popularized in the early 1950s by the disc jockey Alan Freed, when the musical development was essentially an African-American idiom. As a distinctive, popular form, it soon gained authority by the use of the electric guitar, mass-produced by Leo Fender in 1948 and adopted by performers like Les Paul, Jimi Hendrix, Carlos Santana and Eric Clapton. With the introduction of electronic devices like sound boards, synthesizers and microphones using feed-back effects, rock-and-roll was amplified and it captured the audience by the quality of its sound as well as the music itself. The theatrical effect quickly altered the musical, with lighting making an effective complementary element enhancing the rhythm itself. The interplay of performers and audience at what might be called the zone of transition, the edge of the stage, furthered the visible intensity of the performance.

Such concerts gained fame as they aroused concern. They were an expression of a counter-culture: a youth culture disaffected with the political and social order, which they saw as entrenched and materialistic. The student revolts of 1968 (see Chapter 4) were a worldwide expression of this disaffection, which in New England found an outlet in the concert at Woodstock. Described by one commentator as "the most successful fiasco in the history of entertainment" (Kratz 1994: 1), Woodstock was to be a rustic gathering of the young, planned to number about 100,000, at a music festival. The Woodstock Festival of Music and Art ran for three days in August 1969. It was actually held – or at least improvisationally set up – at a farm in Bethel, many miles from Woodstock in upper New York State. The three-day festival was provided with insufficient amenities, policing and camping space for the huge crowd, nearly five times what was anticipated. A constellation of performers that included Jimi Hendrix, Janis Joplin and the Grateful Dead, stood above the bad weather, alcohol, sex and LSD that provided an inchoate atmosphere that was indeed memorable. Moreover, it was seen as the "Woodstock Nation," a spontaneously formed, uninhibited mass of young people disaffected with the bourgeois culture and the political situation, primarily the Vietnam War, and the fight for race, gender, and gay rights surrounding them.

Woodstock was neither the first, nor the last, nor the most successful of rock concert festivals, even though it surely is the best known. Murray Lerner, a documentary film director, saw the end of the early concert movement with the third Isle of Wight concert of August 1970. This small offshore English island had held such concerts in 1968 and 1969, and would continue again in 2000. The 1970 one was the most impressive, with an audience of 600,000 and performances by major figures like Jimi Hendrix, Joni Mitchell and Joan Baez and groups like The Doors, The Who and Jethro Tull. One reviewer of the film wrote: "In the end, what we vividly see is the end of the presumed but unwritten symbiosis between one very serious attempt at social revolution and one of the sweetest eras – if not the sweetest – in rock history" (Wager 2003: 1). Thereafter, the rock concert was heavily commercialized. Whatever their style and venue, the performers wanted "money and power in the legitimate business world," argued one critic (Seabrook 2000: 191) of the rock phenomenon in general.

The rock concert has spread across much of the globe but still remains largely Anglo-American in execution. Rock groups in Myanmar, India and Thailand, for instance, play in their own countries under often severe restrictions concerning content and appearance. Moreover, they do not have the appeal – or the skillful promoters – that assure major groups their international audiences. Even the Rolling Stones, arguably the most famous and foot-loose group in the world, did not tour Singapore, Hong Kong, China and India until 2003. As guitarist Keith Richards said: "It is always nice to go somewhere new and China is very old, but at the same time it will be our first time there, and in India – and it's about time they let us in there anyway" (Hayes 2003: 1). However, because of the SARS – Severe Acute Respiratory Syndrome – epidemic, this portion of the tour was in fact canceled.

In this new phase, the theatricality became a dominant element. The distinctive lighting of rock concerts – bright colors, strobe lights, rapidity of change as a function of mood – was determined and directed on the assumption that the lighting engineer at the electrical console was as much a part of the performance as the singers themselves (Shaw 2001: 1). The singers added intensive theatricality to their own performance as they created their own form of aerobatics and dramatic entrances, often zooming in or descending on to the stage by way of wires and harnesses – or appearing from behind bursts of smoke and fireworks.

No one explored and exploited the advantages of modern, electrically assisted staging more effectively than did Michael Jackson. His world tour of

HIStory, carried out in 1996 and 1997, was record-breaking in number of performances, in attendance and probably in the equipment needed. This equipment weighed 1,200 tons and was carried about on 43 trucks. It was handled by 160 employees, who were a regular part of the tour, assisted by 200 stagehands hired in each location where Jackson performed. The sound system consisted of 200 cabinets or units, and the lighting of 1,000 fixtures. Perhaps most interesting, certainly overwhelming, were the pyrotechnics, 500 pieces fired each night, with noise effects "comparable to a TNT explosion bringing down a three story building" (website "The HIStory world tour" 2003: 4).

Other popular musical environments

In a more modest but no less dynamic environment, the disco entered popular culture after World War Two and reached its dazzling peak of appeal in the 1970s. The disco – or *discothèque,* for its origins were French – substituted recorded for live music and brought a new personality to the entertainment field, the disk jockey who selected and played the records. It was the dual skill of providing continuity between records and choosing appealing performers that gave the DJ commanding authority of the disco scene. If the disco followed the night club, its distinctiveness was its theatricality. Spot lights and strobe lights and loud music pulsated and swirled in seemingly endless patterns as the dancers crowded the floor and enjoyed new dance forms like the 1960s hit "The Twist." Perhaps the most celebrated, some would say infamous venue was Studio 54, located on West 54th Street in New York City, appropriately enough in a former theater and television studio.

Elsewhere, and notably in Europe, clubs of similar spectacular environment appeared, such as the Dorian Gray in Frankfurt and Le Palace in Paris, this one located in an old movie theater. Both clubs were renowned for their state-of-the-art light shows. For the few years in which they were enormously popular – Studio 54 opened in 1977 and closed in 1986 – the discos provided a new night scene in which persons with different tastes, dress and sexual preference mixed in a wide-open atmosphere stimulated by dance, alcohol and drugs. However, the disco has grown to become a worldwide institution and is found in multiples in all major cities.

Perhaps an unexpected complement to the disco scene has been the rave. Emerging in the 1980s in Great Britain and quickly spreading over Europe and the United States, the rave was initially an impromptu musical event, a gathering of the young at a secret and often "non-traditional" site (a field, wharf or warehouse). One young reviewer of the phenomenon in the United States commented on its illegality at the outset: "Spaces were not rented, they were broken into" (website "Raves: history" 2001: 1). Wherever located, the rave was a long night of intense group dancing, frequently accompanied by drug use, and measured by the beat of hard rock, "techno" music, as well as "house" or "garage" music.

Marked by this early spontaneity, raves were soon commercialized and included laser shows that were synchronized with the music. Moreover, the typical participants changed from young adults to teenagers and, in the process, the intensity of participation increased as well. Originally attracting small numbers, raves now include thousands and are cited by authorities as the scene of drug abuse, careless sex and unwanted noise. The common use of the drug Ecstasy has been a major concern. Perhaps the most interesting aspect of this socio-musical development has occurred in Germany with the formation of a "rave nation," a "subculture with similar leisure and consuming habits" and standing as an appealing social alternative to the fragmented society of contemporary daily life (Richard and Kruger 2002: 1–2).

New formats for the traditional musical comedy

The visual excitement of performance and participation at raves, as at rock concerts and discos before them, is also shared by the audiences at the "legitimate theater," notably in the form of the megamusicals of Andrew Lloyd Webber, arguably the most successful of today's musical theater composers who has combined several different musical idioms – rock, opera, English folk – into a style at considerable contrast with the earlier, tuneful New York musicals of composers like Richard Rodgers and Cole Porter. Lloyd Webber's *Phantom of the Opera* has been the most spectacular of his big, long-running shows, among which are *Cats* and *Jesus Christ Superstar.* On several occasions in the 1980s and 1990s, he had three productions running simultaneously in both London and New York, another record in this era of record setting.

The Phantom of the Opera, which first opened in Her Majesty's Theatre Haymarket, London on October 9, 1986, has had over 5,000 performances there and has been presented in 90 cities around the world. Its musical success was enhanced by its staging, which used rock-concert lighting effects along with Hollywood-like dramatic explosiveness. The heavy chandelier, centered above the audience, is seen to be cut from its chain moorings by the enraged phantom and then to come crashing down on the stage, a startling, frisson-producing ending to Act II.

Such theatrical extravaganzas, like molten lava, flow resolutely down the slopes of today's entertainment environment. Electrical and sound engineering, the arena or park as an entertainment venue, wireless microphones, crowds of tens of thousands in rapt attendance, performers disheveled or wildly attired, all conform to our contemporary sense of theater just as much as burgundy plush seats, gilded woodwork and opera glasses created the sense of theater among the wealthy in the nineteenth century. Yet in technical sophistication, preparation and profit, perhaps even purpose, the rock concerts of today are nearly beyond comparison with their wild progenitor known now simply as Woodstock.

A kaleidoscopic vision of things seen electronically

At the start of the twenty-first century, our vision of things is more kaleido-scopic than chaotic. It is electronically controlled, monitored and remembered. Billions of humans see the world daily not through a mirror darkly but through bright images projected on an open lap-top or Smartphone, on an in-flight movie, that compresses the grandeur of the Parthenon or the sweeping vista of Capetown as seen from the top of Table Mountain into a small rectangle of retrievable memory. The most recent development of this state of eye is the televised show in a theater at the visitors' center of the Grand Canyon National Park. There the panoramic and aerial views are seen by many as more breathtaking than those provided by the site itself.

Many critics have examined the "semiotics of tourism," the condition of what the tourist sees as already being invested with the value of familiarity or arrested in space. Put simply, the reproduction authenticates the real. What has been seen in travel brochure, on television, in textbook and magazine, defines and frames what is subsequently seen. The classic example of this cultural phenomenon is the comment of the notorious aesthete Oscar Wilde who, upon looking at a beautiful sunset, remarked that it was "a poor Turner," that painter's sunsets being famously dramatic.

Tourist sites are also carefully packaged. In the United States, the frequently seen highway sign, "Scenic Overlook," alerts the driver to pull off the road at the announced site to see the sight as many have before. Consider the ritualized photographs of the tourist before the Eiffel Tower or in front of the White House. Recall the tour guide's familiar announcement of a five- or ten-minute bus stop to allow a photo opportunity.

The uncertain wonder of travel has now been replaced by the fulfillment of tourist expectation. The American historian Daniel Boorstin, in his pace-setting book *The Image*, recounts the anecdote that Wilhelm II, Emperor of Germany, in the first decade of the twentieth century, excused himself from a state meeting exactly at noon in order to appear on his palace balcony as a military band played. According to Baedeker, the tourist guidebook, the emperor regularly did this. And so he provided confirmation for the awaiting tourist (Boorstin 1992: 103–4). In a like manner today, porpoises, killer whales and elephants in zoos and theme parks join "native dancers" in Kenya and mili-tary tattoos before the castle of Edinburgh, to perform at fixed hours and thus to satisfy tourist schedules and assure on-time delivery of the authentic.

Plato's viewer of reality, expressed in his famous cave scene, can be con-trasted with contemporary conditions as a metaphor of reality. Briefly, the philosopher put it this way: the reality we see is really the shadows reflected from behind us of figures only partially revealed from the other side of the wall. Plato's viewer had an unclear picture of reality; ours sees a clear picture. Plato's viewer sat in quiet contemplation before a flickering fire; ours is entertained thoughtlessly, but with measured time, in a surround of blue luminescence indoors or well-aimed spotlights outdoors.

This distinction may contain a moral imperative, as certainly the two critics just mentioned would assert. An even stronger criticism has been registered by Neal Gabler in his book *Life: The Movie* (1998). Gabler's thesis is simple and direct: in this era of incessantly projected images and media hype, "life has become art, so that the two are indistinguishable ... " His examples are several: the trial for murder of the American athlete O. J. Simpson, the life and death of Princess Diana, and the presidency of Bill Clinton during the Monica Lewinsky affair. "The conversion of life into the medium of entertainment," he continues, requires publicity and the creation of a substitute for the movie star, "the celebrity" (Gabler 1998: 7), about whom Daniel Boorstin had earlier written. While one may find Gabler's statement that life has triumphed over entertainment exaggerated, it is not far amiss. Almost all those activities that are prominent as commercial ventures in the contemporary world seek to amuse and to distract, to arouse and to please, even to inform in a way that is theatrical, not analytical. The two-dimensionality of it all is the reason for the critical concern. It is superficial or, in the apt expression, a "democracy of surfaces."

All the world's a stage, as Shakespeare wrote. But the technological means available to stage everything is what makes entertainment distinctive in contemporary society. Framed, staged, arranged and presented, enhanced by the skills of lighting and sound engineers, provided with an audience transported by vehicle, not necessarily by joy (the latter impossible to attain in a crowded parking lot), modern entertainment is largely an industrial product, a venture capital investment directed to profit.

It hardly could have been otherwise. From the eighteenth century on, when the young Englishman did a grand tour of famous sites on the European continent and, shortly after, when Alexis de Tocqueville and Charles Dickens came to the still freshly minted United States to see what they were all about, travel has been a form of recreation and entertainment. (Dickens' comments about the pigs running all about the streets of Louisville, Kentucky, were clearly meant to be entertaining.) The Royal Hawaiian Band that greeted visitors to Honolulu between 1873 and 1915 served the same purpose. In the center of New York City, P. T. Barnum beguiled a large public with his American Museum that he had purchased in 1841 and converted into a show of the unusual and bizarre, an entertainment that preceded the vaudeville act and the music-hall routine. Every world's fair in the early twentieth century had an entertainment strip (the Midway at the World Columbian Exposition of 1893 perhaps the most famous) – and each and all of them attracted more crowds than did any other fair feature.

To consider such diverse activities is only to assert the historically obvious: our contemporary world, with its many stages, shows a change less in form than in intensity and scale. What had earlier been either infrequent or irregular and unusual has now become daily and familiar. The locale, the electrical technology and the regularity of it, its existence as an industry – these elements, more than the nature of the entertainment, are what amount to the major change. To mark it apart, the term "venue" has entered our popular vocabulary. An eighteenth-century legal term meaning the place and site for a trial, the word in the 1950s became descriptive of different locations for the performing arts. Now it means the site of all managed events, from rock concerts to international conferences.

Venue is a key term in the new geography of entertainment. And that geography is not concerned with topography, the lay of the land, so much as it is concerned with spectacle, what is seen there, on the stage, whatever the location, but certainly arranged with the aid of the ministry of tourism, the lighting and sound engineers, the interior directors of resort and cruise ship, the frequency of low-fare airline flights, the travel agent – and, of course, the leisure time available.

Staging has long been the function of ritual and ceremony, the show of power and authority. When the French King Francis I met the English King Henry VIII at an elaborate pageant and festive ceremony near Calais in 1520, the sumptuousness of it all gave it its historical name "The Field of the Cloth of Gold." Nearly five centuries later, Malcolm Forbes, the famous capitalist, gave himself a seventieth birthday in Tangier, Morocco. He provided jet air transportation, including rental of the new defunct Concorde, to gather some 800 guests at the extravaganza. For an estimated $2.5 million, he entertained royally and with 600 drummers and dancers in performance. Even this sum and this pageant were small in consideration of the $8 million that Salt Lake City paid for the opening ceremonies and the elaborate cauldron at the 2002 Winter Olympics. The entire cost of the games, nearly $2 billion, was rounded out at about $800,000 per competing athlete.

Seeing is believing; today, it is also costly. Popular culture as staged culture is pervasive, spectacular. It would also be extravagant were it not treated as a profitable business, as indeed it often is.

Exterior of new Celebration, Florida home model for customer viewing (© Mark Peterson/CORBIS)

6 Happily spaced out
The topography of pleasure and diversion

No one knew better than Walt Disney the purpose of the new features of the built environment that appeared worldwide in the half century or so after 1950. "To all who come to this happy place: welcome," he declared in his dedication speech at Disneyland on July 17, 1955. The various Disney theme parks are certainly advertised as happy places. But happy space, where people can readily find entertainment and recreation, is not limited to what the Disney Corporation puts up and puts on. It is a major enterprise of land developers around the world and extends from vast enclosed space, such as the 5,000 guest rooms in Las Vegas' MGM Hotel, to vast open space, as certainly are the grounds of the 5,492-yard Royal Malta Golf Course on that Mediterranean island which is only 122 square miles in size. The Millennium Dome in Greenwich, England, a temporary structure, enclosed 800,000 square feet of space, large enough, its boosters said, to accommodate the Eiffel Tower if it were laid on its side.

With the new millennium, roller-coaster statistics have been way out – and up. Nagashima Spaland in Japan announced its "Steel Dragon 2000," the largest and longest roller-coaster in the world. The coaster reaches a height of 312 feet and stretches out track to a length of over 8,000 feet. Yet for sheer height and speed, the new 2003 coaster Top Thrill Dragster at Cedar Point, Ohio, is temporary champion. From a peak of 420 feet, the 16 passenger cars drop at a speed of 120 mph. The coaster is the sixteenth at the park and marked the ninth time one of them had briefly broken the world record.

If one broad generalization can serve to describe the current peppering of the earth's land mass with theme parks and golf courses, with convention centers and shopping malls, with museums and sports arenas, as well as with resorts on the seacoasts and mountainsides, it is this: the countryside is everywhere being reshaped to accommodate recreation, while the city is being reorganized to accommodate entertainment. Pleasure and pleasurable things are now major market items. As the redevelopment of the old Darling Harbor area of Sydney began in the 1980s, the developers of its marketplace seized as their motto the expression "Making Cities Fun."

Negative critics of this development have in effect changed the old adage that the world is going to hell in a hand-basket to read that the world is going to hell in a golf cart. The exchange of goods and services – Adam Smith's argument that humankind has a tendency to truck, barter and trade – is no longer just serious business but also enjoyable entertainment. This calculated coming-together and this jostling of activities that were largely separate and discrete a century or so ago are major elements in postmodernism, where eclecticism and mixed use have replaced the imagined and prescribed rational order of the industrial age, when the ideal was of a world of carefully assembled parts and neatly pigeonholed activities.

This concern to provide a rational order of things was best expressed in the layout of the world's fairs or international expositions of the late nineteenth and early twentieth centuries. Summertime fantasies, largely constructed of non-durable materials that would shape the immense halls and palaces that rose and fell in a matter of months, these expositions were expressions of technological progress and ideological statements about a culture – Western civilization – that prided itself on its appreciation of reason, order, progress and the benefits of consumable goods and inventions.

Translated into desired urban form, the rationalist philosophy reached its height in the construction of the 984-foot Eiffel Tower, held together by 2.5 million rivets, its top observation deck reached by elevator and affording an aerial and panoramic view of the world below which was and is, of course, the urban pattern of Paris. At last the bird's-eye view – which earlier urban designers had imagined and translated into their maps and plans – was a human reality and, when photographed, a means to the refinement of city planning.

On a different scale, the board game Monopoly also reorganized urban space in the pursuit of pleasure – and gain. Created in the United States in 1935, it soon appeared in German, French and British editions. The game board contains neatly arranged rectangles that represent built space in the country's largest city, with some properties more valuable than others. On just about all of them "improvements" can be made by the addition of houses and hotels – in effect real estate like "Park Avenue" (or the "Champs-Elysées" in the French version) where the hapless player who lands there must pay the player–owner a handsome rental fee. The object of the game is to amass wealth by real-estate speculation. It is all done by a roll of the dice, in its own way a statement about the capriciousness of the market.

While avidly played to this day, with an annual international competition bringing representatives of some two dozen nations together, Monopoly emerged at a time when commercial buildings, however congested and inadequately planned, were generally single-function and constructed in styles that announced their purpose. Structures expressing dignity and solidity of purpose, such as banks, libraries and museums, were done up in the neo-classical style with symmetrically arranged columns, imposing façades and splayed stairs that asserted the high authority of the place. Department stores, a French invention of mid-nineteenth century, enticed customers with canopied entranceways and large display windows. Railroad stations and hotels were the most expansive piles of stones, often pretending to past glory: London's St Pancras Station and Midland Hotel (1868) were built in gothic style and the Pennsylvania Railroad Station in New York City (1910) imitated the Baths of Caracalla in Rome. Just as the king was in the counting house, counting all his money, and the queen was in the pantry, eating bread and honey, most commercial activities were conducted in places constructed for one purpose.

All under one roof

The many vast structures that define our urban environment today, however, contain collections of shops and concessions that were previously seldom mixed together, except in the covered arcades that appeared in cities like London, Brussels, Paris and Milan. Often defined as "centers," these contemporary multi-purpose structures, found in every major urban site today, are analogous to nothing so much as the most popular fast-food product of our time: a mouth-stretching hamburger with two patties, cheese, tomatoes and the like. Stacked up, joined together, the ingredients are configured into one desirable object.

Such is the spatial mix of much of the built environment today. The bank in the supermarket, the sandwich shop in the garage station, the climbing wall and the putting green on the cruise ship, the religious service in the soccer stadium, the restaurant in the museum, a mixture of things stuck together in the shopping mall or the convention center – they seem to hold together as well as the fast food just mentioned; and the combination seems to have exceptional appeal.

What would have been considered spatially incongruous or disorderly a century ago is the accepted order of things today. To appreciate the contrast, consider two examples. One is from Charles Dickens' novel *Hard Times* (1854); the other from a book on the architecture of a famous firm that designs resorts, *The Hospitality and Leisure Architecture of Wimberly, Allison, Tong and Goo* (1995). In the first, Mr M'Chokumchild, obviously a disciplinarian, asks a class of students if they would wallpaper a room with figures of horses. Half reply "yes," and half reply "no." M'Chokumchild then pronounces that they would never paper a room in that manner. "Do you ever see horses walking up and down the walls of a room in reality – in fact?"

In the second text, the commentary on a resort called the "Lost City," a theme park in the Republic of Botswana, South Africa, states that the park was built solidly on a "mythical story" of a great earthquake. This manufactured "legend" tells of the earthquake changing the course of a river. The visitor will now find on the site "the largest combination of grand-scale water features found anywhere on earth," and situated in an arid valley that was accordingly "transformed into a man-made tropical jungle with over 1.6 million trees, plants, and shrubs." To provide sufficient local color to the legend, one of the two golf courses on the property, for instance, has live crocodiles that are "a permanent hazard on the 13th hole" (Naisbitt 1995: 130).

The horses not allowed on the wallpaper and the crocodiles found around the thirteenth hole are testimony to the different attitudes toward built space then (1854) and more recently (1997). Put otherwise, Mr. M'Chokum-child could never have found employment as a groundskeeper in the "Lost City." And yet it was in the time of Dickens that the production of pleasure and pleasurable things as commodities began as an urban phenomenon, one directed by and to the new moneyed classes of the nineteenth century, the urban middle classes or the bourgeoisie.

The arcade and the music hall, the public park and the museum, the carousel and the city football stadium provided fixed environments in which could be spent the new leisure time that allowed many to become spectators as well as *flâneurs*, those who strolled along the new boulevards and stared at shop windows or admired, as they did with some perplexity in the famous cartoons of Daumier, ancient Greek statues standing on pedestals in French museums. Even baseball, which has entered American myth as a rural sport, was and remains urban-bound, and never were its most successful teams located in a field of dreams (as the arcadian movie treatment of the film bearing that name attempted to prove in 1989). In the late twentieth century the city contained many "stately pleasure domes," to slightly modify Coleridge.

Lasting urban effects of temporary recreational activities

Insufficient credit for this urban reordering has been assigned to two major and spectacular developments that were initiated in the nineteenth century: international expositions ("world's fairs" in the American idiom) and the Olympic Games. Predicated on the principle of international goodwill and cooperation, these two activities were initially summertime ephemera, here today and gone five months later (for the international expositions) or a few weeks later (for the Olympic Games). However, from the perspective of the city sponsors, they were soon seen as possible sources of new revenue and the acquisition of additional urban amenities. They became what were later called "mega-events," of such magnitude to attract world attention and investment monies directed to urban development.

Their popularity, therefore, came from the condition of their being show-cases, displaying international achievement and talent, local advantage and hospitality. It is therefore fitting that the first occurrence of this showcasing took place in the Crystal Palace, the glass-and-iron building in which London's Great Exhibition of 1851 was held. The Olympic Games were conjured up from their Greek past by a non-athletic French nobleman, Baron Pierre de Coubertin, in 1896. The fact that the Olympics and the fairs often coincided (Paris, 1900; Saint Louis, 1904; London, 1908; Montreal, 1976; and a fair in Seville when the games were in Barcelona, in 1992) suggests the importance of both in the eyes of city planners and boosters.

Much has been written about both of these recreational and spectator-designed activities as expressions of high ideals and the desire for human betterment, just as much has been written about them as expressions of a capitalist ideology, reworking the older human tendencies to barter and play into newer and (as anticipated but seldom realized) more profitable ones. Yet the ritualized fun and games they provided were seen as appealing means by which the local power elites could gain international urban advantage: investment in infrastructure, increase in tourism and assured widespread publicity through sponsorship.

As if offering a variant of the old expression that all roads lead to Rome, those marketing the fairs and the games wanted to prove, however briefly, that all roads (and major railroads and, later, airlines) led to Athens in 1896 or London in 2012 – and, during that more than one hundred-year span, to about three dozen other cities, as geographically far apart as Osaka, Japan and Vienna, Austria.

Yet much, if not all, of the permanent construction for these former grand events is forgotten. The distracted crowds now rushing through the city, with individuals wrapped in their thoughts and asserting their anonymity, hurry unknowingly into or past urban features that owe their existence and placement to the world's fairs or the Olympic Games. Transportation hubs like railroad stations (in Paris, the Gare St Lazare – its fame in some measure assured because its form was captured on canvas by Claude Monet – was constructed for the 1867 Paris International Exposition) and airports (the major expansion of Hartsfield Airport in Atlanta, that helped allow it to become the busiest airport in the United States, was done for the 1996 Summer Olympics held in that city), grew to assure effective processing of thousands of visitors to these events.

New hotels were constructed (the first modern hotel in Paris, the Hotel du Louvre, was built for the 1867 international exposition and the first modular hotel constructed in the United States was the Hyatt Regency, built in seven months, for the 1968 world's fair in San Antonio, Texas). New art museums appeared (that of Saint Louis was built as part of the 1904 world's fair and in Paris the Museum of Modern Art was built for the 1937 international exposition) and bridges were thrust over rivers (the ever-so-frequently photographed Pont Alexander III in Paris for the 1900 International Exposition; and, most recently, the daring Almillo Bridge, designed by Santiago Calatravo, was constructed for the 1992 Seville World's Fair). Add to the mix sports arenas, parks, street improvements, plazas, fountains and urban transportation systems (the famous Paris Metro was built for the 1900 Paris International Exposition) and the enduring effects of these grand cultural ephemera can only be considered stunning.

Perhaps the permanent effects of such fairs are most easily seen in the structural exclamation point expressive of local self-satisfaction: the modern city tower. The first of the series remains the most famous, the Eiffel Tower, signature structure of the 1889 Paris International Exposition and, until recently, the world's most popular tourist site. After it came the Space Needle in Seattle (1962), the Hemisphere Tower in San Antonio (1968) and the

Sunsphere in Knoxville, Tennessee (1982). Many other towers went up and down quickly at major fairs, all well-illuminated at night in praise of the twentieth century's motivating source, electricity.

Today, the observation tower is a commonplace tourist attraction. They rise high above the city skyline in Cairo, Vancouver, Kobe, Kuala Lumpur, Shanghai, Toronto and Moscow, to name the most prominent of such structures; and many have revolving restaurants, while almost all also serve as transmission outlets for modern communications. The Eiffel Tower set the communications precedent when, during World War One, it sent and received radio messages to and from the Western Front. The first revolving restaurant proposed was to be featured in a huge, globe-like tower, the Friede Aerial Globe, suggested for the St Louis Exposition of 1904. The structure was not built, however.

The epitome of tower development no doubt is the Stratosphere Casino and Hotel, located in Las Vegas. At 1,149 feet in height, it layers modern entertainment: seven revolving restaurants, three wedding chapels, a "triple-twist" roller coaster, among other features. The complex, in imitation of something else, as is most of contemporary Vegas architecture, was inspired by world's fair towers. As one of the officers of the complex said: "[We] realized that just about every famous tower was associated with a World's Fair" (Botello 1998: n.p.).

As if the tower were not enough as a major world's fair attraction, George Gale Ferris, an Illinois engineer, gave it a spin. He constructed the Ferris Wheel for the 1893 Columbian Exposition in Chicago. After an immensely popular run, the wheel was disassembled at the fair's end and reconstructed for the 1904 St. Louis Exposition. Since then, such wheels have been erected all over the world. Ferris wheels (the name "Ferris" becoming a generic term) now curve skyward as announcements of the city as site of entertainment in Yokohama, Japan; Vienna, Austria, as well as Dallas, Texas and Chicago, Illinois.

In 1999, the British decided to outdo all others and constructed a giant wheel on the River Thames as part of the nation's millennium celebrations. At 1,392 feet in circumference and 443 feet in height, it dominates the Thames scene. For reasons that are self-evident, this particular playtime structure has been called the London Eye. What it oversees are the House of Parliament and even Buckingham Palace, where concern was expressed that photo-ops at that venerable site of pomp and circumstance might now include the high and wide brim of the wheel as well as that of the queen's hat.

The sports arena

Not wheels but circles – the five interlocking ones representing the five continents – symbolize the global extent of today's Olympics, and these circles, each in a distinctive color placed on a flag with a field of innocent white, fly over the accommodating structures of the host city and its surrounding territory. They also announce urban entertainment of lasting value. The stadium built on the then-new campus of Washington University in Saint Louis for the Olympics that coincided with the 1904 World's Fair, is still used by that school's athletics teams. Sports facilities, such as this early one, have since that time been the principal contribution of Olympic Games to urban growth in the entertainment sector. Arenas, swimming pools, ice rinks, tracks have all largely moved indoors and have also gained a homogeneous shape as these competitive events are essentially races against time in pre-configured space. The now universally found Olympic-size swimming pool is the obvious spillover of this concern and demand. As basketball has advanced as an Olympic sport, its rigidly determined court size has advanced the regularization of the sports arena.

The most recent urban sport feature is the sports dome. The oldest and arguably the most famous of the lot is the Astrodome in Texas, opened in 1966 and then described by its owner with a hyperbole that matched the structure's size (710 feet in diameter) as the "eighth wonder of the world." Variants of this dome have become the most obvious Olympics' contribution to popular culture in cities as scattered as Montreal (1976), Atlanta (1996) and Sydney (2000). The Sydney Super Dome was, from its inception, designed to be "the largest indoor live entertainment and sporting arena in Australia." Its very first use was as a concert site for the great Italian tenor Luciano Pavarotti.

Modern arenas, indoor and out, have become multi-media venues. Whether constructed as part of an Olympics meet or to accommodate a large sports franchise or a national team – football (including soccer) and basketball being the principal spectator sports in residence – these huge facilities, capable of containing tens of thousands of spectators, have often served other purposes. They have been one of the principal sites of rock concerts. In the year 1998, for instance, ten of the top concerts in terms of attendance figures and box-office receipts were those given by the Rolling Stones. They were all held in arenas and stadiums, including the Tokyo Dome, the Osaka Dome and the Olympia Stadium in Munich. In 2012 Lady Gaga boasted a world "stadium" tour promoting her album, *Born This Way*. The tour took her to stadiums ranging from Rajamangala National Stadium, Bangkok, Thailand to the Rod Laver Stadium in Brisbane, Australia.

Stadiums have also been used as the site for political and religious rallies. No two religious figures have made the stadium or arena more their personal turf than Pope John Paul II and Billy Graham. Both men, devout believers in the chemistry of personal appearance regardless of the distance between speaker and audience, have drawn crowds in unprecedented numbers. As early as 1982, Pope John Paul II attracted 27,000 when he spoke in London's Crystal Palace National Sports Centre. In 1989, Billy Graham broke that record when 29,000 gathered there to hear his message. The pope has celebrated Mass at Mile-High Stadium in Denver in 1993, with 87,000 in attendance; in the America's Center Dome in St Louis the same year, with 100,000 in attendance; and in Aztica Stadium in Mexico City in 1999 with 110,000 in attendance. Billy Graham averaged a nightly audience of 55,000 at Alltel Stadium in Jacksonville, Florida, during his stay, November 2–5, 2000. Sport and religion joined in happy familiarity on October 29, 2000 in Rome's Olympic Stadium, when the Pope celebrated a Mass dedicated to the "gift of sport." The report of the event by CNN stated that the pope got the "wave," perhaps best defined as a secular form of group benediction, from the sports spectators.

With the advent of television, the stadium and arena serve as convenient theatrical settings for this medium. Multiple cameras strategically placed (the television network, NBC, used 60 cameras including one on a helicopter and another in a blimp for televising the Summer Olympics in 2000) have made such sports events electronic equivalents of Byzantine mosaics. The opening and closing ceremonies of the Olympics and the halftime shows of American football games have become something of an art form unto themselves, in the tradition of the Hollywood extravaganzas of the 1930s. It certainly was no coincidence that the opening and closing ceremonies of the 1984 Summer Olympics in Los Angeles were arranged by David L. Wolper. One of Hollywood's most successful producers of film and television documentaries, Wolper is perhaps best remembered as the person who brought Alex Haley's *Roots* to television as a seven-part mini-series in 1976.

Appointed by Mayor Tom Bradley of Los Angeles to the Olympic Committee, Wolper not only arranged television rights for a cool $250 million but also brought his flair to bear on the ceremonies. For the opening night he arranged 84 grand pianos (one for each of the last two digits of the particular Olympic year) that joined in an incredibly well synchronized performance of George Gershwin's *Rhapsody in Blue*. Writing of this opening recently, one journalist suggested that both the opening and closing events of this particular Olympiad were "perhaps the most stunning live-televised events ever" (Peterson 1999: 3).

The Summer Olympics held in Sydney increased the musical instrumentality at the Los Angeles Stadium by a factor of about 24. A 2,000 piece band, to match the figure for the new millennium, played the unofficial Australian national anthem "Waltzing Matilda" at the opening ceremonies. Obviously, in our era of sports entertainment, statistical advantage is not only measured in hundredths of a second at the Olympic Games. Nor has entertainment been restricted to fixed-seating events. The ambulatory nature of entertainment, the walk-by and stroll-through activity of the late nineteenth- and early twentieth-century city – given a certain immortality in the lyrics of Irving Berlin's "Easter Parade" – has been recapitulated in the long expanses of the shopping mall.

The shopping mall

Yet another American-designed institution, the shopping mall has become an urban pandemic. Now found in the environs of every major American city and many small towns, the mall can also be found as far afield as George-town, Penang in Malyasia; Norwich, England; Capetown, South Africa; Chennai, India; and Vienna, Austria. In downtown Manila, the Philippines, there are six prominent malls offering the stroller and the shopper most of the merchandise and amenities that can be found elsewhere. The Megamall, considered Asia's largest at nearly one million square feet when opened in 1991, is a statistical enormity: 550 retail shops and dining places, 12 cinemas accommodating 11,074 spectators, a 45-lane bowling center, 50 food-court outlets, parking space for 3,000 cars. It is described, on its website, as "the pride of Philippine shopping ... " (website "SM Megamall" 2000: 1).

The parking facilities are the obvious indication of the modern shopping mall's place in the urban and suburban environment. Just as the department store was situated in a world transported by steam train and electric tram, the mall is essentially a creature of the automobile. However, its interior was made possible by air conditioning, then a new feature of urban living and one that allowed a regulated environment that could remain all year at a temperature that inspired shopping.

The mall emerged in the United States in the 1950s, the time that the nation's vast federal highway system was being designed and constructed, the time when the two-car family was becoming reality and shopping was in itself becoming a major enterprise. Perhaps first marked by the construction of the Southdale Mall in Minnesota in 1956, the mall moved the center of com-merce from downtown to city periphery and also to the suburbs. For this reason, it has been described as "anti-urban." Its careful articulation and arrangement of the products it sells and the services it provides has led to critical examination of the psychology of purchase that it encourages. Its chief originator was the Viennese-born but Los Angeles-based architect Victor Gruen, who designed the Southdale Mall. He has been credited with for-mulating the concept of the "Gruen Transfer," the unpredictable but critical moment when the "focused" buyer – set on getting a pair of socks, an electric can opener or a stereophonic sound system – changes pace and purpose to become the "impulse buyer," suddenly enticed by the display of something she (or he, of course) had not previously considered.

The mall also creates an ambience that combines what is for sale with what is displayed or arranged for distraction from intended purpose. The now widespread food courts and movie theaters, the occasional petting zoo and the "signature amusement" – the large skating rink in the Galleria in Dallas, Texas, or the one in Manila's Megamall, for instance – add to the mall's functions as a pseudo-civic center and theater of pop culture. Nowhere are those functions more grandly presented and set out with such sweeping gestures of eclectic flair than in the West Edmonton Mall in Edmonton, Canada, and the Mall of America in Minnesota. Huge in size (the one encompassing 5.2 million square feet, the other 4.2 million square feet), these two malls, both created by the same developers, are extravaganzas of marketing in an amusement park environment.

The website for the Mall of America features brightly colored animation and the slogan "There's a place for fun in your life." This mall's centerpiece, a seven-acre indoor theme park featuring 28 rides, confirms the reality of the slogan. To list the indoor features of both malls is to catalog the features listed in city guidebooks: numerous dining facilities, hundreds of retail outlets, hotels, wave pools, gyms, lagoons and zoo-like attractions containing penguins, dolphins, sharks and tigers. In the words of Nader Ghermezian, one of the two brothers responsible for both these malls: "What we have done means that you don't have to go to New York or to Paris or to Disneyland or to Hawaii. We have it all here for you in one place, in Edmonton, Alberta, Canada!" (Crawford 1992: 4). In its expression of self-congratulation, the Mall of America website publicity declares: "Mall of America is one of the most visited destinations in the United States, attracting more visitors annually than Disney World, Graceland and the Grand Canyon combined."

Embracing so many commercial activities and offering such a wide variety of entertainment and enjoyable distractions, the modern shopping mall has made a mixed salad of nearly all the ingredients that existed separately in the early twentieth-century city. Yet what is distinctive in the shopping mall is not exclusively situated there. The Dutch architect Rem Koolhaas, known as much for his trenchant writing as for his daring architecture, has seen the shopping mall as a formative and deformative development in the urban environment. Declaring it to be "the last remaining form of public activity," he also sees it as colonizing every other feature of urban life.

Two major contemporary urban institutions, neither originally directed toward product consumption nor intended to be sites of fun or entertainment, also exhibit something of the riotous diversity of the shopping mall. These are the museum and the convention center, the one an old and venerable institution, the other a development of the air age.

The museum opens its doors wider

Crusty in its early nineteenth-century origins, the museum became a temple of high culture by the end of that century, a place for observation of and instruction in aesthetics and good taste by means of the declared "masterpieces" arranged on the walls. A city, to enjoy esteem as a seat of civilization, required an art museum, it was widely averred. Many major world's fairs or expositions left such museums behind. The tenor of praise for this activity was most resonant in the intentions of the organizers of the St. Louis Exposition of 1904. David R. Francis, director-general of the exposition, writing of the value of a permanent art exhibition building, said that its existence would prove that the United States "is now able to compete with assurance, pride and honor, holding a position of dignity and respect before the art world."

As the twentieth century rolled on with technological progress and exploded in two world wars, museums started to house and honor other than what were traditionally determined to be art masterpieces. Museums of science and industry became very popular, as did history museums and then sports museums: "95 per cent of museums postdate the Second World War," the geographer David Lowenthal has asserted (Lowenthal 1996: 3).

Many of these are housed in refitted buildings, such as Tate Modern, the new gallery of the Tate Art Collection in London, located in the Bankside power plant designed in the 1920s to generate electrical power for the city. The Andy Warhol Museum in Pittsburgh is located in an old 1920s warehouse. A particularly striking adaptation is the Orsay Museum in Paris, housing the nineteenth-century art taken from the crowded Louvre, and handsomely as well as effectively displayed in this old railroad station – designed as part of the urban development coincidental with the 1900 Paris International Exposition.

Perhaps the most daring and extensive architectural re-adaptation has occurred with the old Fiat Automobile Factory in Turin, originally a dazzling work-space commissioned by Giovanni Agnelli, Fiat's founder, as the structure to allow mass-assembly manufacturing of his automobiles, much in the manner of Ford's River Rouge plant near Detroit. Praised in its time by architects and engineers, Le Corbusier chief among them, the two major Fiat buildings making up the complex were best known for the test track that ran around the roofs of both.

It was Renzo Piano, now one of the world's most renowned architects, who was assigned the task to rehabilitate the old buildings once automobile production ceased there in 1958. Piano devised what he described as a "city within a city" (Newhouse 1998: 200), not greatly dissimilar in designation and purpose from the modern shopping mall. Its unusual quality, however, was a huge exhibition area, formerly the body stamping shop, to which is joined an art gallery. The exhibition area serves as space for trade shows, temporary art exhibits and other visual presentations. Along with this facility, the old buildings include restaurants, shops and a concert hall. Such use of space provides kinetic qualities, a sense of constant animation, characteristics of city plazas in the eighteenth and nineteenth centuries.

Most museums are neither so expansive nor so divergent from old purposes as is the re-animated Fiat factory. Yet few museums any longer would be denounced by anti-elitists as suffering from cultural constipation where everything is tightly held in. Older museum architecture – often palatial and stark in its monumentality, thus reinforcing the notion of high culture, susceptible of appreciation only by an élite – has given way to a calculated openness and a daring form that attracts widespread attention and announces the building itself as a work of art, certainly as an attention-getter. Something of a rage of new museums is sweeping across the globe. In 2012 in the United States alone, hundreds of new museums are under construction or in the planning stage, including those designed by cutting edge architects such as

Londoner Farshid Moussavi, designer of the newly expanded Museum of Contemporary Art in Cleveland, Ohio, and those dedicated to pop culture icons such as Johnny Cash, in Nashville, Tennessee. They join the impressive number that has added to the world's art and culture spaces since the 1970s.

Perhaps the first example of the divergently bold and iconoclastic architecture was the National Center of Art and Culture Georges Pompidou. Part of the plan of urban renewal in the old and depressed area of the Marais, where the central market of Paris once stood, this is the structure that began the very successful careers of Renzo Piano and Richard Rogers, who won the international competition for the building and site in 1971. To assure maximum and flexible interior space, an ideal and requirement since Le Corbusier's time in the 1920s, the architects placed the "guts" of the building, its mechanical and service components, on the exterior and even emphasized this arrangement by color-coding it brightly in blues, reds and yellows. The escalators were placed in glass tubes allowing riders to look out at the cityscape and observers of the building to look in at the escalator riders. As museum and library, as video center and theater, the Center was arranged to appeal to a wide and diverse audience. Set on an open plaza that continues the street life and carnivalesque activity long associated with the area, the building and its setting have become major tourist attractions in the city.

If the center aroused excitement and criticism for its riotous re-interpretation of traditional rectangular museum architecture, the Guggenheim Museum in Bilbao, Spain, has denied all such previous form in favor of the polymorphic. Its form sweeps and turns as if unsettled, in a calculated way reminiscent of the maritime history of the city. Designed and structurally tested before it was built by use of the computer software program intended for the production of French airforce fighter planes, the building is coated with sheaths of titanium that add a luster and tonal quality that vary according to time of day and the weather. The building's central exhibit space is a hall 400 feet long and 100 feet high, grand enough to accommodate sculptures that others cannot exhibit, like Frank Serra's *Snake*, weighing in at 15 tons and extending 150 feet in length, not monumental but gigantic.

Barely was this building in place than Gehry designed the new EMP (Experience Music Project) that "swoops" around the site of the Seattle Exposition of the Twenty-First Century, a world's fair of 1962, now famous for the Space Needle. The verb "swoop" is appropriate. It was the term used by Paul Allen to describe the form and appearance of the building he wanted. Cofounder of Microsoft and a man with billions of dollars to his name, Allen was a rock-music buff and a longtime fan of the Seattle musician who provided to his medium what has been called the Northwestern sound: Jimi Hendrix, widely considered the world's best electric guitar player. Beginning with the purchase of one of Hendrix's hats, Allen amassed a major rock-and-roll collection that took on museum dimensions. But, master of software, Allen wanted a state-of-the-computer art museum. The exhibits are electronically controlled allowing the individual armed with a magic wand (a palm-held computer) to proceed through the museum at individual pace and with idio-syncratic purpose. As a showcase is electronically zapped, the exhibit is explained and snippets of music (copyright restrictions forbid more than 29 seconds) place the exhibit in its musical context.

The central "nave," as it might be called, is a concert hall giving body to Hendrix's dream of a "sky church" where music could be appreciated by large groups. Most dramatic and entertaining of all is the special and spectacular "Artist's Journey," an electronic variation of the traditional amusement park fun house that takes the rider, by means of hydraulic lifts that suggest swift movement, back to the early years of rock-and-roll. Derisively called "the blob," the EMP is of a computer-generated design, like the Guggenheim of Bilbao, and decked out in the colors of Fender electric guitars. As the sun sets – as it does even in foggy Seattle – the purple texture of the building glows as if it were part of the landscape of Mars.

Gehry's dash and daring have been matched by the dramatic architectural presentations of Santiago Calatrava, the Spaniard hitherto best known for his bridges. Calatrava, a native of Valencia, is a master artisan of concrete, a material that he likens to "a supple and malleable rock" (Calatrava 2001: n.p.). Yet Calatrava has said that "frequently my designs recall the form of skeletons or other forms derived from nature" (Calatrava 2001: n.p.). His Museum of Science in Valencia does indeed look like the assembled skeletal remains of a vast vertebrate, while his addition to the Milwaukee Art Museum is dominated by a giant *brise-soleil*. This sun screen is nothing less than a well-designed bird wing that dazzles as its vanes open and close elec-tronically according to the outside light. Most compelling of all may well be the Planetarium he has designed in Valencia, which looks like a giant eye, conforming to his desire to abstract from nature, which explains his "longtime obsession to make a building like an eye...." The architecture critic Paul Goldberger said of the Milwaukee Art Museum addition that "it has nothing to do with the display of art and everything to do with getting crowds to come to the museum" (Goldberger 2001: 98). It is, as they say about the theatrical, "a show-stopper."

Such a comment is consistent with the opinion of Glenn Lowry, director of New York's Museum of Modern Art. For him the museum of the near future will provide "a loud, cacophonous environment in which fun is had by all" (Newhouse 1998: 191). No one will then any longer hear the traditional museum sound: the squeaking of floorboards. When, in 1998, the Guggenheim in New York City, housed in a famous spiral structure designed by Frank Lloyd Wright, offered an unusual display of 140 motorcycles of a variety of makes and covering more than a hundred years, the event clearly marked the end of the feather-duster era of museum display. Staid patrons and critics objected; people who had never been in a museum, let alone the Guggenheim, flocked in crowds. "The Art of the Motorcycle" was the museum's most successful show.

The museum director, the energetic and bold-minded Thomas Krens, who was the inspiration behind the Guggenheim Museum in Bilbao, justified the

show in crisp terms. He wrote: "If the institution's original mission is interpreted as a mandate to present paintings and drawings, then motorcycles have
no place on the Guggenheim's ramp. But the contemporary museum is no
longer simply a sanctuary for sacred objects" (Krens 2001: n.p.) Nor,
according to Krens, need the museum be placed on high cultural ground.
In 2001 the Guggenheim, in conjunction with the famous Hermitage of
St Petersburg, Russia, opened a museum in Las Vegas as part of the Venetian
Hotel, currently the world's largest. A special gallery in the hotel housed the
art works, while an adjoining building, designed for more varied exhibits,
reprised the earlier New York Guggenheim "Art of the Motorcycle" show.
The museum, however, closed in 2003, a victim of increasing costs and a
decline in tourism.

Exhibits in other than art museums are also departing far from the con-
ventional. The Museum of London produced a show in 1999 that celebrated
"Five Hundred Years of Capital Dining," the subtitle of the exhibition being
"London Eats Out." With ancient utensils, modern menus, paintings and
furniture on display – and with a special section devoted to roast beef – the
show was an exercise in extended and expansive London gastronomy. A historical object, much commented on, was a bun stamped with a crown and
dating from the coronation of King George IV in 1821.

One of the most successful of museum displays was "Titanic: The Exhibition."
Of less intrinsic artistic value than many objects that could be found in better
condition in an antique shop, as one art reviewer remarked, these displays of
silverware, eyeglasses and bottles were significant for their narrative function
because they "move the story along." And then this reviewer added: "The
elitist nature of many art shows is not present" (Marger 1997: 3). Between
1997 and 2001, the show successfully set sail to a variety of American cities
from St. Petersburg, Florida to Memphis, Tennessee; then on to Chicago,
Illinois, and farther on to Kansas City, Missouri, and Seattle, Washington.
The Chicago presentation had its newsworthy aspect: the front doors of the
Science and Industry Museum had to be removed to allow entrance of the
13-ton chunk of the Titanic's hull. "Titanic: The Exhibition" was viewed by
more than 7,000,000 persons. So much for the persistent romance of a vessel
that never reached its intended destination on its maiden and last voyage.
(Of course, the exhibit had benefited from the blockbuster film *Titanic*,
released in 1997.)

Ships have also settled permanently in museums, with just about
every country bordering on the sea having a maritime museum. Specialized
museums are almost countless and include some seven Coca-Cola museums
(one in Brazil, another in Taiwan), an equal number of comic-book museums
(one in France). Finland has a spy museum, the Netherlands a computer
museum. There is a lawn-mower museum in Southport, England, and a
sewing-machine museum in Arlington, Texas.

Museums are now more than just displays: the museum is yet another
multiple-attraction day-trip destination. Restaurants, bookstores and shops,

offering reproductions of this work of art or that in multiple forms from posters to postcards, from playing cards to paper napkins, are integral features of the current museum experience. One can only imagine how many scarab earrings and brooches were sold when the earthly possessions of long-dead King Tut (the popular nickname for Tutankhamun) did their extended world tour between 1961 and 1981, even though these ancient goods were originally intended, not for display in the here-and-now, but to be available to the king who had moved on to the Afterlife.

In 2003 a cartoon in the magazine *New Yorker* showed a somewhat perplexed visitor, strolling along an art museum gallery, suddenly looking down and seeing on the floor an arrow affixed to a sign reading "To the museum store." At the renovated entrance to the Louvre in Paris and the Armand Hammer Art Museum in Los Angeles, and many other museums such a sign is unnecessary. The museum book and retail stores are at the entrance, strategically situated to assure impulse buying at the beginning or at the end of a museum visit.

There is nothing fishy about the recent growth of public aquariums. The first such structure was put up in Regents Park, London in 1853, but by 1928 there were only 45 worldwide. In recent years the number has floated upward into the hundreds. The figures are quite staggering: 57 in the United States, 47 in Japan, 26 in the United Kingdom – and Russia, the Czech Republic, Singapore, China and South Africa are also among the nations supporting aquariums. Like zoos, of which they are often a part, aquariums add a new dimension to exotic tourist sites. The major part of the globe, the unseen depths of seas and oceans, is now laid open to humans who need not hold their breath but can gasp at the grace, beauty and frightening appearance of creatures of the deep.

With recent improvements in filtering systems and the strength of glass holding tanks several stories high and forming glass tube passageways, visitors to the aquarium are only tourists moving through – but not in – another medium. The AZA (Association of Zoos and Aquariums) reports that for the year 2000 their 30 member aquariums in the United States had 75 million visitors. In the form of an extensive resort hotel aquarium, the Atlantis in the Bahamas has the largest exhibit: some 50,000 sea animals in 11 exhibit lagoons, described as "second only to Mother Nature," on the hotel's website (www.atlantis.com).

Hospitality and leisure architecture

In this new and highly kinetic environment, where museums are multiplying and diversifying their functions and where entertainment is cozying up to enlightenment as a major museum purpose, it is not surprising to find that architects have expanded their portfolio to include "hospitality architecture" and "leisure architecture," forms that accommodate both the newer meetings industry and the older tourist industry. Hospitality architecture is expansive and embraces the developments that once centered on the city hotel. Leisure or destination architecture means the resort that is in and of itself the object of one's travel. Such additions to the built environment are now among the most obvious of popular culture.

Originally conceived in the late eighteenth century as a collection of sleeping rooms for persons on business in the city, the hotel soon was outfitted with a restaurant and then a ballroom. Its public space was limited and highly functional. By the late nineteenth century, the resort hotel (in the mountains or on the shore) and the colonial hotel (in the port city) added new dimensions and interior space with new purposes. The bar and the lounge, the winter garden and the billiards room were such features. Extended porches and balconies, tennis courts and gardens added to the array of features.

The modern resort hotel, so familiar in its turn-of-the-century appearance in Miami and Monte Carlo, was, like the colonial hotel, generally situated in an appealing environment and standing as a grand retreat from the hustle-and-bustle swirling around it. The Hotel Astor in New York or Claridge's in London or George V in Paris, Raffles in Singapore, and the Huntington in Pasadena, California, still function. They enjoy long-established reputations as places where the famous and wealthy, not always one and the same, holed up and watered down in the interwar period. Today, most of these places have been renovated to accommodate tourists who dream of other days, when liveried servants moved swiftly and silently to satisfy the inconsequential demands of guests whose principal activities were changing clothes for the next occasion of the day: tennis or croquet, lunch or dinner, drinking, eating and exchanging gossip.

Perhaps the quintessential tropical hotel and one that quickly gained world renown is the Royal Hawaiian, the second of the resort hotels on Waikiki, opened in 1927 and soon revered as the "Pink Palace" because of the color of its stucco exterior. That it was renovated right after World War Two, when it had ceased serving as a recreational spot for American troops in the Pacific, is an interesting fact. The person responsible for this undertaking was George J. Wimberly. Today, the firm he founded – Wimberly, Allison, Tong and Goo – is the largest in such architecture and has designed several hundred facilities around the world, particularly in today's Pacific Rim countries. In designing the Four Seasons Hotel in Mexico City, the firm's intention was "to create a secluded retreat in the center of this enormous, vibrant city" and to assure a quality of execution "that would attract high-level executives and professionals traveling to Mexico City on business" as well as providing "an elegant social setting for affluent local residents" (Naisbitt 1995: 22).

Airline and travel magazines regularly carry advertisements for variants of this hotel, all suggesting it as an escape or respite from the frenetic pace of the workaday world. Courtyards, fountains, marble-floored and spacious lobbies, high ceilings, arches and colonnades are standard architectural elements, fixed rhythmic forms that reinforce the idea of leisure, comfort and grace. Hospitality architecture is well-named. Leisure architecture is a variant of the older term "resort architecture." It is also, as mentioned above, widely referred to as destination architecture. In this last term is declared its real purpose: a place that serves as the desired end – or fulfillment – of a trip. Not quite Shangri-la, perhaps, but an environment calculated to suggest that the temporary resident is at or in the vicinity of the mythic and romantic Isles of the Blessed.

Somehow mixed up in this set of hotel blueprints is one significant sub-category: entertainment or narrative hotel design. Such design is intended to provide the hotel guest with new diversion, something more than traditional service. The decor therefore may be arranged by colors or patterns that suggest progression as the guest moves through the hotel. Karen Daroff, a leading exponent of such interior design in restaurants as well as hotels, speaks of it as providing "three-dimensional cinematic experiences" (Daroff 2003). Less dramatic forms of entertainment hotel architecture attract attention by reworking commonplace features. And so, the use of stools designed to resemble gold molars (yes, teeth) in the lobby of the St Martin's Lane Hotel in London; or the dramatic – and amusing – "wine tower" in the Mandalay Hotel in Las Vegas. Forty-two feet high, glass-encased, the tower requires that wine stewards be hoisted in a harness to the proper level to get the particular vintage desired by the customer at table below. A current Vegas specialty is replicature architecture, allowing hotels to take on the characteristics of a city: Paris, Venice or New York, as three of the hotels suggest. The Parisian Hotel lobby is dominated by three legs of the three-quarters-scale Eiffel Tower, the scene bathed in the equivalent of perpetual twilight; the Venetian Hotel has a canal upon which float gondolas.

Whatever its nomenclature, the resulting architecture is intended to assure realization of the tourist's or vacationer's objective to be immersed in an environment that is neither urban nor businesslike. The aim is, to use the popular term, to "get away." The challenge to the architect, and to the resort's owners, is to provide the appearance of a gateway or threshold into the local culture, while assuring the comforts and conveniences that are found in the home culture, usually that of the industrialized and wealthy nations from which most of the resort guests come. Generally designed as a collection of multiple, but complementary units, the resort creates the illusion of a self-contained village where the guest has temporary residence.

Arguably the first to establish the pattern was the *Club Méditerranée* or Club Med, as it is popularly called. Founded in 1950 as a tent complex in Spain on the coast from which it derived its name, it gained its reputation as a sun-and-surf place. To help generate a sense of inclusion among its guests, the Club Med referred to its facilities as a village and labeled its personnel GOs (Gentle Organizers) and its guests GMs (Gentle Members). The resort chain grew rapidly: the young and the single of the yuppie generation saw it as a place to *bouffer, bronzer et baiser* (eat, tan and kiss – although the last term is somewhat more suggestive in French vernacular). However, changing tourist habits, competition from other resort corporations and more liberal attitudes toward sex caused the 130 locations in 30 countries to suffer an attrition of GMs and, hence, income at the turn of the century.

Business tourism and the convention center

Another change in tourism is the growth of the meetings and hospitality industry, primarily serving businessmen. The rather barren traveling-salesman meetings held in bleak hotels – as described in terms of self-importance by Willy Loman to his sons in Arthur Miller's famous play *Death of a Salesman* – are everywhere gone. Today, as Hans Rissmann, Chief Executive of the Edinburgh International Conference Centre, asserts, "our top priority at the EICC continues to be to provide a top-quality product and achieve total customer delight" (Rissmann 2001: n.p.). That state of being is achieved in considerable measure by the site and its attendant distractions. The EICC is within sight of Edinburgh Castle, a major attraction in a tourist city.

The hundreds of convention and conference centers that sparkle on the earth's surfaces are of many forms: palaces, like that of the Prince-Archbishop of Salzburg, Austria; campuses like that of Cambridge University; tourist or golf resorts like that at Coeur d'Alene, Idaho, which boasts of being the only golf course in the world where one green is on a floating island. Both more significant and more spacious, however, are the purpose-built conference and convention centers. The one at Edinburgh, opened in 1995, is circular, appearing as a set of poker chips surmounted by a coaster. The arrangement allows the interior to be segmented or joined, much as an orange is, thus accommodating various-size meetings within its 22,700 square feet of public space.

Similar to it in form and purpose, but oval rather than circular, is the glass-encased convention center on the resort area of Jejeu Island, off the coast of South Korea. Although not exceptionally large, the center, situated in the popular Jungmun Resort, contains classrooms for 3,500 and a banquet hall for 2,400. Moreover, by 2005 it was one of four major convention centers in Korea collectively able to cater to 16,800 people.

Convention centers first became prominent in the United States in the 1980s and are now an international industry bringing in considerable revenue. It has been said that one night's residence by a convention-goer in Korea has the same economic effect as the export of nine television sets. In some cities, of which Denver and Atlanta are prominent examples, convention space has been doubled or is currently being doubled to take advantage of this new growth industry. In a 1999 ballot the citizens of Denver approved an expenditure of $268 million to increase the center's usable public space from 292,000 to 584,000 square feet. In light of this expansion, a new private hotel to have 1,100 rooms is being built as the "convention headquarters hotel," directly across the street from the expanded convention center. In varying dimensions of vast, usable space, from a conference of ten people to a Papal Mass of 100,000, America's Center in St. Louis is highly flexible, even if statistically super-muscled: exhibit halls, 340,000 square feet in size; a ball-room, 28,000 square feet in size and capable of seating 2,200 guests; while the concrete domed stadium, in which the Pope offered his 1999 Mass, is measured in acres: 32.

Publicity for the Edinburgh International Conference Centre has declared it to be "at the heart of the economic revitalization" of the center of the city. Many cities in the United States have made the same claim. Like the sports arena, the convention center is considered a necessary characteristic of the global city. Atlanta gave proof to that contention in 2000 when it hosted the annual meeting of the International Amusement Park and Attractions Industry (IAPA) Convention: 28,000 delegates from 101 countries moved through the displays of 1,303 exhibitors. The IAPA "is in the business of fun," an official statement avers, and fun includes convention-going.

The growth of the hospitality and meetings industry – even with its varying architecture – has not been matched by diversity in the arrangement of the features and conveniences of the guest rooms. Sameness is the key to success. The neatly folded edges of the roll of toilet paper in the hotel bathroom, whether in New York or New Delhi, are part of the comforting familiarity that visitors enjoy and expect. For instance, when American business people or travelers – suffering from jet lag – descend from the wide-body jet, they find such familiar details comforting.

What was unique or at least strange and exotic a century ago has been absorbed into a global culture with its universal road signs, ubiquitous plastic bags and television sets, and corporate signatures: a smiling Kentucky colonel selling chicken, golden arches announcing a place to quickly enjoy hamburgers, a wreathed "S" suggesting the elegance of a Sheraton Hotel, or an atrium many floors high, the centerpiece of the Hyatt hotel chain.

Disneyfication

Fear for the fate of the particular and the traditional has been expressed by critics who see a bright sameness corroding other cultures. This is "Disneyfication." The term is derisive, employed to suggest rigorous organization, fanciful history, idealization of urban living – a mythical American Main Street – and effective salesmanship. Disneyfication is commodification passing as entertainment wrapped in a nostalgia for what never was ("the good old days") and seeking conformity of behavior in a tightly controlled environment.

The Disney theme park is defined as a "land" or "world," complete in itself and exhibiting none of the unpleasantness of daily life: uncollected garbage, chewing gum and dog feces, fender benders, road rage and muggings. Only long waits in line remind the visitor of the real world outside the theme park's gates.

Disneyland opened in Anaheim, California in 1955. Walt Disney and his collaborators translated the two-dimensional world of animated cartoons to the three-dimensional creation of a carefully themed park situated in cheaply purchased real estate. The project was given shape by some of Disney's most talented personnel, soon named "imagineers." They designed the structural features of the park as a series of coherent ensembles including Main Street, Adventureland, Frontierland and Tomorrowland, each a highly sanitized and loosely interpreted part of American culture set out in three interlocked time zones: past, present and future.

What the clever Disney imagineers did was create spatial configurations that are both unhistorical and anti-urban. As one critic has asserted, the Disney theme parks assert a political ethic that "represents the tyranny of engineered happiness and consensus" (Ghirardo 1996: 62). The imagineers also engineered a "Main Street" of illusion in which there is no dissent, no "lonely crowds." The only sounds heard are those of parades and happy shoppers, with nothing worse than an occasional balloon popping, a minor event quickly accompanied by the wail of childhood grief.

Variants of such spatial organization, carefully planned and corporately controlled, as well as often patrolled, have also changed residential patterns. Gated communities, an American practice of restricted access to other than residents and internal regulation of property development, have emerged in the last three decades and provide the appearance of tidy conformity. The practice is now spreading elsewhere. Even in the officially Communist People's Republic of China, such communities are mushrooming on the outskirts of Shanghai, now the biggest city in the country. They are handsomely walled and elegantly named in English: Long Beach, Sun Island, Holiday Cottages, Shanghai International Elite Villas. The growth of golf communities in the United States, now questioned by land preservationists as an extravagant use of land, also impose strict building codes while providing residents with the sort of meadow views nowhere else available in most big-city suburbs.

Historic preservation and tourism

As more land is consumed for recreation, other land is put aside, preserved. Historic preservation is a widespread activity today and an effort to assure that our collective, fixed memory – the buildings around us that date from other times – are not razed. In their fixity, in their being there, such buildings inform us of cultural continuity. To visit a historical site is to be haunted by the past, to sense the atmosphere and the arrangement or another day, of activity once important, now useless. The forge, the spinning wheel, the clock weights in Jefferson's home at Monticello, the Hall of Mirrors in the Palace of Versailles, the prison cell in which Nelson Mandela was confined on Robben Island, these are the thresholds across which we make our secular pilgrimage back through time.

Yet historic preservation itself has no long history. Several efforts to assure historic preservation were made early in the nineteenth century, but the major concerted efforts occurred later in Great Britain and France. The National Trust, which concerns England, Wales and Northern Ireland, was established in 1895 as the result of three wealthy Victorians seeking to save important monuments and land from unregulated development. Its achievements have been notable in the century since its founding: over 200 buildings saved, 6,500 miles of coastline and 612,000 acres of countryside protected against further development. Dependent on private funding, the trust charges admission fees to its properties and even rents out rooms in some of its buildings. France moved in to achieve even more spectacular results through governmental action. Through two laws passed in 1913, one pertaining to structures like the Palace of Versailles and the other to historic sites like Mont-Saint-Michel, some 40,000 buildings and properties are now protected. In 1976, a private initiative, the National Association for the Preservation of Sites and Monumental Structures, was formed to coordinate local and regional efforts to protect places not on the national list.

The United States – whose citizenry have long used the greeting "What's New?" – was late in coordinated efforts at historic preservation. The National Trust for Historic Preservation was established in 1949 to encourage pre-servation of buildings under the jurisdiction of the National Park Service, as were Mount Vernon and Monticello, for instance. With the passing of federal legislation in 1976, the Federal Historic Rehabilitation Tax Credit, some 30,000 such places are annually added to the list and preserved for further service through the enticement of a 20 percent tax credit for any renovation project approved by the Park Service.

In the United States, as in many other countries, interest in preservation is not always unalloyed. As the rewards for historic tourism grow, sites once ignored or severely encroached upon by urban development are now being rehabilitated. The model for such procedures is America's oldest and most successful re-creation of the past on site: Williamsburg, Virginia. "Partly restored and partly re-created," a tour guide says of the place, it is "a step back in time to the eighteenth century as costumed interpreters ... go about their everyday duties" (website *Mid-Atlantic tourbook* 2001: 291). The restoration was the vision of a local resident, W. A. R. Goodwin, rector of a local church, and supported financially by John D. Rockefeller. When work on Williamsburg was begun in 1926, Mickey Mouse was still two years away from his appearance in *Steamboat Willie*. If the site is therefore pre-Disney, it nonetheless offered the same sanitized, spatialized segment of American his-tory that the Disney Imagineers would later make famous. Here was a version of the colonial American town where the walkways are unpaved, as they once were in real time, but where no sheep dung or horse manure bothers the tourist and where, until very recently, no African Americans walked the streets as they once would have done as slaves.

"Imageability" and the city

Since Williamsburg's re-creation, other such examples of outdoor historic theater – where the buildings and site are animated by interpreters or actors – have added to the landscape of entertainment. Similar developments have occurred in major cities as the importance of "imageability" has been added to the qualities that make a city distinctive, both to residents and tourists. What Paris and New Orleans have as a genuine part of their urban fabric, other cities have been seeking to acquire by urban renewal tinctured by the past. Even a city as unusually appealing as San Francisco has redone Ghiradelli Square centered on the old Ghirardelli chocolate factory, a well-known landmark, to provide it with a mall-like atmosphere appealing to tourists, particularly in their role of shoppers seeking the locally produced or the particularly defined.

At the other side of the United States, in New York, downtown districts have undergone a similar, but much more extensive and theatrical modification. Times Square and Broadway had deteriorated from being the "Crossroads of the World" and the "Great White Way" of the interwar period to the bleak center of sleaze, their brisk traffic in the 1960s and 1970s being pornography and drugs. Revitalization began amidst fanfare and glitz, particularly with the decision of the Disney Corporation to renovate the New Amsterdam Theater on 42nd Street, once the home of the Ziegfeld Follies. Its reopening with *The Lion King* in 1993 was a spectacular success. Other corporations and the Times Square Business Improvement District, funded by taxes on local businesses, have given the site more than its original glitz. Neon prevails, turning the night scene into the appearance of a (nearly, but never quite) setting tropical sun.

Here, as in the South Street Seaport project at the tip of Manhattan, academic critics have complained of the sanitized and ahistorical nature of the project. The sounds and sights of the past, rowdy, tawdry and unhealthy, have been banished. In Times Square, a gaudily announced presentation of acceptable entertainment prevails, while South Street Seaport, once the site of lively maritime activity, is now isolated in time and in place, set apart by good restaurants and boutiques that attract tourists and well-to-do locals to an atmosphere resembling a theme park without the rides.

And so it is elsewhere. The re-creation of once busy seaports, now overflown by global airlines and outmoded by container ships that require none of the elaborate storage and management facilities of wharf-and-pier ports, is one of the most widespread and strikingly similar activities of the postmodernist urban scene. London, Singapore, Baltimore, Sydney, San Francisco, Vancouver and Capetown have each attempted to make the waterfront the new playground. The once ship-cluttered port cities that appeared on Mercator-projection maps serving as the points of contact of the maritime empires of the late nineteenth century have been re-romanced, with festival atmosphere replacing the grime and grim appearance of the wharf environment that shrouded the novels of Arthur Conan Doyle, Joseph Conrad and Graham Greene.

The London Docklands plan, spread out in the 1980s from Tower Bridge down the Thames River to Greenwich, was one of the most ambitious and contentious undertaken: an effort to convert the vast maritime area that once briskly served the British Empire, into a super-modern financial, commercial and residential area. The compelling vision was less one of the imperial past than that of a soon-to-be Manhattan-on-the-Thames. As skyscrapers and vast office blocks were proposed and initiated, the plan was designed to revitalize and decongest London. Tourism was added as a major factor in the early 1990s with major visitor destinations like Tower Bridge and the West India Dock made over as entertainment spots with shops, restaurants, hotels and night clubs arranged to attract sightseers. Docklands was distinctive in scale and in the range of modern building. The massive Canada Tower in Canary Wharf, a bulked-up skyscraper with a pyramid roof, became the second tallest building in Europe and dominated the London cityscape, a structure of glowing prominence as the sun set and the visitor looked across the Thames from the Greenwich Observatory.

Baltimore, a long time ago part of the British maritime scheme of things, also lost its purpose. It was invested with a new one in the 1960s, when the Inner Harbor project was initiated. A conference center was constructed, the waterfront was opened to the public with attractive walkways. Harborplace, a shopping mall, was constructed. A large aquarium was opened; a major hotel settled in. Tourists abounded: the aquarium quickly hosted one million visitors a year. What happened in Baltimore also happened with Darling Harbor in Sydney and, on a more modest scale, with the Victoria and Alfred dock complex in Capetown, South Africa. Darling Harbor restoration, hurried along to attract visitors to the Summer 2000 Olympics, had a shopping center complex, a conference center and an aquarium. As with many other aspiring entertainment venues, it also had a large-scale Imax theater.

The Victoria and Alfred (V&A) project followed what appears to be the standard plan. In point of fact, the head of the company charged with V&A development, David Jack, had been a student at the University of California at Los Angeles (UCLA). He had closely studied American waterfront development and used that as the base for what took place in Capetown. With its wide range of restaurants, its two on-site hotels (one in a renovated warehouse), its Imax theatre and its large super-modern shopping mall, the V&A complex has brought "Anywhere" to one of its most southerly points.

Thus, these port cities, re-designed to serve the tourist interests of the air age, now resemble one another in the same way they did in the late nineteenth century when they served shipping of an international sort. The past of the port can also be rehabilitated, "commodified" as a tourist attraction, even when it is a stony silent reminder of the external dominance and presumed superiority of one people – the sort of people George Bernard Shaw ridiculed when he said the world is divided into two groups: Englishmen and foreigners.

In Shanghai, the late nineteenth-century Bund (the transposed Hindu term meaning a fortified or protected area) was extraterritorial space occupied by foreign merchants, first British and French, later joined by Americans. As they prospered, they built grand edifices celebrating their banking and commercial activities along the bank of the Huangpu River. In recent years, the Communist government of China, interested in both modernizing the city and erasing the European imperial past, started razing these buildings. This procedure was recently halted in view of the appeal that the buildings have as tourist attractions. Whatever their ultimate future, the string of Bund buildings now glow brightly as part of Shanghai's spectacular night display.

Perhaps most ironic of all is the rehabilitation of the French colonial heritage in Ho Chi Minh City. Once called Saigon – and still so called by many city residents – the city was to be a showpiece of French colonial power in the form of outsized buildings. The huge governor's palace, the grand city post office, the public theater, even the Roman Catholic cathedral were nineteenth-century confections heaped up in some measure to fulfill the admonition of the great French colonial administrator Joseph Gallieni who had served in Annam, now Vietnam. He stated: "batir en dur," build in durable materials to show the locals that the French would be on the scene for time to come. In the last several years, the Communist regime has been rehabilitating these buildings, turning the once colonial heritage into a tourist advantage.

Fields of pleasure and entertainment

Here, then, is another example of changing purposes and, consequently, patterns of land usage. Yet the space that has been preserved is much less than that which has been reallocated. The British National Trust now cares for 612,00 acres of countryside. The global golf industry occupies some 10 million acres, or about half the area of Scotland where the game was devised some five centuries ago. Golf, however, does no more than join all the other recreational and entertainment venues, from racecar tracks, to stadiums, to theme parks, to convention centers, to resorts and shopping malls, which have reconfigured the real estate of the contemporary world.

The vast majority of the world's population has no more gained entrance to these entertainment and recreational sites in city and countryside than did their ancestors have access to the urban delights of nineteenth-century Europe or the royal court diversions of Tudor England or Bourbon France. Nonetheless, resorts and shopping centers, as well as the other institutions previously described, are increasing in number and in economic effect. They are able to do so with the spread of consumerism and the consequent commodification of the built environment.

Entertainment, with travel included as a major component, is the world's major industry today. Architecture and urban planning are globally attuned to this fact. It would be difficult, even in this age of the quick-minded computer, to calculate the amount of space occupied by the structures serving the leisure, travel, meeting and entertainment industries. However, if the square footage of just three – the West Edmonton Mall, the Mall of America, and the Megamall in Manila – were joined together, the resulting enclosed space would be just about half the size of Monaco. Of course, these figures pale in comparison to the land mass given over to resorts and theme parks. Disneyland and Disney World, added together, would between them provide enough land to contain 60 states of Monaco. The 39 parks in North America, Latin America and Europe owned by Six Flags, the largest of theme park corporations, would add up to another 70 states of Monaco. On an even grander scale, if all the acreage of resorts, shopping malls, golf courses and theme parks around the world were added together, they would offer a land surface into which the United Kingdom could probably squeeze.

Never in history has so much land been devoted so long to a single activity as currently has been turned over to the various fields of entertainment. Only battlefields serve for comparison. And yet, for instance, the shifting battlegrounds of the Thirty Years' War in Europe (1618–48) were more far-ranging than any combination of today's theme parks but in no way either so large or concentrated. Moreover, the Thirty Years' War had a shorter run than either or both of Disney's American parks, the one now 57 years old, the other 41.

The multiple functions of such land use are also new, only found previously in temporary form at the world's fairs. However, world's fairs were not successful business ventures, in terms of receipts over expenditures. The entertainment industry is, and it achieves this success by trying as much as possible to achieve what Disney World does. According to a former Disney vice-president: "The Orlando philosophy is to get you there, keep you there, and to make sure you spend all your money with them" (Grover 2001: 1).

Land has always been coveted; buildings have always been constructed to serve as symbols of power. However, never has property been so regularly and extensively directed to serve as the well-prepared site of pleasure palaces and fun get-aways. It's as if the famous Potemkin Villages, hastily arranged in eighteenth-century Russia to provide the touring Empress Catherine with cheering crowds supposedly happily settled there, have now been built more substantially but also require admission charge or room rent of those they greet.

The world of waste: the sloop *Clearwater*, built to promote the anti-pollution cause, sails down the Hudson River past a junkyard in Newburgh, New York State, on its way to attend an Earth Day event in 1970 (© Bettmann/CORBIS)

7 The unintended outcomes

Some measure of the enormity of unintended outcomes of contemporary popular culture was the "10-mile-wide flotilla" of six million plastic bags found floating in the Pacific Ocean in 2002. Fallen from a container ship, the bags became a vast pollutant instead of packaging for purchases at fast-food restaurants in California (Hayden 2002: 58). Many of the institutions, instruments and practices that have defined contemporary popular culture have led to questionable, even disastrous effects, such as this one. Automobile accidents and their resulting deaths are daily news in most countries. Air pollution and the profligate use of non-renewable resources have given rise to new agencies of protest, like the Green Party in Germany and the Sierra Club in the United States. In the "throw-away" economy, waste management has ironically become a new growth industry in most of the developed world. Critics have urged a shift to a sustainable economy or what Worldwatch has called a "reuse/recycle economy" (website "Worldwatch" 1998: 1).

The issue has become more acute in the last two decades with the emergence of IT (information technology) where the rapidity of advance quickly makes products obsolescent.

E-waste

In 2003, a baseball fan of a losing team reportedly threw a cell phone at the right fielder of the rival and winning team. This act was an unusual example of a common problem, ineffective e-waste management. That was one of about 55 million handsets discarded or recycled in the United States in 2003, a statistic that has nearly doubled within a decade, as 100 million mobile devices were replaced in 2011 (website "Recycling Programs" 2012). Recognizing the enormous problem globally, the major manufacturers of cell phones met in Basel, Switzerland in January 2003 and established the Initiative for a Sustainable Partnership on Environmentally Sound Management of End-of-Life Mobile Phones. The title is long for a problem aggravated by the product's short life. Currently, cell phones become obsolete in less than a year, outmoded by new models ever more appealing in their range of features.

In 1997, according to an American Environmental Protection Agency (EPA) report, e-waste in general – television sets, computers and cell phones – amounted to 3.2 million tons annually. Similar statistics representing similar waste management problems for products ranging from toys to cars could be easily mustered. Few are the items like the 1975 Barbie doll and the well-kept 1935 Ford phaeton that have gained new value as collectibles or antiques.

Plastics

In the film that launched the remarkable career of Dustin Hoffman, *The Graduate* (1967), one of the older business types at the family graduation party offers quick professional advice to the young Princeton graduate whom Hoffman plays. "Plastics!" he whispers. Plastic products are basic in our throw-away society in which novelty, convenience and pleasure bear brand names printed on plastic bags and Styrofoam containers that are quickly and often randomly discarded. Plastic contains much of popular culture: it records its music and videos, it facilitates the serving of fast food, it rings in the pro-verbial six-pack, it forms much of the automobile body, it holds groceries and serves, almost ironically, as the material of garbage cans and their liners.

Used plastic containers form part of the worldwide litter scene, found in the aisles of American movie theaters, in barbed-wire residential fences in Kenya, among the hedgerows of England and France, and in street gutters just about everywhere. In the United States, the adopt-a-highway project has volunteers cleaning up the debris cast out of car windows. In a recent act intended to have dramatic effect, the Irish government has imposed a 13-cent use tax on each plastic shopping bag.

Such litter has debased the current coastal scene. On the beaches and in the water, ingested by sea life and found ensnaring the necks of porpoises and seagulls, it has replaced the traditional flotsam of seaweed, driftwood, rope and cork that marked the passage of ships in the age of sail. The worst effects have been in the Caribbean and the Inside Passage of Alaska where cruise ships have caused major environmental problems, not surprising in view of the 200 or so cruises each month in the Caribbean and the estimate that each cruise passenger produces onboard between five and six times the waste that he or she produces when at home.

The MARPOL international convention of 1973, established "to eliminate the pollution of the sea" caused by the discharge of toxic materials, contained a clause that specified the North Sea and "the wider Caribbean" as "special areas" requiring more severe limitations on the discharge of ship-generated waste. Violations of the terms of this convention and ones established by the United States for its coastal waters led to 87 law suits against cruise lines between 1993 and 1998.

To this particular instance of water pollution, now being addressed by the cruise lines through refined onboard processing of waste material, may be added the pollution of streams, lakes and rivers as sites for waste discharge. In the more developed nations, largely responsible for this problem, strict environmental laws have assured much clean-up (fishing is again now possible in the Great Lakes and the River Thames, for instance).

While much of this material, like parts of the cell phone and the plastic supermarket bag, is recyclable, the waste management problem is aggravated by the waste products not yet disposed of. Again, the EPA estimates that three-quarters of all the computers sold in the United States have simply been shelved in garages, cellars and attics as new models have been purchased. Joined to this problem, or heavily weighed down by it, is the junked automobile. Ten million meet this fate annually in the United States; even in Poland, where an automobile's on-the-road existence is ten to fifteen years long, some 500,000 automobiles are annually junked. The Germans are the most successful in recycling parts: 85 percent of parts from their junked automobiles are used again, as compared to 75 percent in the United States. Still, the remaining amount ends up in domestic landfills, a highly undesirable but growing landscape feature.

The major concern in all recycling efforts is what is called source reduction. The focus is not so much on disposal of waste but on reducing the quantity, by less wasteful use of materials, of which packaging is the most obvious. With the growth of air freight and the introduction of e-commerce, standardized and durable packaging has become the norm, making the tote and string bag of earlier days now just a relic. To reduce the one-time use of packaging materials, the current goal in the European Union is to reach 90 percent use of recycled materials. To this end an "eco-label" in the shape of a daisy – and resembling the star cluster that is the symbol of the European Union – was devised and introduced in 1992 (TED 2003: 1).

Noise

A serious issue is the noise that has accompanied the intensification of means of communication, except text messaging, of course. Noise pollution is the outcome. It has become an urban problem in which unwanted and intense sound disrupts daily living, generating stress and fatigue. Jet aircraft taking off have generated the most widely recognized noise problem. The situation in the area of Heathrow Airport, on the edge of London, where 461,000 airplanes annually take off and land, has not only disturbed the sleep of residents but disrupted schooling and led to learning impairment (website "Local Authorities Aircraft Noise Council" 2012). A similar result has been found for the areas surrounding O'Hare Airport in Chicago, where one teacher claimed that children just stopped listening every time a plane took off, on average every three minutes.

Schools and houses near Heathrow and O'Hare – along with houses in the flight pattern of San Francisco International Airport – have been soundproofed with two layers of glass. Consequently, reducing the noise hazard leads to the environmentally problematic need for air-conditioning.

Whether along the once quiet banks of the Seine in Paris or on the streets of Rome, the automobile has polluted the world's urban environment. Its increase seemingly never-ending, road traffic pollutes by sheer numbers as well as noxious fumes and noise. In the United States, the steady stream of automobile noise on major roadways on the edge of residential districts has led to the introduction of sound walls, usually conspicuous and unattractive reinforced-concrete structures, found in almost all large American cities. Ohio and New Jersey experimented with "vegetative walls," high mounds of dirt and mulch, or berms, surmounted by tightly clustered trees and perennial flowers.

Car stereo systems and "boom boxes" (portable radios) force noise on everyone around. Of lesser volume, but no less noticeable, is now the disrupting effect of the cell phone. Its intensive use in cars has prompted concern about road safety, both because of the motorist's hand being off the steering wheel to hold the phone and the possible distraction from attention to the road that use of the phone may cause. Texting exacerbates an already dangerous situation, and in 2010 AT&T initiated a documentary on the perils of driving while texting featuring interviews with first responders to teen car accidents and friends of young people killed in texting-while-driving incidents. Ireland, Great Britain and Israel have banned phone use from moving cars, as has the state of New York; ironically, however, many states and municipalities passed laws early on banning cell phone use while driving, which did not portend the pervasiveness of the texting, which is often more distracting than talking. Moreover, cell phones are used in almost every social environment, and they have frequently elevated monologue to a disturbing form of theatrics. The sudden sound of someone speaking to an unseen and unheard party has a jarring effect and the sound of impoliteness.

Thus intrusive use of the cell phone has been banned in certain places, like theaters and libraries, where it would be very distracting. *Wired News* reported in its online issue of February 5, 2003 that the actor Kevin Spacey interrupted a stage performance to holler at a member of the audience whose cell phone was ringing: "Tell them you're busy." The *Sacramento Bee*, a California newspaper, carried an article on the subject in its online edition of April 6, 2003, in which a moviegoer complained that a person arriving late at the theater phoned the friends he was to have met as he walked down the aisle in order to determine where they were sitting.

Light

In the last decades of the twentieth century, light pollution was added to the list of environmental hazards. The glitz of urban sites aglow from London to Las Vegas and on to Seoul, as well as the huge light pods for night sports events contribute to the problem. In response, organizations like the International Dark-Sky Association have appeared with the intention of arousing public concern about light pollution.

Major causes of light pollution are poorly designed public light fixtures but also include all-night gasoline stations, fast-food shops, motels and billboards. Such recreational activities as night baseball and tennis add to the problem and to the 25 percent of all electricity now directed to lighting. Cities in the United States, Britain, Canada and Australia have passed ordinances controlling night lighting

Land use

In 1994 the Disney Corporation proposed to build a new park, strictly historical in theme, called DisneyAmerica, in the vicinity of the Manassas National Battlefield Park, commemorating the opening battle of the Civil War. A coalition of academic historians and preservationists vigorously protested. Disney backed away; the theme park was not built. Less than ten years later, a golf course flanked by residences was being constructed on the same land.

This rather new relationship between sport and community, sharing land, is most obvious in the spread of golf communities in the United States. They have often become retirement communities, particularly as the "baby boomers" are retiring and wish a more relaxing combination of residence and activity. As the online explanation of DC Ranch in Scottsdale, Arizona, put it, "this golf community is a connected community focussed on the neighbourhood" (website "az-golfhomes" 2003, n.p.). Golf communities are found in Jamaica, the Dominican Republic, Spain and Australia, some suggestion of the growing popularity of this residential form.

More dramatic has been the new shift on the ski slopes of Colorado. As the ski resort business has declined – because of several seasons with poor weather conditions and an aging population that skis less – the large corporate interests that control these resorts have made their major business into real-estate development. "In the process," wrote one critic, "the sport of skiing morphed from a more or less environmentally outdoor experience into a destructive, extractive industry" (Clifford 2003: 35). This means the cutting down of forest areas, the disruption of wildlife and the intensifying use of natural resources like water.

Similar concern has been expressed worldwide over the appearance of shopping centers and "big boxes," the sort of structure found in supermarkets such as the mega-corporation Wal-Mart. In the United States, such development has caused a dramatic shift in commerce from city centers to the suburbs, or to major highway junctions where land is available at cheaper rates. Elsewhere, there is growing concern that the American pattern will be replicated, particularly in Eastern Europe. There, the shift from a state-controlled economy to a market one has made visible not only the consumer goods hitherto denied but also something of the consumer attitude prevalent in the United States. In 2003 Viktor Trebicky of the Institute for Environmental Policy in Prague, Czech Republic said, "We are making the mistakes the West made 20 years ago." His colleague Eva Kruzikova said that the new availability of consumer goods has made any discussion of a sustainable economy difficult (Maher 2003: 2). While Wal-Mart has not yet made a foray into the Czech Republic, as of 2012 4,068 of the company's big box stores can be found across the globe in 14 countries including Mexico (1,479 stores), China (284 stores), Guatemala (164 stores), and most recently, India, which has one retail outlet.

There is, however, a choice irony in recent shopping mall development. It is the disillusionment with the idea of its founding genius Viktor Grünbaum, a Viennese who immigrated to the United States in the Nazi era and there changed his name to Victor Gruen. It was Gruen (see p. 125) who developed the first mall in Southdale Center, Minnesota in 1956. What he wished to do was provide the myriad suburbias appearing in the United States with a new core, a sort of encased downtown that would replicate the best features of that earlier urban form but with the convenience of proximity. Although the mall has become something of a surrogate gathering place that would encourage community, it remains primarily a shopping and entertainment place without the civic spirit Gruen had hoped to see flourish there. In a telling statement, he later remarked "I refuse to pay alimony for those bastard developments" (Unferth 2002: 3).

One wonders what Gruen would think of the newest iteration of shopping "communities" that are springing up throughout the US, with names like "Legacy Village" and "Crocker Park" in the Cleveland, Ohio Metropolitan Area and "Mountain Brook Village" and "Cahaba Village" near Birmingham, Alabama. These environments meld everyday living with conspicuous consumption as, particularly in the case of Cleveland's Crocker Park, people can live amid high-end chain stores such as Abercrombie and Fitch, Banana Republic, Barnes & Noble, and Urban Outfitters. Indeed, residents' lives become centered on consumption, as ordinary activities such as walking the dog puts them into the center of marketing and commerce – they leave their private spaces and enter into a fully commercialized space, manufactured as "neighborhood." Devoid of blemishes and authentic character, these sites epitomize what Jean Baudrillard described as "hyperreal," a space that is a map without a history, a "desert of the real itself" (website, "The Precession of the Simulacra" 2012).

Moreover Gruen would have found unpalatable the many food courts now located in the malls, bringing together many of the fast-food shops that once stood separately. Fast food, certainly one of the most prevalent and criticized popular cultural developments of the second half of the twentieth century, has become the center of a new global concern: obesity.

Nutrition and obesity

In their quest to reach new or different demos, marketing researchers have encouraged a new "prepubescent Pop" music for the 6–11 age group and are also working on age-targeted food products. Appealing to the young, H. J. Heinz, the food company in Pittsburgh, gave ketchup a couple of new splashes of color a year ago by turning the tomato-red substance into purple and green. The young approved and so this year the company is trying to add color to french fries by introducing a Kool Blue variety. "We asked the kids what would make them want to eat more french fries," a company executive stated when Kool Blue and other french-fry varieties were announced (Spangler 2002: c2).

As the above remark suggests, American consumption of french fries dropped in 2001, the first time in over a decade. Analysts believe this is in part the result of consumer concern over fatty foods. Concern with obesity – with an estimated 17 percent of the young overweight – may be having some effect in the United States, but on the world scene obesity has become the ironic complement of starvation, in the major problem of malnutrition. A Worldwatch News Release stated in 2000: "For the first time in human history, the number of overweight people rivals the number of underweight people ... " (website "Worldwatch" 2002: 1). The World Health Organization, declaring that obesity is one of "today's most blatantly visible yet most neglected public health problems," coined the word "globesity" to describe the condition (WHO 2003). In the US one in three people is obese and the increase in the use of corn syrup (an expensive sweetener made from corn, the biggest crop of US farms) has contributed to an epidemic of type-2 diabetes; as of 2011 26 million children and adults were living with the disease (website "New Diabetes Statistics Highlight Need for Prevention" 2012).

Terrorism

Car bombing, aircraft hijacking, hostage-taking have become all too familiar news items. Their horrendous proportions were brought home to people in the United States on April 19, 1995 when the Murrah Federal Building in Oklahoma City was destroyed. The detonation of a bomb placed in a truck parked in front of the building killed 168 people. The explosion occurred at about 9:03 a.m. Ten minutes and several years later, on the morning of September 11, 2001, United Airlines Flight 175 crashed into the South Tower of the World Trade Center in New York City, a fiery explosion of 12 tons of jet fuel. Less than a half-hour earlier American Airlines Flight 11 had struck the North Tower.

The destruction of the Murrah Federal Building was an act of domestic terrorism. The destruction of the two World Trade Center (WTC) towers was an act of international terrorism. Moreover, the terrorist organization held responsible for the New York tragedy (as well as a comparable act that heavily damaged the Pentagon in Washington on the same morning) is one with a loose network of cells in over 40 countries, an indication of frightening potential. The "terrorist spectacular," of which the destruction of the WTC complex is the most stunning example, is designed by its perpetrators to be a media spectacle.

The dramatic horror the terrorist inflicts can be quickly and vividly displayed on television screens because of the ubiquity and portability of television equipment. Accordingly, tens, even hundreds of millions of viewers become eyewitnesses to the tragedy, even though they are elsewhere in reality. Even more than eyewitnesses, they are repeat viewers of the act as it is projected over and over again. The crash of United Airlines Flight 175 into the South Tower, vividly recorded on videotape, was shown repeatedly on every American television network as well as around the world on that fateful day.

Acts of terrorism are that: crude, cruel acts of the theater of the horrendous, Grand Guignol expressed at its worst. They become most spectacular when they are most horrendous. The day-long television coverage of the destruction of the twin WTC towers is the dreadful proof of the compelling force of the dreadful relationship. "For hijackers, hijacking television is usually part of their plan" wrote the senior news commentator Daniel Shorr (Shorr 2001: 11, section 1). Television assures a multiplier effect, an extension and a prolonging of the act, a deepening of its impact on the viewing public. In a not dissimilar way, the creator of the crime may move from elusive figure on the scene to celebrity on the screen (Gabler 1998: 181). Seen by few in life, Mohammed Atta, believed to be the key figure in the September 11 bombing, now joins Osama Bin Laden, Timothy McVeigh, and others before him whose images fascinate as their crimes repel. Notoriety is just the dark side of celebrity.

Yet terrorism thrives more often on personal anonymity. For the perpetrators, the cause, not the person is important. The shrouded or unseen attacker is as anonymous as is his or her victim. "It wasn't a personal vendetta," commented a Palestinian terrorist who had wounded an American in Israel. "It was public relations. It was like telling the media to pay attention to us," he said in conversation with an American journalist (Blumenfeld 2002: 38).

Almost twelve thousand terrorist acts were recorded between 1981 and 2002. Among them were 182 airplane hijackings in 50 countries, in which many of the passengers were tourists. Since the 9/11 attacks, numerous acts of terror varying in range of casualties, method, and purpose have been committed. Some of the more horrific include the October 26, 2002 hostage taking and attempted rescue in a theater in Moscow, Russia, which resulted in 170 deaths (including the 41 terrorists), and, more recently, the March 11, 2004 bombing of four trains in Madrid, Spain, where 191 people were killed, the October 28, 2009 bombing at a marketplace in Pakistan, which took 118 lives, and the October 2, 2006 school shooting at the Amish-run West Nickel Mines School in Lancaster County, Pennsylvania, where 10 girls aged 6 to 12 were tied up and shot by Charles Carl Roberts, who then shot himself (five girls were murdered). The latter case reveals the complexities involved in defining terrorism; some scholars assert that the Roberts case is one of misogyny as terrorism (website "Global Terrorism" 2012).

There is not even an approximate figure for the muggings and thefts of tourists, so commonplace have they become and so unlikely of solution that many are not even reported, much less defined as terrorism. Tourists have been hijacked, kidnapped and killed for personal gain and for political retaliation. One of the most dreadful incidents reported by Reuters as occurring between 1992 and 1997 took place in Egypt. The terrorist organization al-Gama'at al-Islamiyya on November 17, 1997 carried out a devastating act in which 59 tourists and 4 Egyptian guides were killed by 6 gunmen who also soon lost their lives at Karnak. The radical group which perpetrated the crime was opposed to the Egyptian government and wanted to destabilize it by destroying its tourist trade, the major source of the country's foreign currency.

Other terrorist attacks have been made frequently against the presence, home and abroad, of the corporations and business practices that define the American consumer economy. Abroad, the most prevalent have been the bombings and other destructive attacks against McDonald's restaurants. Since the early 1990s, McDonald's restaurants have been blown up or otherwise destroyed in Brazil, France, China, Chile, Greece, Belgium, Bosnia, Russia and South Africa.

The most blatant domestic acts have been committed by environmental activists who practice "monkey wrench ecotage." This term, describing assaults on property and equipment of corporations exploiting the land, but with no intention of direct personal harm, is derived from Edward Abbey's novel *The Monkey Wrench Gang* (1975), in which an odd gang of four protest what they see as wanton destruction of the natural environment for the sake of profits. "A planetary industrialism ... growing like a cancer. Growth for the sake of growth." Such are the words spoken by Dr S. K. Sarvis, the unlikely leader of the gang and expressing the sentiments of activists who later turned fiction into fact.

Trees in forests intended to serve as lumber have been spiked to render them useless. New homes in a formerly pristine tract of land on Long Island were burned. The most dramatic and costly example of "monkey wrench ecotage" was the destruction by arson of the newly built and not yet opened Blue Sky Basin building complex, a ski resort in Colorado. This act of violence resulted in $12 million of property damage. A highly secretive and cell-based organization with the acronym ELF (Earth Liberation Front) laid claim to this assault.

Language and culture

Above these changes the United States still looms. Its large population, its dominant economy and its privileged position in software production (operating systems for computers, blockbuster movies and exported television programs) assure its continuation as the heartland of popular culture. Add to this combination the primacy of English as the language of international communication, and the formidable position of the United States is undeniable, as are the reasons for concern. The unintended threat to other cultures is palpable. Currently, most books published in the Netherlands and a large number in Germany are published in English in order to reach a wider audience. The Kenyan author Ngugi wa Thiong'o in *Decolonizing the Mind* (1986) has bitterly complained about this sort of development as a continuation of the colonial mentality imposed by the European conquerors.

Yet the preponderance of English in contemporary scientific and business discourse, to say nothing of the popular culture of music and film, makes facility in it something of a cultural imperative. Rigorous study of the language is now mandated in almost every European country. Tourist guides around the world now learn English to further their trade not only because Americans are the largest single national group of tourists but also because other tourists frequently use English to negotiate abroad when they are not home, say, in Denmark, or Italy, or Brazil.

Faced with international support of open markets and the deleterious effect of the importation of cultural products, such as movie films and television programs, the French argued for the "cultural exception" in trade negotiations. UNESCO sponsored a conference on the matter in Stockholm in 1998. The topic was: "Culture: a form of merchandise like no other?" The conclusion was that culture was indeed a distinctive product. In an article she wrote for the prestigious Parisian newspaper *Le Monde*, the French Minister of Culture and Communications, Cathérine Trautman, spoke forcefully on the subject. "Cultural assets are not merchandise like others." Referring to several film makers, such as Alain Resnais and Martin Scorsese, she asks: "Where does the power of their films come from, if not from their exploration of their own world anchored in their own culture and irreducible to formulas?" She supported her argument with telling statistics: nearly 75 percent of the films shown in European movie theaters and on European television are American, but only 3 percent of films shown in the United States come from Europe (website "Europe Strives to Catch Up with Digital Hollywood" 2012).

An argument that Mme Trautman did not address, but one that concerns others is "convergence," an industry term for the merger or acquisition of media corporations to form conglomerates that direct the production, distribution and exhibition or sales of the major media: publishing, movies, television and the internet. Today there are six such giants that control vast empires broader in reach and deeper in influence than that of the British Empire, upon which, it was said in the late nineteenth century, the sun never set. A resident in one part of what was then that empire, Rupert Murdoch, born in Australia but now an American citizen, remarked of his News Corporation in his 1999 annual report; "Virtually every moment of the day, in every time zone in the planet, people are watching, reading and interacting with our product" (Murdoch 1999: 13).

In 2012 these giants were AOL Time Warner, the Walt Disney Company, Bertelsmann AG, Viacom, News Corporation and Vivendi Universal. Three are American-based, one is German, another French and the last Australian (Murdoch's News Corporation still has its headquarters in Australia). To list the business assets of any one of these would require counting on all fingers and toes of a family of five – at least. Magazines, publishing houses, newspapers, theme parks, radio and television stations, movie theaters and sports teams are all part of the various empires. Media companies' annual revenues are staggering; Bertelsmann's 2011 earnings were £15.3 billion and Viacom earned $14.91 billion. Given the size and influence of these corporations, the term "cultural imperialism" has been used by opponents of the corporate convergences that override national interests and divergent culture areas. Even today, a half century since it was first aired, the *I Love Lucy* situation comedy series is seen in over forty countries. It has been said that in its high moments of success, the drama series *Dallas* was viewed by both British and Spanish royal families, some measure of the show's widespread appeal, on a vertical as well as a horizontal basis. The cost of such a production is prohibitive for most nations, an obvious reason for the success of American exports. Moreover, the situation of most sitcoms and dramas is nearly universal in its effect, more commonplace than unusual among the urbanized populations of today. Dubbing or use of subtitles allows such shows to segue into other cultural environments with little difficulty. The question remains, however, whether this is good or bad, a means to further entertainment and extended appreciation of the human comedy or to greater profits and deeper penetration of Western culture, American in particular. As Madam Trautman argued, cultural products are unlike other forms of merchandise.

Language diversity and popular culture

In an interestingly titled paper on the continuing disappearance of languages, "Endangered languages: the crumbling of the linguistic ecosystem," Professor Osahito Miyaoka remarked that the effort to save the famous Japanese crane or ibis from extinction was widely reported in Japanese newspapers but the disappearance of the Sakhalin dialect of the Ainu language in 1994 went unnoticed (Miyaoka 2003: 1). Quoting from another source, he indicates that, of the roughly 6,000 languages in the world today, fewer than half will survive the twenty-first century. As is obvious, the development of modern media and their combined boundlessness and intrusiveness mean that once sheltered and self-sufficient linguistic communities of small scale have become an anomaly.

Moreover, the global trend in book publishing is toward consolidation in multimedia conglomerates, so that smaller national publishers in countries like Scotland and the Netherlands face extinction, absorption or the dreadful expense of publishing books for a very small readership. Few large publishers, for instance, negotiate to publishing rights in Dutch as most citizens of the Netherlands read English. Two other current indications of this linguistic state of affairs are, first, the instruction booklet for any electronic device in which English, French, Spanish and Japanese are the usual languages provided; and, second, the displacement of French by English as the day-to-day language of bureaucrats in the European Union.

American dominance

Today, according to a United Nations report, 85–90 percent of the films shown worldwide are American. Wal-Mart is today the number one corporation in terms of both sales and profit in the world. Cyberenglish is the most significant form of communication in that medium. And in 1951 the International Commercial Aviation Institute accepted English as the language for all international flights. In facts such as these are rooted both the admiration and resentment found worldwide of American economic dominance in the communications industries. In his book *America*, Jean Baudrillard wrote that the United States was "the original version of modernity." Europe he called "the dubbed or subtitled version" (Baudrillard 1988: 76). That remains the condition and the problem.

Conclusion
Reconditioning the human condition

On a grander scale – on the level of the human condition – critics are expressing concern over the changing perception and organization of reality. Landscape, it has been said, is an act of human mediation with nature. It is the outward look and the presence of the viewer that determine perspective, one's angle on what is outside, beyond us. Previously, we reached into and organized what was at arm's length or at the distance of a stride. We determined our place from within our home, our shelter. From its windows, through its doors, we entered the natural world. The French philosopher Paul Bachelard phrased it nicely in his book *The Poetics of Space* (1958) with his chapter title, "The house and the universe."

Today this condition has been altered. The shelter has given way to the screen. Automobile windshield (windscreen in British terminology), movie screen, television screen, computer screen and even the small screen on the cell phone – the screen is the current mediating agent, the unopenable window on the world. (A segment of an American CBS nightly news program is called "Eye on America.")

The historical development of this condition, the one by which we are now screened from reality, reaches back to the nineteenth century. As mentioned in the introduction of this book, the railroad coach first encased the individuals who watched a passing panorama in which they participated only visually. What was seen depended not at all on any physical exertion, any move physically into the environment. The automobile continued to refine this new relationship, particularly when completely enclosed sedans replaced the open cars of the first automobile age. Then followed the movie screen: the pseudo-reality of two dimensions given imaginary depth by the bright light projected and then reflected. Railroad coach, automobile and movie theater were all "away," external to the shelter of the home.

With the electronic revolution in the second half of the twentieth century, screened reality was domesticated. The individual no longer went out into the world; the world came in. It was reduced to small dimensions and conveniently seen in living room, bedroom, bathroom and kitchen on the television screen. The experience was and is essentially passive, not dissimilar to the movies, other than the viewer's ability to change from one program to another. Then came the computer and in 1989 the World Wide Web, which allowed pictorial as well as textual information to be accessed by computer from any part of the world by means of a browser. With the advent of the PDA or Smartphone, more images than are contained in the greatest of world museums and more sights than those seen by all of the world's explorers combined are at the user's fingertips. Only the imagination seems to be the limiting factor. In 2012, the estimated number of internet users worldwide is two billion, with a majority presented in the English language.

Although the now infamous dot.com economic collapse of 2000 has proved how hastily organized and quickly overextended were the companies in the United States designed to sell everything from pet food to automobiles on the Web, the problem was not considered fundamental to the global consumer economy. Whatever the outcome of the dot.com downturn, there seems little likelihood that the consumer economy will continue to undergo any major changes in the near future. The avalanche of stuff that Frank Gehry saw as "coming right at you" is still considered good policy, not impending catastrophe. At a national political meeting in early 2002, the premier of China made a speech in which he was quoted as saying: "We need to encourage people to spend more on housing, tourism, automobiles, telecommunications, cultural activities, sport and other services and develop new focuses of consumer spending" (Dorgan 2002: a3).

Unlike any other previous widespread development, popular culture has an internal dynamism of rapid change. "I was almost kept waiting," once remarked Louis XIV as he attended the arrival of a coach. Now Louis XIV's purported words can be uttered by anyone, titled or not, holding a ticket for train or plane, or having access to an automobile. And yet one can also argue that time has not freed us but has tied us up and held us down, first with telephone wire and on railroad tracks, now with optical fiber and on asphalt airport runways. The Czech author Milan Kundera wrote a charming sort of manifesto against this condition in his novella *Slowness*. "Why has the pleasure of slowness disappeared?" he asks early on. He answers succinctly toward the end of the book: our age "gives over to the demon of speed" (Kundera 1995: 3, 135).

As if in unintended confirmation, the term "waiting room" – popularized in the railroad age – has all but disappeared from the public scene. And it is highly doubtful that the once popular Coca-Cola slogan "The pause that refreshes" will ever be re-used. Even American universities are ending that period of anxiety undergone by new applicants who waited at the mailbox for word of acceptance: the news is now delivered by e-mail. Overnight delivery, now assured globally by jet-flying freight companies, has further reduced the once daily or weekly excitement of anticipation. Fast-food companies now measure success in terms of delivering food to their customers more quickly than their rival companies can do.

If other cultures preceding ours sought to move swiftly (think only of the wing-footed messenger of the gods whose Roman name is that of an

American automobile model, Mercury), none was able to organize so many of its activities as are we to the pulse of a cursor, a pacemaker, a digital stop watch (on the face of our Smartphones).

To those professing a global vision and a far-reaching cultural awareness, since the 1950s the human condition has been undergoing a major change in the meaning and form of community. From the first reference made to a "global village" by the popular theorist, Canadian academic Marshall McLuhan to films like *Clockwork Orange* (1971) and *Blade Runner* (1982) that are set in an anti-civic and anti-urban environment, the question is how to create a viable and meaningful community. Public space and public discourse have been threatened by the automobile and the electronic media. "Cordoning us from community life," writes Jane Holtz Kay in her popular study *Asphalt Nation* (Kay 1997: 51), "the car accentuates an environment of exclusion." The strong critic of contemporary urbanization Mike Davis sees the city as having turned in on itself. "The public spaces of the new mega-structures and supermalls have supplanted traditional streets and disciplined their spontaneity" (Davis 1992: 155). And Neil Postman discussing "public discourse in the age of show business" (the subtitle of his widely read *Amusing Ourselves to Death*), contends that "television ... is transforming our culture into one vast arena for show business" (Postman 1985: 80). The intensifying threat of terrorism – and governmental reactions to it – have gravely constrained the use of public space, and have begun to diminish public discourse.

Popular culture is the first cultural form to compress so many activities previously considered distinct, to engage diverse groups and classes of people so widely in a common environment: in front of the television screen, at the theme park, in the shopping mall, on the computer. These are the new four corners of the world, all within easy reach, not scattered years and cultures apart. The development, still ongoing but less than a century old, has not been premeditated, but it was assured by its two most distinctive characteristics: the proliferation of images and stuff, the intensification of the means of communication and distribution. Add to these two the prevalence of its mood that is entertainment, and the global effects of popular culture are all bunched together.

There are, however, few statements that can be made with the certainty that they will endure the test of time. Tomorrow's blog, online "newspaper," and television news hour will report some piece of information that will change or modify something that has been written here. For unlike the Warner Brothers' *Looney Tunes* made more than a half century ago, no study of popular culture can possibly conclude with Porky Pig's immortal words: "That's all, folks!"

Bibliography

A note

The broad study of contemporary popular culture invites, almost requires, some sort of joining of the historical with the journalistic. Popular culture is indeed newsworthy; it is often of the glittering moment, but its personalities and excitement often quickly recede into a past of little particular consequence. Yet the enduring trends and developments are the attractions that merit attention because they have reshaped our cultural environment. The theme parks and animated cartoons, the crowded shopping malls and busy airports are as much a mark of our contemporary civilization as the long enduring pyramids of Giza are of the days of the pharaohs. In analyzing these features, the historian of necessity and out of curiosity turns to the popular press as well as to the monograph.

Much of the information that appears in this bibliography comes from websites. There is no doubt that popular culture and the Web have a strong if recent marriage of convenience consummated in cyberspace. The openness and availability of websites allow a concentrated examination of subjects that have not yet made their way into print literature or a detailed comparison that also is not readily available otherwise. For instance, the fascinating topic of *son et lumière* shows, about which I have been interested for some four decades, was brought to my computer screen from sites as far flung as Egypt, India, New Zealand, South Africa and England (as well as many locations in France where I have seen several such shows).

Moreover, access to journal and newspaper articles was greatly facilitated by online editions, many of which would not have been available in any research library close to hand. Lastly, the Web has been an invaluable means of corroboration; it has served as if the reference section of a university library. Website references are followed (here) by the date they were accessed.

Abbey, E. (1976) *The Monkey Wrench Gang*, New York: Avon.
ABC News. "Cyber-Bullying a Factor in Suicide of Massachusetts Teen Irish Immigrant." Online. HTTP: http://abcnews.go.com/Health/cyber-bullying-factor-suicide-massachusetts-teen-irish-immigrant/story?id=9660938 (May 1, 2012).
——. "Cruise Ship Wreck Search Suspended." Online. HTTP: http://abcnews.go.com/International/cruise-ship-wreck-search-suspended-ship-moves/story?id=15383588 (May 9, 2012).
ABI Research. "More than Seven Trillion SMS Messages Will Be Sent in 2011." Online. Available HTTP: http://www.abiresearch.com/press/3584-More+than+Seven+Trillion+SMS+Messages+Will+Be+Sent+in+2011 (April 18, 2012).

Aéroport de Paris Charles de Gaulle. "Statistiques annuelles." Online. Available HTTP: http://www.aeroport.fr/les-aeroports-de-l-uaf/stats-paris-charles-de-gaulle.php (March 26, 2012).

Airports Council International (ACI). "Year to Date Passenger Traffic." Online. Available HTTP: http://www.airports.org/cda/aci_common/display/main/aci_content07_c.jsp?zn=aci&cp=1-5-212-218-222_666_2_ (March 26, 2012).

Ali, T. and Watkins, S. (1998) *Marching in the Streets*, New York: Free Press.

American Diabetes Association. "New Diabetes Statistics Highlight Need for Prevention." Online. HTTP: http://www.diabetes.org/for-media/2011/new-diabetes-statistics-highlight-need-for-prevention.html (May 11, 2012).

American Society for Plastic Surgeons. "138 Million Cosmetic Plastic Surgery Procedures Performed in 2011." Online. Available HTTP: http://www.plasticsurgery.org/News-and-Resources/138-Million-Cosmetic-Plastic-Surgery-Procedures-Performed-in-2011.html (May 7, 2012).

AMS. "Ad Exposures." Online. Available HTTP: https://ams.aaaa.org/eweb/upload/faqs/adexposures.pdf (May 5, 2012).

Anderson, K. (1991) "Is Seaside too good to be true?" in Mohney, D. and Easterling, K. (eds) *Seaside,* New York: Princeton Architectural Press.

Aquila, R. (1989) *That Old Time Rock & Roll, A Chronicle of an Era: 1954–1963*, New York: Schirmer Books.

Arlen, M. J. (1969) *Living Room War*, New York: Viking.

Aron, C. S. (1999) *Working at Play: A History of Vacations in the United States*, New York: Oxford University Press.

Attia, S. "25 years later, Egypt's tourism landscape is inspiring," *Egyptian Gazette* (October 5, 1998): 6.

Bailey, C. "So you thought you'd like to go to the show? ... " *Floydian Slip.* Online. Available HTTP: http://www.floydianslip.com/discs/walllive.htm (January 11, 2001).

Bale, J. (1994) *Landscapes of Modern Sport*, Leicester: University of Leicester Press.

Barnes, J. "Plane Tree Massacre," *New Yorker* (July 23, 2001): 26.

Barthes, R. (1999) "On Cinemascope," trans. J. Rosenbaum (first published in *Les lettres nouvelles*, February 1954). Online. Available HTTP: http://social.chass.ncsu.edu/ jouvert/v3i3/barth.htm (February 1, 2002).

Baudrillard, J. (1988) *America*, trans. Chris Turner, New York: Verso.

—— (1996) *Disneyworld company*, trans. François Debrix. Online. Available HTTP: http://www.uta.edu/english/apt/collab/texts/disneyworld.html (February 23, 2002).

—— "The Precession of the Simulacra." Trans. Sheila Faria Glaser. Online. Available HTTP: http://www.egs.edu/faculty/jean-baudrillard/articles/simulacra-and-simulations-i-the-precession-of-simulacra/ (May 14, 2012).

Beauvoir, S. de (1976) *The Second Sex*, trans. and ed. H. M. Parshle, New York: Knopf.

Bennett, M. J. (1996) *When Dreams Came True: The GI Bill and the Making of Modern America*, Washington: Brassey's.

Berger, J. (1972) *Ways of Seeing*, London: Penguin.

Blumenfeld, L. (2002) "The apology: letters from a terrorist," *New Yorker* (March 4, 2002): 37–40.

Bly, Elizabeth. (2010) *Generation X and the Invention of a Third Feminist Wave.* Case Western Reserve University, 2010. Online. Available HTTP: http://etd.ohiolink.edu/send-pdf.cgi/Bly%20Elizabeth%20Ann.pdf?case1259803398 (May 22, 2012).

Bond, P. "Look back in anger by john osborne." Online. Available HTTP: http:www.wsws.org/articles/1999/sep1999/look-s14_prn.shtml (May 2003).

Boniface, P. and Fowler, P. J. (1993) *Heritage and Tourism in the "Global Village,"* London: Routledge.

Boorstin, D. J. (1992) *The Image: A Guide to Pseudo-Events in America*, New York: Vintage.

Botello, A. "The world's largest souvenir?" Online. Available HTTP: http://www.metropolismag.com/july.96/insites.html (February 4, 1998).

Boyer, C. M. (1992) "Cities for sale: merchandising history on South Street Seaport," in Sorkin, M. (ed.) *Variations on a Theme Park: The New American City and the End of Public Space*, New York: Hill and Wang.

Brohm, J.-M. (1978) *Sport – Prison of Measured Time*, trans. Ian Fraser, London: Ink Links.

Browell, N. (2000) *Tomorrow Never Knows: Rock and Psychedelics in the 1960s*, Chicago: University of Chicago Press.

Brown, L. B. "Paving the planet: cars and crops competing for land." Online. Available HTTP: http://www.worldwatch.org/chairman/issue/010214.html (February 14, 2001).

Buchanan, P. (1997) *Kansai International Airport Terminal*, in *Renzo Piano Building Workshop*, Vol. III, London: Phaidon Press: 128–220.

Bush, D. (1975) *The Streamlined Decade*, New York: George Braziler.

Caccia, B. "'Rock around the clock' celebrates its 45th anniversary." Online. Available HTTP: http://oldies.about.com/library/blclock.htm (February 8, 2002).

Calatrava, S. "Design approach." Online. Available HTTP: http://www.calatrava/1/1_2.html (November 3, 2001).

Campanella, T. J. "Jin Mao, Shanghai," *Architectural Record* (January 2000): 82–89.

Campbell, C. (1990) *The VW Beetle*, Stanford, CT: Longmeadow Press.

Campbell, K. "The end of the world as we knew it." Online. Available HTTP: http://www.csmonitor.com/durable/2001/07/27/text/p13s1.html (January 12, 2001).

Campisano, J. (2000) *American Muscle Cars*, New York: MetroBooks.

CAPA Centre for Aviation. "World Airport Rankings 2010." Online. HTTP: http://www.centreforaviation.com/analysis/world-airport-rankings-2010-hong-kong-eclipses-memphis-as-the-worlds-busiest-cargo-hub-47887 (April 16, 2012).

Carter, Bill. "Olympic Hockey Finale Drew Huge Ratings." Online. Available HTTP: http://mediadecoder.blogs.nytimes.com/2010/03/01/olympic-hockey-finale-drew-huge-ratings/ (February 10, 2012).

Celi, Z., Favor, D. and Ingersoll, R. (eds) (1994) *Streets: Critical Perspectives on Public Space*, Berkeley: University of California Press.

Christgau, R. (2000) *Any Old Way You Choose It: Rock and Other Pop Music, 1967–1973*, New York: Cooper Square Press.

Clark, D. (1996) *Urban World, Global City*, London: Routledge.

Clifford, Hal, "Downhill slide," *Sierra* (January–February 2003): 35–39.

Cling, C., "Triple threat: three tenors performance a showcase for distinctive styles" (reprinted from *Las Vegas Review-Journal*, April 21, 2000). Online. HTTP: http://www.tenorissimo.com/domingo/articles/lasvegas042100.htm (November 13, 2001).

CNN Travel. "New terrorism alert system will offer specific warnings." Online. Available HTTP: http://articles.cnn.com/2011-04-20/travel/terrorism.advisory.system_1_alert-levels-terrorist-threat-warnings?_s=PM:TRAVEL (April 16, 2012).

Cohen, K., *The Beatles' Yellow Submarine turns 30: John Coates and Norman Kauffman look back. Animation World Magazine*, issue 3/4 July 1998. Online. HTTP: http://www.awm.com/mag/issue3.4/3.4pages/cohen.html (June 7, 2002).

Conner, S. (1995) *Postmodern Culture*, Oxford: Blackwell.

Cooke, A. (1978) *Six Men*, New York: Berkeley Books.

Corliss, R. *The first angry man: John Osborne 1929–1994*. Online. Available HTTP: http://www.time.com/time/magazine/archive/1995/950109.obituary.html (January 3, 2002).

Council on Foreign Relations. "Targets for Terrorists: Post-9/11 Aviation Security." Online. Available HTTP: http://www.cfr.org/air-transportation-security/targets-terror ists-post-911-aviation-security/p11397 (April 8, 2012).

Crawford, M. (1992) "The world as a shopping mall" in Sorkin, M. (ed.) *Variations on a Theme Park: The New American City and the End of Public Space*, New York: Hill and Wang.

Curtis, H. (2001) *Hotel Interior Structures*, Chichester: Wiley-Academy.

Daily Mail Online. "Father's outrage as TSA subjects his wheelchair-bound three-year-old son to humiliating search … on his way to Disney." Online. Available HTTP: http://www.dailymail.co.uk/news/article-2116881/TSA-subject-child-wheelchair-inva sive-airport-security-tests-Chicago.html (April 8, 2012).

Daley, C. "Review of New Zealand film." Online. Available HTTP: http://www.jcu.eduau/aff/history/reviews/martin edwards.htm (March 29, 2003).

Daroff, K. (2003) "Rotterdam Film Festival speech." Online. Available HTTP: http://www.daroffdesign.com/pr/rotterdam/index.html (October 26, 2003).

Das, Andrew. "M.L.S. Salary Figures Released." Online. Available HTTP: http://goal.blogs.nytimes.com/2011/05/10/m-l-s-salary-figures-released/ (February 10, 2012).

David, D. "Grand Prix history." Online. Available HTTP: http://www.ddavid.com/formula1 (June 16, 2001).

Davis, M. (1992) "Fortress Los Angeles: the militarization of urban space," in Sorkin, M. (ed.) *Variations on a Theme Park*, New York: Hill and Wang.

Deford, F. (1971) *The Life and Times of Miss America*, New York: Viking Press.

Dick, B. (1966) *The Star-Spangled Screen*, Lexington: University Press of Kentucky.

Dobrin, P. "Classical 'Carmen,' arena-rocking stage." Online. Available HTTP: http://inq.philly.com/content/inquirer/2001/06/18/magazine/CARMEN18.htm (November 1, 2001).

Dorgan, M. "Beijing leader pledges to raise incomes as boost for economy," *Lexington Herald-Leader* (March 11, 2002): a3 and a7.

Duncan, A. (1998) *Art Deco*, London: Thames and Hudson.

Edgerton, G. R. and Rollins, P. C. (eds) (2001) *Television Histories: Shaping Collective Memory in the Media Age*, Lexington: University Press of Kentucky.

Edgerton, R. "History of the Scopitone." Online. Available HTTP: http://www.stim.com/stim-x/9.4/scopitone/scopitone.html (February 1, 2002).

Ehrman, E., Forsyth, H. *et al.* (1999) *London Eats Out: 500 years of capital dining*, London: Philip Wilson.

Ewen, S. (1988) *All Consuming Images: The Politics of Style in Contemporary Culture*, New York: Basic Books.

Fink, C., Gassert, P. and Junker, D. (eds) (1998) *1968: The World Transformed*, Cambridge: Cambridge University Press.

Foster, H. "Bigness." Online. Available HTTP: http:www.lrb.co.uk/ (April 30, 2003).

Franken, S. "Pittsburgh's FedEx ground delivering *Harry Potter*." Online. Available HTTP: http://www.post-gazette.com/businessnews/20000707fedex1.asp (August 20, 2001).

Fraser, R. (1988) *1968: A Generation in Revolt*, New York: Pantheon.

Freeland, M. (1998) *Bob Hope*, London: André Deutsch.

Friedan, B. (1963) *The Feminine Mystique*, New York: W. W. Norton.

Friedman, T. L. (2000) *The Lexus and the Olive Tree*, New York: Vantage.

Friedrich, O. (1986) *City of Nets: A Portrait of Hollywood in the 1940's*, New York: Harper and Row.

Fullbrook, E. and Fullbrook, K. (2008) *Sex and Philosophy: Rethinking De Beauvoir and Sartre*, London and New York: Continuum International Publishing Group.

Gabler, N. (1998) *Life: the Movie: How Entertainment Conquered Reality*, New York: Vintage.

Gaines, C. and Butler, G. (1981) *Pumping Iron: The Art and Sport of Bodybuilding*, New York: Simon and Schuster.

Garratt, S. "Toy story." Online. Available HTTP: http://shopping.guardian.co.uk/christmas/story/0,8167,404030,00.html (February 3, 2002).

Gartner. "Spending on Gaming to Exceed \$74 Billion in 2011." Online. HTTP: http://www.gartner.com/it/page.jsp?id=1737414 (May 9, 2012).

Gebhard, D. (1996) *The National Trust Guide to Art Deco in America*, New York: John Wiley.

Geddes, N. B. (1932) *Horizons*, Boston: Little, Brown.

Gehlawat, A. "Playback as mass fantasy: the Hindi film experience." Online. Available HTTP: http://www.indiastar.com/Gehlawat.html (March 10, 2000).

Gessen, Keith. "Letter from Moscow: Stuck. The meaning of the city's traffic nightmare." The New Yorker. Online. Available HTTP: http://www.newyorker.com/reporting/2010/08/02/100802fa_fact_gessen#ixzz1vbocM0zf (March 26, 2012).

Ghirardo, D. (1996) *Architecture After Modernism*, London: Thames and Hudson.

Gleick, J. (1999) *Faster*, New York: Pantheon.

Gluckman, R. (2002) "The Americanization of China." Online. Available HTTP: http://www.gluckman.com/Americanization.html (January 19, 2002).

Goldberger, P. "The skyline: new museums in the midwest," *New Yorker* (November 5, 2001): 96–98.

Good, Jonathan. "How Many Photos Have Ever Been Taken?" Online. Available HTTP: http://blog.1000memories.com/94-number-of-photos-ever-taken-digital-and-analog-in-shoebox (May 5, 2012).

Goodman, E. "Retrofitting the male image," Lexington, *Lexington Herald-Leader* (January 19, 2002).

Greenleigh, P. (1988) *Ephemeral Vistas: The Expositions Universelles, Great Exhibitions and World's Fairs, 1851–1939*, Manchester: Manchester University Press.

Grover, R. "Now Disneyland won't seem so Mickey Mouse." Online. Available HTTP: http://www.businessweek.com/2001/01_05/b3717097.htm (July 7, 2001).

Gurin, D. "Traffic controls in cities abroad." Online. Available HTTP: http://www.panix.com/~danielc/world/autoredq.htm (August 1, 2001).

Hackett, A. J. (1999) "Queenstown bungy jumping." Online. Available HTTP: http://www.ajhackett.com/history.htm (July 10, 2001).

Hall, C. M. and Paige, S. J. (1999) *The Geography of Tourism and Recreation: Environment, Place and Space*, London: Routledge.

Hartley, J. (1992) *The Politics of Pictures: The Creation of the Public in the Age of Popular Media*, London: Routledge.

Haslam, D. "What the Twist did for the Peppermint Lounge," *London Review of Books*, vol. 22, no. 1 (January 6, 2000). Online. Available HTTP: http//www.lrb.uk.v22.n01/hasl02_.html (October 23, 2003).

Hayden, T. "Trashing the ocean," *U.S. News & World Report* (November 4, 2002): 58–60.

Hayes, D. "Rolling Stones ready to rock and roll around Asia." Online. Available HTTP: http://quickstart.clari.net/qs_se/webnews/dt/Qjapan-britain-music.RF8KDM7. html (April 24, 2003).

Hewison, R. (1986) *Too Much: Art and Society in the Sixties*, London: Methuen.

Hicks, R. "The NHS and cosmetic surgery." Online. Available HTTP: http://www.bbc. co.uk/health/features/cosmetic_surgery.shtml (December 19, 2001).

Hind, S. "Michael Jackson biography." Online. Available HTTP:http://www.rollingstone. com/artists/bio.asp?oid=1650& cf = 1650 (July 1, 2002).

Hodgson, G. (1998) *People's Century: From the Dawn of the Century to the Eve of the Millennium*, New York: Times Books.

Hovagimyan, G. H. "Laterday." Online. Available HTTP: http://artnetweb.com/gh/ laterday.html (February 22, 2002).

Huffington Post. "TSA's 'Get Your Freak On Girl' Worker To Be Fired." Online. Available HTTP: http://www.huffingtonpost.com/2011/10/28/tsas-get-your-freak-on-gi_n_1064451.html (April 8, 2012).

Ito, T. "The space of Asiatic light in an ephemeral city," *Architectural Design*: *Light and Architecture*, vol. 67, nos. 3–4 (1997): 32.

Iyer, P. (2000) *The Global Soul*, New York: Knopf.

James, L. "Congressional testimony by Dr. Leon James on road rage and aggressive drivers." Online. Available HTTP: http://www.aloha.net/~dyc/articles/ testimony.htm (May 15, 2000 / February 2, 2002).

Jameson, F. (1998) "Notes on globalization as a philosophical issue," in Jameson, F. and Miyoshi, M. (eds) *The Culture of Globalization*, Durham: Duke University Press.

Johnson, H. and Gwertzmann, B. M. (1968) *Fulbright the Dissenter*, New York: Doubleday.

Johnston's Archive. "Global Terrorism." Online. HTTP: http://www.johnstonsarchive. net/terrorism/globalterrorism1.html (May 11, 2012).

Jones, P. M. "Plastic surgeries changing the face of an eager Brazil." Online. Available HTTP: http://www.hucff.ufrj.br/hospital_Midia/chicago.html (July 9, 2001).

JSG. "Low riders – A contemporary folk art form." Online. Available HTTP: http: www.library.arizona.edu/images/folkarts/lowriders.html (April 19, 2003).

Kay, J. H. (1997) *Asphalt Nation*, New York: Crown Publishers.

Kerouac, J. (2003) *On the Road*, New York: Penguin Classics, p. 134.

Khan, H. (1999) "The tourism explosion: policy decisions facing Singapore," in Tyler, D., Guerrier, Y. and Robinson, M. (eds) *Managing Tourism in Cities: Policy, Processes, and Practices*. New York: John Wiley.

Klein, N. (2001) *No Logo: Taking Aim at the Brand Bullies*, New York: Picador.

Kratz, G. I. (1994) "Woodstock at 25." Online. Available HTTP: http://www.pub liccom.com/14850/9407//coverstory.html (February 2, 2002).

Krens, T. "The art of the motorcycle." Online. Available HTTP: http://www.whole pop.com/features/motorcycles/guggenheim.htm (November 10, 2001).

Kundera, M. (1995) *Slowness*, trans. Linda Asher, New York: HarperCollins.

Kunstler, J. (1994) *The Geography of Nowhere*, New York: Touchstone.

Kwan-Seok, L. "Korea's Convention Strategy." Online. Available HTTP: http://www. kt-i.com/jan_feb_01/economy/focus/focus.htm (January 3, 2001).

Le Corbusier (1986) *Towards a New Architecture*, trans. F. Etchells, New York: Dover.

Licklider, J. and Taylor, R. "The computer as a communication device." Online. Available HTTP: http://www.kurzweileai.net/articles/art0353.html?printable=1 (April 19, 2003).

Livingstone, M. (ed.) (1991) *Pop Art: An International Perspective*, London: Rizzoli.
Local Authorities Aircraft Noise Council. "Statistics." Online. HTTP: http://www. laanc.org.uk/ (May 10, 2012).
Longman, P. "No sex, s'il vous plait. We're club med." Online. Available HTTP: http://www.usnews.com/usnews/issue/09/08/97med.htm (July 23, 2001).
Lowenthal, D. (1996) *Possessed by the Past*, New York: The Free Press.
McCarthy, D. (2000) *Pop Art*, Cambridge: Cambridge University Press.
Maher, H. "Ex-East block grows, but at a cost?" Online. Available HTTP: http://www. msnbc.com/news/7394448.asp (April 4, 2003).
Marger, M. A. (1997) "Human element vividly recreated." Online. Available HTTP: http://www21.sptimes/titanic/show_review.htm (February 21, 2002).
Mid-Atlantic Tourbook (2001). AAA: Heathrow, Florida.
Mirzoeff, N. (ed.) (1998) *The Visual Cultural Reader*, London: Routledge.
Mitchell, E. (1996) "The bikini turns 50." Online. Available HTTP: http://www.time. com/time/international/1996/960701/fashion.html (December 12, 2001).
Miyaoka, O. "Endangered languages: the crumbling of the linguistic ecosystem." Online. Available HTTP: http.www.elpr.bun.kyoy-u.ac.jp/essay/miyaoka01.htm (April 29, 2003).
Mobithinking. "Global Mobile Statistics 2012." Online. Available HTTP: http:// mobithinking.com/mobile-marketing-tools/latest-mobile-stats (April 18, 2012).
Morgan, J. "Golf sprawl," *Preservation* (May–June 2001): 39–47.
Munoz, F. "Historic evolution and urban planning typology of olympic village." Online. Available HTTP: http://www.blues.uab.es/olympic.studies/viles/munoz.html (June 12, 2001).
Murdoch, R. (1999) "Chief Executive report." Online. Available HTTP: http://www. newscorp.com/report99/chief1.html (October 26, 2003).
Naisbitt, John (1995) *The Hospitality and Leisure Architecture of Wimberly Allison Tong & Goo*, Rockport, MA: Rockport Publishers, 1995.
The New York Times. "Pottermore: How Rich is J.K. Rowling?" Online. Available HTTP: http://www.ibtimes.com/articles/168445/20110623/pottermore-jk-rowling-harry-potter-e-book.htm (February 10, 2012).
Newhouse, V. (1998) *Towards a New Architecture*, New York: Monacello Press.
Ngugi wa Thiongo (1986) *Decolonizing the Mind: The Politics of Language in African Literature*, London: J. Currey.
No Place for Sheep. "Labiaplasty. Baudrillard. That is All." Online. Available HTTP: http://noplaceforsheep.com/2012/04/03/labiaplasty-baudrillard-that-is-all (May 7, 2012).
Norr, H. "Drowning in e-waste." Online. Available HTTP: http://www.a21.org/ewaste_ SFChronicle (April 28, 2003).
The Numbers. "Top Selling DVDs of 2012." Online. Available HTTP: http://www.the-numbers.com/dvd/charts/annual/2012.php (May 5, 2012).
O'Hanlon, S. "Douglas, Zeta-Jones win court fight over photos." Online. Available HTTP: http://dailynews.att.net/cgi_bin/news?e=pri&dt=news&st=newspeopledouglas dc&view (April 11, 2003).
Owen, D. "Swinging in Morocco: golf diplomacy and the last North African kingdom," *New Yorker* (May 21, 2001): 51, 53–59.
Patten, Fred, "A Capsule History of Anime." Online. Available. HTTP: http://www. awn.com/mag/issue1.5/articles/patten1.5 (2002)
Peiss, K. (1998) *Hope in a Jar: The Making of America's Beauty Culture*, New York: Metropolitan Books.

Peterson, B. "David Wolper L.A. influential." Online. Available HTTP: http://www.usc.edu/dept/pubrel/trojan_family/autumn99/Wolper/wolper.html (July 16, 2001).

Pew Research Center. "Americans and Text Messaging." Online. Available HTTP: http://pewinternet.org/~/media/Files/Reports/2011/Americans%20and%20Text%20Messaging.pdf (April 18, 2012).

Pfanner, Eric. "Europe Strives to Catch Up with Digital Hollywood." *The New York Times.* Online. HTTP: http://www.nytimes.com/2010/05/13/technology/13iht-film.html (May 11, 2012).

Phillips, I. "Club Med." Online. Available HTTP: http://www.deeperblue.net/content/1998/travel/clubmed/1.shtml (July 23, 2001).

Politico.com. "111.3 Million People Watched the Super Bowl." Online. Available HTTP: http://www.politico.com/blogs/media/2012/02/million-people-watched-super-bowl-113632.html (May 5, 2012).

Polley, M. (1998) *Moving the Goalposts: A History of Sport and Society Since 1945*, London: Routledge.

Postman, N. (1985) *Amusing Ourselves to Death*, New York: Penguin.

Powell, C. "The American GI." Online. Available HTTP: http://www.time.com/time100/heroes/profile/gi02.html (January 27, 2002).

Progressive Insurance. "Progressive Corporate Art Department." Online. Available HTTP: http://art.progressive.com/art_popup.asp (May 5, 2012).

Rabac, B. "Looking good via surgery a subjective selective process." Online. Available HTTP: http://sanjose.bizjournals.com/sanjose/stories/2001/06/11/focus2.html (December 19, 2001).

Raz, A. E. (2000) "Domesticating Disney: onstage strategies of adaptation in Tokyo Disneyland." *Journal of Popular Culture*, 33/4: 77–99

Reid, C. "Hong Kong fight greats change face of Hollywood." Online. Available HTTP: http://www.dailynews.att.net/ (October 24, 2001).

Richard, B. and Kruger, H.-H. "'Shut up and dance,' a transformation in the attitudes and aesthetics of German youth culture." Online. Available HTTP: http://www.uni-frankfurt.de/f609/kunstpaed/indexweb/publikationen.shutup.htm (June 30, 2002).

Ringer, G. (ed.) (1998) *Destinations: Cultural Landscapes of Tourism*, London: Routledge.

Rissmann, H. "Press release, 25 April 2001 six-year mission." Online. Available HTTP: http://www.eixx.co/uk/newstart.html (July 7, 2001).

Ritchie, Karen. "Get ready for 'Generation X': Soon the primary market, and very unlike aging Boomers." *Advertising Age* (November 9, 1992), 21.

Robinett, J. and Brown, R. "A bumpy road building the European theme park industry." Online. Available HTTP: http://www.hotel-online.com/Neo/Trends/ERA/ERAEuropeanThemeParks.html (July 9, 2002).

Roden, L. "London tackles its traffic woes." *Lexington Herald-Leader* (July 23, 2001, reprinted from *Los Angeles Times* [January 19, 2001]).

Roy, A. (1997) *The God of Small Things*, New York: Random House.

Rusli, Evelyn M. "Talks with Instagram Suggest a $104 Billion Valuation for Facebook." Online. Available HTTP: http://dealbook.nytimes.com/2012/04/18/with-instagram-deal-facebook-shows-its-worth/ (May 1, 2012).

Savan, L. (1994) *The Sponsored Life: Ads, TV and American Culture*, Philadelphia: Temple University Press.

Saywell, T. (November 9, 2000) "Will soaps wash in China?" Online. Available HTTP: http://www.chinatopnews.com/BBS/Square/messages/904.html (October 23, 2003): 1.

Scheuer, J. (1999) *The Sound Bite Society: Television and the American Mind*, New York: Four Doors Eight Windows.

Schiphol Airport. "Amsterdam Airport Schiphol's Network and Market Share in 2011." Online. Available HTTP: http://www.schiphol.nl/SchipholGroup/NewsMedia/Press releaseItem/AmsterdamAirportSchipholsNetworkAndMarketShareGrowIn2011.htm (April 16, 2012).

Schivelbusch, W. (1986) *The Railway Journey*, Berkeley: University of California Press.

Schlosser, E. (2001) *Fast Food Nation*, Boston: Houghton Mifflin.

Schorr, J. (1991) *The Overworked American*, New York: Basic Books.

Seabrook, J. (2000) *Nobrow: The Culture of Marketing Culture*, New York: Knopf.

Seiler, Andy, "'Astro Boy' Zooms Back with a Movie," DVD. Online. Available HTTP: http://www.usatoday.com/life/movies/2002/2002-01-16astroboy.html (2002).

Severson, Kim. "A Killing (a First) in a Town Produced by Disney." *The New York Times.* Online. Available HTTP: http://www.nytimes.com/2010/12/03/us/03celebration.html?_r=2 (April 4, 2012).

Shaw, K. "Kevin Shaw lighting design: Rock and roll lighting techniques." Online. Available HTTP: http://www.lightingresource.com/lcenter/kevin/Rock-n-Roll.asp (December 12, 2001).

Shields, R. (ed.) (1992) *Lifestyle Shopping: The Subject of Consumption*, London: Routledge.

Shorr, D. (2001) "Television, tool for terror." Online. Available HTTP: http://www.csmonitor.com/2001/1019/p11s1-cods.html (February 27, 2002).

Smith, P. (1997) *Millennial Dreams: Contemporary Culture and Capital in the North*, London: Verso.

Sorkin, M. (ed.) (1992) *Variations on a Theme Park*, New York: Hill and Wang.

Spangler, T. "Heinz gets 'funky' with frozen fries." *Lexington Herald-Leader* (February 12, 2002): c2.

Specter, M. "The Blunderdome." *New Yorker* (January 29, 2001): 46–51.

Stewart, D. "Times Square Reborn," *Smithsonian*, vol. 28, no. 11 (February 1998): 36–44.

Stockholm International Peace Research Institute. "Military Expenditure." Online. Available HTTP: http://www.sipri.org/research/armaments/milex (February 10, 2012).

Strauss, Gary. "X marks advertisers' spots: Discerning post-boomers elusive target." *USA Today* (June 7, 1993), Money Section, 1B.

Suarez, R. and Schnidman, F. "Talk of the nation: land and public policy, March 10, 1999." Online. Available HTTP: http://www.nthp.org/news/docs/19990310_speech.html (August 1, 2001).

TED (2003) Online. Available HTTP: http://www.american.edu/TED/eulabel.htm (April 29, 2003).

Tesoro, J. "Asia says Japan is top of the pops." Online. Available HTTP: http://www.asiaweek.com/asiaweek/96/0105/feat1.html (November 15, 2001).

Tobin, J. (ed.) (1992) *Re-Made in Japan: Everyday Life and Consumer Taste in a Changing Society*, New Haven: Yale University Press.

Tomlinson, J. (1999) *Globalization and Culture*, Chicago: University of Chicago Press.

Trautman, C. (1999) "L'exception culturelle n'est pas négociable," *Le Monde* (10–11 octobre 1999). Online. Available HTTP: http://www.culture.fr/culture/actualités/politique, diversité/lemonde.htm (April 20, 2002).

Tully, M. "Lovable relic of the 'permit raj'." Online. Available HTTP: http://www.ft.com/reports/z1c7b2.htm (January 7, 2001).

Turner, L. and Ash, J. (1975) *The Golden Hordes: International Tourism and the Pleasure Periphery*, New York: St. Martin's Press.

Twitchell, J. (2000) *Twenty Ads That Shook the World*, New York: Crown Publishers.

Unferth, D. (2002) "The corruption of the shopping mall." Online. Available HTTP: http://www.consciouschoice.com/issues/cc1510/corruptshoppingmall1510.html (April 28, 2003).

UNESCO. "Analysis of Cinema Production." Online. Available HTTP: http://www.uis.unesco.org/culture/Documents/ib8-analysis-cinema-production-2012-en2.pdf (May 5, 2012).

United States Census Bureau (2000) *Statistical Abstract of the United States*, Washington: United States Government.

—— (2012) "WorldPOP Clock Projection." Online. Available HTTP: http://www.census.gov/population/popclockworld.html (February 10, 2012).

Updike, J. "The Prodigal Sun." *Allure* (October 1997): 192–98.

Venturi, R., Brown, D., and Izenhour, S. (2001) *Learning From Las Vegas: The Forgotten Symbolism of Architectural Form*, Boston: MIT Press.

Wager, G. "Murray Lerner's film of the Isle of Wight festival." August 1970. Online. Available HTTP: http://www.doors.com/magazine/dcm9.html (April 9, 2003).

Waitt, G. "Consuming heritage: received historical authenticity." *Annals of Tourism Research*, 27/4: 2000.

Warhol, A. and Hackett, P. (1980) *Popism: The Warhol Sixties*, New York: Harvest Books, Harcourt Brace.

The Washington Post. "Number of Active Users of Facebook Over the Years." Online. Available HTTP: http://www.washingtonpost.com/national/number-of-active-users-at-facebook-over-the-years/2012/02/01/gIQArZYmiQ_story.html (February 10, 2012).

Waters, R. "The wall live in Berlin." Online. Available HTTP: http://www.roger waters.org/about_berlin.html (January 11, 2001).

Watson, B. "A rally to remember." *Smithsonian*, vol. 33, no. 5 (May 2002).

WHO (2003) "Obesity." Online. Available HTTP: http://www.who/int/nut/obs.htm (October 23, 2003).

Wilson, J. "Heavy cruiser." *Popular Mechanics* (May 2001): 66–70.

Wirefly. "Recycling Programs." Online. HTTP: http://www.wirefly.org/programs/ (May 10, 2012).

World Tourism Organization. "Facts and Figures." Online. Available HTTP: http://www.unwto.org/facts/menu.html (May 9, 2012).

White, K. "Guggenheim to play the Strip." Online. Available HTTP: http://www.lvrj.com/lvrj_home/2000/Oct-21-Sat-2000/news/14653795.html (October 10, 2001).

World Tourist Organization (1999) *Compendium of Tourist Statistics, 1995–1997*, Madrid: WTO.

Zakaria, F. "The arrogant empire." *Newsweek* (March 24, 2003): 18–39.

Other websites cited

"About Albert Lasker." Online. Available HTTP: http://www.laskerfoundation.org/aboutthefoundation.html (October 14, 2003).

az-golfhomes (2003) Online. Available HTTP: http://www.forsaleinarizona.com/dcranch.htm (October 25, 2003).

"About air shows." Online. Available HTTP: http://www.airshows.org/aboutairshows.htm (August 2, 2001).

"About world trade centers association." Online. Available HTTP: http://iserve.wtca. org/awtc/about.html (July 7, 2001).

"Airplane noise pollution." Online. Available HTTP: http://www.eces.org/ ec/pollution/ noise.shtml (September 1, 2001).

"Amusement and theme parks." Online. Available HTTP: http://www.users.stargate. net/~rollocst/a_park.html (November 1, 2001).

"An emerging 'thumb culture'." Online. Available HTTP: http://www.jinjapan.org/ trends/article/030110fea_r.html (April 16, 2003).

"An introduction to anime." Online. Available HTTP: http://www.rightstuf.com/ introduction (February 6, 2002).

"Astrodome." Online. Available HTTP: http://www.ballparks.com/baseball/national/ astrod.htm (June 12, 2001).

"Boys will be girls." Online. Available HTTP: http://jin.jcic.or.jp/trends98/honbun/ ntj980619.html (January 6, 2002).

"Chronic hunger and obesity epidemic eroding global progress." Online. Available HTTP: http://www.worldwatch.org/alerts/000304.html (February 20, 2002).

"Color trends." Online. Available HTTP: http://www.dupont.com/finishes/na/color. html (January 13, 2002).

"Denver meeting planner: convention center expansion plans." Online. Available HTTP: http://www.denver.org/plannerw/cce.htm (June 22, 2001).

"EC eco-labelling." Online. Available HTTP: http://www.american.edu/TED/EULA BEL.HTM (April 29, 2003).

"Elvisology." Online. Available HTTP: http://www.elvis.com/elvisology/ (January 1, 2002).

"European golf industry facing new challenges." Online. Available HTTP: http://www. asiagolf.com/news/1999/1/111999euro.htm (February 13, 2001).

"Everett struck by fan's thrown cell phone." Online. Available HTTP: http://reds. enquirer.com/2003/04/20/www.red4notes20.html (April 27, 2003).

"Fantasycamp." Online. Available HTTP: http://www.timesunion.com/promo/winter experience/fantasy.asp (August 4, 2001).

"Fédération nationale des associations de sauvegarde des sites et des ensembles monumentaux." Online. Available HTTP: http://www.patrimoine-etpaysages.org/ somedito.htm (July 1, 2001).

"FIVA general." Online. Available HTTP: http://www.fiva.org/eng/fiva_general.htm (November 23, 2001).

"General aviation aircraft." Online. Available HTTP: http://www.generalaviation.org/ databook/20000.html (August 2, 2001).

"Gold and platinum awards." Online. Available HTTP: http://www.riaa.orggold-history-2. cfm (January 1, 2002).

"Harry Potter conjures magic video debut" (9 June 2002). Online. Available HTTP: http//:www.starswelove.com/scriptsphp/news.php?newsid=488 (October 20, 2003).

"History channel great race." Online. Available HTTP: http://www.digrc.org/press/ releases.htm (July 28, 2001).

"History of the international aerospace exhibition ILA." Online. Available HTTP: http://www.ila-berlin.com/vers2/topics/daten/comment4.htm (August 2, 2001).

"The HIStory world tour." Online. Available: HTTP: http://www.suchart.com/ michaeljackson/tourhistory.html (April 24, 2003).

"Hong Kong Disneyland." Online. Available HTTP: http://www.info.gov.hk/ disneyland/ indexe.htm (February 20, 2002).

"How much information?" Online. Available HTTP: http://www.sims.berkeley.edu/ research/projects/how-much-info/ (January 2, 2000).

"IAAPA 2000 annual convention." Online. Available HTTP: http://headlines.amuse mentparknet.com/inf/$headline.exe/amusementpark/viewmessage?8059 (August 1, 2001).

"IFPA mission statement." Online. Available HTTP: http://www.ifpa.ie/about/ mission.html (August 1, 2001).

"IMAX fact sheet." Online. Available HTTP: http://www.imax.com/corporate/facts. html (March 1, 2002).

"Information bulletin – raves." Online. Available HTTP: http://www.usdoj.gov/ndic/ pubs/656/6567.htm (July 30, 2001).

"Isle of Wight festival history." Online. Available HTTP: http://www.iwight.com/home/ festival_history.asp (April 9, 2003).

"It's in the Bag." Online. Available HTTP: http://www.ufojeans/56/history_2.htm (October 17, 2003).

"Magic of Walt Disney engineering." Online. Available HTTP: http://www.wdimagic. com/history.html (June 28, 2001).

"Low riders grow up." Online. Available HTTP: http://www.acfnewsource.org/cgi-bin/ printer.cgi?376 (April 19, 2003).

"Mall of America." Online. Available HTTP: http://www.mallofamerica.com (July 18, 2001).

"National Trust." Online. Available HTTP: http://www.great-britain.nationaltrust.org. uk/main/ (January 8, 2004).

"Raves: history." Online. Available HTTP: http://www. phantasmagoria. f2s.com/writings/ rave1body.htm (July 30, 2002).

"Pope gets cheers at packed sports jubilee." Online. Available HTTP: http://sports illustrated.cnn.com/soccer/news/2000/10/29/vatican_jubilee_ap/index.html (July 14, 2001).

"Proceed with caution: growth in the global motor fleet." World Resources Institute. Online. Available HTTP: http://www.igc.org/wri/trends/autos2.html (August 2, 2001).

"Recycling cell phones." Online. Available HTTP: http://www.worldwise.com/reccelphon. html (April 27, 2003).

"Road rage report." Online. Available HTTP: http://www.reportroadrage.co.uk/incidents3. htm (August 31, 2001).

"Salzburg." Online. Available HTTP: http://www.image-t.com/salzburg/4005.htm (January 27, 2002).

"Selling America's kids: commercial pressures on kids of the 90's." Online. Available HTTP: http://www.consunion.org/other/sellingkids/index.htm (February 3, 2002).

"Short message service changes youth culture." Online. Available HTTP: http://english. peopledaily.com.cn200303/16/english200316_11382.shtml (April 17, 2003).

"SM Megamall." Online. Available HTTP: http://www.smprime.com.ph/smprime/ megamall.htm (January 6, 2003).

"Son et lumière: battlefields." Online. Available HTTP: http://www.battlefields.co.39/ dcentenary/2000/htm (June 12, 2001).

"Son et lumière: Christchurch." Online. Available HTTP: http://www.ccc.govt.nz/ MediaReleases/2000/December/SonEtLumiere.asp (June 12, 2001).

"Son et lumière: Giza." Online. Available HTTP: http://www.egyptvoyager.com/pyramids_ giza.htm (June 12, 2001).

"spaceimaging." Online. Available HTTP: http://www.spaceimaging.com/newsroom/ 2001_singapore.htm (October 23, 2003).

"Tax credit called most effective in history: study calls 25-year-old preservation program a national success." Online. Available HTTP: http://www.nationaltrust.org/news/docs/20010627_tax_credit.html (August 1, 2001).

"Theme parks popular in China." Online. Available HTTP: http://www.chinavista.com/travel/travelnews/en/tc0615-2.html (November 3, 2001).

"A timeline of television history." Online. Available HTTP: http://www.civilization.ca/hist/tv/tv02eng.html (December 21, 2001).

"Weakest link 'bad for Thai youth'." Online. Available HTTP: http://news.bbc.uk/hi/english/entertainment/tv_and_radio/newsid_18300000/1830100.stm (March 10, 2002).

"The words of Winston Churchill bring light and life to Blenheim Palace." Online. Available HTTP: http://www.winstonchurchill.org/eblwick.htm (June 12, 2001).

"Worldwatch" (1998) Online. Available HTTP: http://www.worldwatch.org/press.news/1998/01/10 (April 28, 2003).

"Worldwatch news release: chronic hunger and obesity epidemic eroding global progress." Online. Available HTTP: http://www.worldwatch.org/alerts/000304.html (February 20, 2002).

"Youth power." Online. Available HTTP: http://www.esomar.nl/Publications/234_youth_99.htm (March 1, 2002).

Index